W9-APJ-934

Unix Network Management Tools

McGraw-Hill Unix Series Titles:

Maxwell	*Unix Network Management Tools*	0-07-913782-2
Medinets	*Unix Shell Programming Tools*	0-07-913790-3
Ross	*Unix System Security Tools*	0-07-913788-1

To order or receive additional information on these or any other McGraw-Hill titles, in the United States please call 1-800-722-4726, or visit us at www.computing.mcgraw-hill.com. In other countries, contact your McGraw-Hill representative.

Unix Network Management Tools

Steve Maxwell

McGraw-Hill

New York • San Francisco • Washington, D.C. • Auckland • Bogotá • Caracas
Lisbon • London • Madrid • Mexico City • Milan • Montreal • New Delhi
San Juan • Singapore • Sydney • Tokyo • Toronto

Library of Congress Cataloging-in-Publication Data

Maxwell, Steven.
UNIX network management tools / Steven Maxwell.
p. cm.
Includes index.
ISBN 0-07-913782-2
1. UNIX (Computer file) 2. Computer networks—Management.
I. Title.
QA76.76.063M3734 1999
005.7'12768—dc21 99-17145
CIP

McGraw-Hill

Copyright © 1999 by The McGraw-Hill Companies, Inc. All rights reserved. Printed in the United States of America. Except as permitted under the United States Copyright Act of 1976, no part of this publication may be reproduced or distributed in any form or by any means, or stored in a data base or retrieval system, without the prior written permission of the publisher.

1 2 3 4 5 6 7 8 9 0 AGM/AGM 9 0 4 3 2 1 0 9

P/N 041132-8

Part of ISBN 0-07-913782-2

*The sponsoring editor for this book was Simon Yates, and the production supervisor was Clare Stanley. It was set in Sabon by **TIPS** Technical Publishing.*

Printed and bound by Quebecor/Martinsburg.

McGraw-Hill books are available at special quantity discounts to use as premiums and sales promotions, or for use in corporate training programs. For more information, please write to the Director of Special Sales, McGraw-Hill, 11 West 19th Street, New York, NY 10011. Or contact your local bookstore.

Information contained in this work has been obtained by The McGraw-Hill Companies, Inc. ("McGraw-Hill") from sources believed to be reliable. However, neither McGraw-Hill nor its authors guarantee the accuracy or completeness of any information published herein and neither McGraw-Hill nor its authors shall be responsible for any errors, omissions, or damages arising out of use of this information. This work is published with the understanding that McGraw-Hill and its authors are supplying information, but are not attempting to render engineering or other professional services. If such services are required, the assistance of an appropriate professional should be sought.

This book is printed on recycled, acid-free paper containing a minimum of 50% recycled, de-inked fiber.

Contents

List of Figures

List of Tables

Code Listings

Preface

This book addresses network management from a tools perspective and is meant to be a guide to effective management of an enterprise network that may consist of Unix workstations, servers, and other networking components such as switches, routers, and hubs.

During the past few years, enterprise networks have become the critical link and integral component of the information systems landscape. Gone are the days when connectivity between users was optional and network failures were a normal part of computing. In many corporations and institutions, a network outage or delay can have serious implications on the organization's ability to conduct normal business activities or communicate with their customers. In the financial community, even a relatively short network outage can result in significant financial impact.

Today's corporate and institutional networks are characterized by significant growth in the diversity and number of systems attached to these networks. This is known as *heterogeneous networking* and is quite common. It is difficult to effectively manage the many different computers, peripherals, and core devices because much of it must be done manually. A critical system or network failure can significantly impact the use of corporate services and affect the day-to-day operations of an organization. Many networks have also been deployed with very little regard concerning their manageability or upgrade capabilities. This makes the task of network management that much harder due to the added requirements of legacy systems.

Also, with the widespread acceptance of the Internet as the primary external communication vehicle for many companies, maintaining network up-time is even more critical because users and customers are accustomed to instant access to information and services. With the small number of steps involved in accessing a site from any location in the world, a disconnection from the Internet could mean lost revenue opportunities if customers choose a competitor's site.

Due to the explosive growth in the networking industry, the computing landscape is filled with various computing platforms and systems from many different vendors. Thanks to the TCP/IP protocol suite, many kinds of computing systems and devices can be connected to the network ranging from large mainframe systems to small hand-held devices. With TCP/IP many of these systems share common services and provide a standard framework for connectivity. Also, with common implementation of network management protocols among these systems, a standard network management model can be deployed.

This book will give you the knowledge of critical tools and necessary skills to aid in systems and enterprise network management. The fundamental importance and goal of this book is to provide information on using public domain tools and related-system utilities to manage a TCP/IP enterprise.

Audience

The primary audience for this book is the network manager and system administrator. However, others will find the book useful because it deals with both fundamentals of network management and specific networking management protocols. Although the book isn't a complete introductory text, it does provide a launching point for those faced with supporting Unix networks in the real world. The text focuses more on tools than detailed descriptions of protocol operations, network management design, or architecture. At a minimum, the reader should be familiar with the basics of the Unix operating system and feel comfortable executing commands and accessing special system files. Users unfamiliar with these subjects might consider examining the other titles in the series. A basic understanding of networking is also assumed.

Unix Versions

All of the tools discussed and examples provided have been used on the Solaris 2.5, 2.6, and 2.7 Unix operating systems. Because many of the Unix tools are available across a wide variety of Unix versions, the reader will have little difficulty adapting and using the tools on his version of Unix. The tools for the most popular Unix versions can be found on the CD-ROM contained in this book.

Acknowledgments

Special thanks to my wife Virginia for her help and witty supportive satire during the entire book development process. Also to Lisa, Matthew, and Joshua for understanding the time requirements and giving me the opportunity to complete the manuscript even while the weather was great for outdoor fun. The author wishes to thank the McGraw-Hill production staff for their outstanding efforts in preparing the manuscript and to Simon Yates, Senior Editor, for managing the entire Unix tools series. Thanks go to the technical and copy editors, Sandra Henry-Stocker and Carol Bowers, for reviewing and providing valuable (and sometimes humorous) feedback, to Paulette Miley for her critical review and attention to detail, to Bruce Bicknell for composing clean pages on a tight schedule, and to Karen Brown for indexing. Thanks also to Bob Kern for his leadership for getting the book to press.

About the Author

For the last 12 years, Steve Maxwell has been involved with the design, deployment, and management of enterprise networks in a variety of companies and institutions. Having been involved with delivering network management products while at 3Com, he has gained insight into the fundamentals and strategies needed to effectively address the network management requirements of Unix networks. Maxwell lives in the Orlando, Florida area with his wife, Virginia, and their three children.

01

Overview of Network Management

On a conceptual level, a network management system addresses three fundamental areas: performance monitoring, configuration management, and diagnostic management. Some network management systems provide all these services while most individual tools address only one or two.

Each of these areas is part of an overall puzzle, as shown in Figure 1.1. A network management system must function in all three areas and provide the tools necessary to implement effective network management. If one of the areas is not covered, the network management picture is incomplete and the solution is inadequate. That is to say, without tools to support critical network management functions, the overall network management effort will be hindered. These three functions are so basic to network management that every tool and utility discussed in this book implements one or more of them. One of the goals of this book is to address each of these areas by describing tools that implement one or more of these management functions. However, because some of the tools presented are not commercial products, not all areas will be covered by an appropriate network management tool.

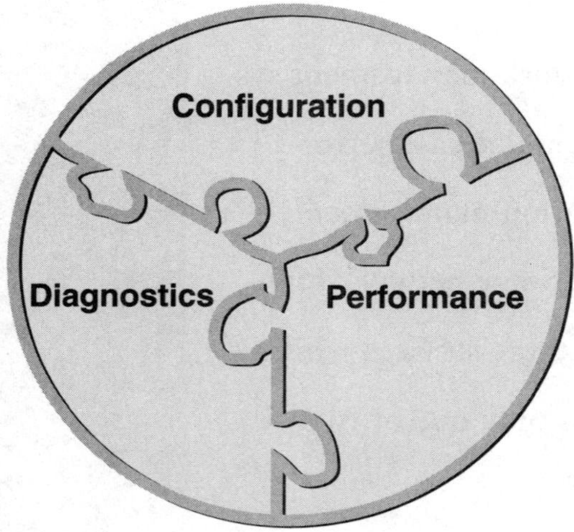

Figure 1.1 *Three Elements of Network Management.*

Performance monitoring includes the ability to keep tabs on the general efficiency or health of the network from the perspective of an enterprise or an individual device. It involves the collection and subsequent analysis of traffic patterns to alleviate network performance bottlenecks and solve related problems. Given adequate historical performance information, performance monitoring tools provide trend analysis as well. By proactively conducting performance reviews, the network administrator or designer can plan for network growth in a more consistent, timely, and strategic fashion.

Network configuration management involves ensuring that each network device or system contains the appropriate configuration and correct version of operating system software. Sometimes, changes are made to individual devices while, at other times, changes are propagated to a large number of systems. In these cases, the network management system must ensure that these changes are made correctly and efficiently.

Diagnostic management involves troubleshooting network failures, software problems, and other issues and problems that affect normal operation of the network or its components. It also involves effectively managing the many different types of problems and issues that result from software—and hardware—related failures. Network problems vary in complexity and can range from a simple hardware failure to a protocol-related problem. It is the goal of the network management system to isolate, describe, and in some cases, repair the problem.

A significant challenge in network management is keeping pace with improvements and advances in network technology as a whole. With the deployment of virtual local area networks (VLANs), where network topologies can be defined and modified very quickly and individual devices and workstations are moved around the network logically rather than physically, the need for robust and functional management is critical. With the migration from standard wide area network (WAN) topologies to virtual private networks (VPNs) where a public network is used as the basis for networking infrastructure, network management must again play an important role in shaping the administration, support, and day-to-day operations of the network.

With these factors in mind, a review of the major components of a network management system with an emphasis on specific system functionality is presented.

Network Management Components

To understand how a network management system functions, we must first consider the individual elements that make up such a system. A network management system consists of the following four components:

- Managers
- Agents
- Management Information Bases (MIBs)
- Proxies

Generally speaking, the first three components are required elements in most networking management systems. The remaining element, proxies, is optional because proxy functionality is very specialized and might not be required in all network environments.

Managers

Network management software includes important functionality to assist the network manager or administrator in the day-to-day tasks for managing the network or individual devices. Network manager software queries agent entities on a regular basis to collect vital device information. A manager might *poll* many agents on a regular basis to collect a host of information regarding the operating state, present configuration, or performance data. Figure 1.2 shows the relationship between a manager and an agent from a high level standpoint. The information collected by the manager is used to determine the general health of individual network devices, a portion of the network, or the network as a whole.

Figure 1.2 *Manager/Agent Relationship.*

Agents

Network management agents are software modules that reside in network devices such as Unix workstations, network printers, and other networking devices. Agents have access to the operational state, device characteristics, system configuration, and other related information as shown in Figure 1.3. Agents are the information brokers for each managed network device; they respond to requests for specific information and are usually polled by one or more network managers. Agents are responsible for the interface between the management software and the device in which the agent resides. Agents can control the functions of network devices by manipulating the database of information stored in the management information base (MIB) contained within the device.

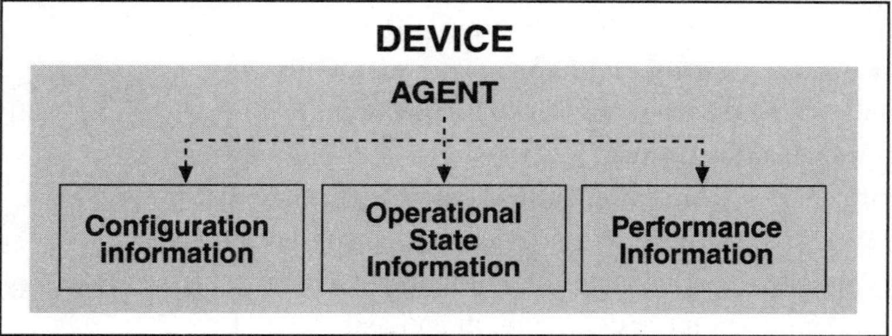

Figure 1.3 *Manager/Agent Relationship.*

The external behavior of network management agents is the same across different vendor products if the agent supports a standard protocol like SNMP. SNMP agents understand both the language and the type of questions a manager can ask. It is possible to deploy a network management system from one vendor, third-party network applications from another, and agents from a host of additional vendors and ensure communication among all components. SNMP provides the framework to permit communication and understanding among many disparate devices, software, and systems.

The internals of many networking devices—such as routers, switches, and hubs—are proprietary by design, and the agent component is provided by the network equipment manufacturer as part of the base system or as an optional upgrade module. In many cases the agent is embedded in the operating system of the device and usually provides minimal configuration options. This is in sharp contrast to computer operating systems such as Unix, where the agent is provided as a stand-alone system program and the user has much more control over the system's operation and configuration. Under the Unix system, several agents are available from both commercial vendors and the public domain. In contrast, no public domain agents are available for most networking hardware products.

It is the responsibility of a network management agent to convert the network manager's request from a standard network format, retrieve the desired information, and send back a valid response. In some situations, the manager might request the agent to perform some action by setting the value of a MIB object. For example, if an agent receives a request to reboot a device, no return message will be sent, but the agent will attempt to satisfy the request, provided the security requirements are met. Only with additional polls to the device would the manager actually know whether the device was restarted.

Equipment vendors define which objects their agents can manipulate, which poses some interesting problems for agent developers. How does a vendor determine agent functionality? Generally, he does this by seeking customer advice and, in an ideal world, by attempting to mimic hardware functions. However, this second goal isn't always practical or attainable; hardware designs generally change too quickly and agent software might not keep pace with hardware improvements. Also, network management as a whole is still in its infancy and not all equipment vendors behave as if agent development is as critical as hardware product development.

Management Information Base (MIB)

The MIB defines a database of objects that can be retrieved or manipulated by a network management system. Figure 1.4 shows the relationship of the agent and MIB objects. The MIB is a storehouse of information and can contain literally thousands of objects that the network manager can use to control, configure, and monitor devices by manipulating the objects directly. MIB objects are made available to a network management system via the agent. It is the responsibility of the agent to maintain the MIB object consistency regardless of the number of objects.

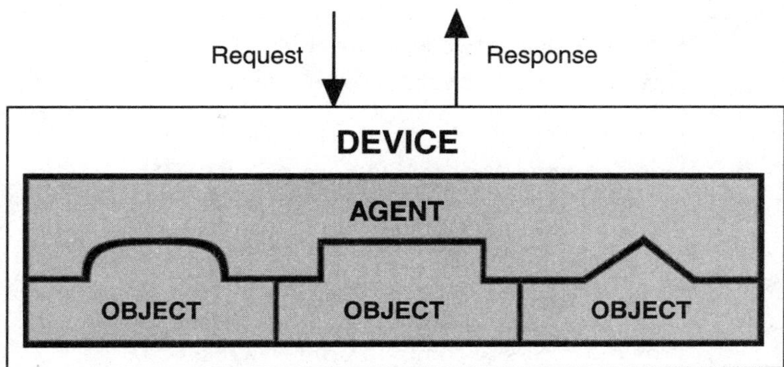

Figure 1.4 *SNMP Agent and MIB Objects.*

Several common standard MIBs have been defined, which include specific objects that must be supported in networking devices so that they are compatible with the SNMP protocol. The most widely implemented and common MIB is MIB-II. Many additional MIBs have been developed and documented in Request for Comments (RFCs) to address different networking components and technologies. Table 1.1 shows a sample list of these MIBs. As you can see, MIBs are available for a diverse collection of services, networking protocols, and architectures.

Table 1.1 *List of Standard MIBs*

MIB	Description
FDDI MIB	Provides access to Fiber Data Distribution Interface (FDDI) network management functions.
Host Resource MIB	Provides access to system objects that are related to memory, disk, processes, and other system related information.

(Cont'd)

Table 1.1 *List of Standard MIBs (Cont'd)*

MIB	Description
ISDN MIB	Used to provide management of Integrated Service Digital Network (ISDN) nodes
DNS Resolver and Server MIB	Provides management capabilities for the Domain Name Service (DNS)
MIB-II	Provides access to system level objects that include network protocols, network interfaces, and generic system information
Printer MIB	Provides access to common printer management functions

Additionally, many vendors have developed their own proprietary MIBs. These MIBs have been developed mainly to address additional functionality not found in the standard MIBs. Many networking product vendors like Cisco, 3Com, Bay, and Cabletron, as well as computer manufacturers like Sun, IBM, and HP, have developed their own MIBs.

Proxies

Proxy[1] devices are used to bridge the gap between standard network protocol managers and legacy systems that do not directly support such standards. Figure 1.5 shows the basic functions of a proxy-based system. Proxies can also be used to provide a migration path from older standard protocols to newer versions without upgrading the entire network. For instance, a significant amount of work has been focused on establishing improvements to the SNMP protocol. When a new version of SNMP is available, all existing network devices are affected. When these enhancements are made available from equipment vendors, it is reasonable to assume that not all products will be changed to support the new protocols.

---

1. This term proxy here is not related to the proxy servers that are used today in many enterprise networks which provide protocol filtering and other related services to hide the details of an internal network to the outside world.

Some vendors will provide upgrades while others will not; it is a matter of product viability and economics. It is also entirely possible that certain devices will be upgraded while other products will be made obsolete. As a result, organizations must address the issue of supporting different versions of SNMP for the foreseeable future. The proxy mechanism is one way to deal with any migration concerns.

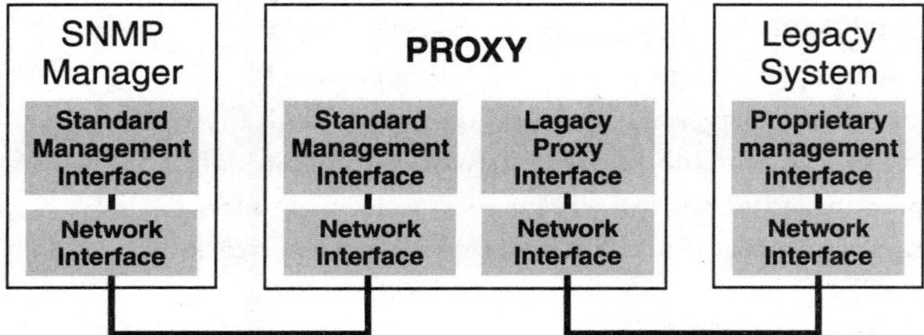

Figure 1.5 *Proxy-Based System.*

It is interesting to note that a proxy-based system might even provide network connectivity to systems that do not support any standard network protocols (such as TCP/IP) and, thus, provide gateway services as well.

Manager Functions

Managers today offer a host of services to address the needs of an expanding heterogeneous enterprise network. The services provided can come from the basic management system itself or from third-party application providers, or they can be developed in-house to address some specific unique requirements. The capabilities and functions of a network manager can be grouped into three sections that include:

- Architecture
- Core Services
- Applications

Architecture

The architecture describes the basic framework and model of how the manager operates and implements the basic services needed to accomplish network management tasks. It should include:

An Open and Extensible Framework—Managers are designed around an open standards-based framework, which can support enhancements to existing protocols and emerging technologies. An open network manager supports standards-based network management protocols such as SNMP and CMIP. Today, the network management protocol of choice is the Simple Network Management Protocol (SNMP). A network management system that doesn't support an open architecture and standard protocols should be viewed with suspicion because it could be difficult for the software to support enhancements in network protocols, databases, and operating system software. Managers must also support the TCP/IP Internet protocol suite and other proprietary networking protocols.

An open management system also provides integration tools and applications programming interfaces (APIs) for third-party developers to *layer* additional software solutions over the management framework. These solutions provide specialized application functions that are usually not available with the basic network management system. Depending on the level of integration, the user might not be aware of the different vendors' solutions contained within the management system.

Support for Distributed/Centralized Monitoring—Network management systems should have the ability to be deployed in a distributed or a centralized architecture. This is also known as the client/server approach and provides the means for the network management system to scale up and address additional network management requirements. In many situations, it is advisable to deploy one or more dedicated computer systems to handle the overhead associated with managing a large network. Although vendors don't specifically require more than one system for management tasks, it is unreasonable to assume that a single network management system can handle and support a network that consists of tens of thousands of devices. If, for the sake of argument, the platform selected could monitor that many devices, some practical considerations would warrant against using a single system.

First, in a centralized approach, the manager is polling each device from a single segment or subnetwork. This can cause serious traffic congestion for that portion of the network and significantly reduce the ability of the other devices on that segment to communicate with the rest of the network. Second, the network management system itself may be so occupied with the task of polling that it might not be able to respond to the GUI or other related management tasks. Third, using a centralized system is problematic with respect to general availability and uptime. Should the main management station fail due to a hardware or software problem that renders the system unusable, the network will be without a management platform until the system can be repaired. This may be an unacceptable situation in computing environments where system uptime and availability are critical.

Support for Common Platforms—To provide the most choices for customers, vendors of network management systems provide cross system support on the most popular operating systems and hardware platforms. Many vendors support both the Unix and Windows NT operating systems. However, Unix is still the most popular platform for vendors of network management systems and will continue to play an important role in the future. Among the most popular and supported Unix platforms are Solaris, AIX, and HP-UX.

Core Services

A network management system should provide basic services that address a certain portion of the network management requirements. These core services are typically considered the minimum amount of functionality that a network management system should provide. As such, it may be assumed these capabilities are available in most enterprise management systems. To a large degree, vendors compete in the industry by providing more significant core service offerings and by ensuring availability of third-party products. Core services may be supplied with the basic system or as additional optional components. Many networks require the following services:

Fault Detection and Resolution—Network faults are problems or conditions that occur in the network. These include configuration problems, overloaded devices, devices that have crashed due to software or hardware problems, and many other network related problems. Due to the large size and complexity of many enterprise networks, the management software must provide a mechanism to detect, report, filter, and in some situations, resolve network failures and problems. For example, when a critical system depletes the available disk space, the network management system should attempt to address the problem by executing a system utility to remove unnecessary files. Also, as with most enterprise networks, the number of networking faults is directly proportional to the number of monitored devices, which can be quite large. Inadequate handling of these faults can impact the ability of the network support staff to respond to the problem.

Alarm Notifications and Processing—Along with fault detection and resolution, a manager should provide a mechanism to respond to detected errors and conditions. An alarm is a programmed response to a network condition. Alarms are used to connect the network condition to some action that will address the problem. For example, an alarm is generated when a critical server becomes unavailable to the network and activates the pager of the system administrator, providing notification of the failure. Events, on the other hand, are specific conditions that are not always considered critical and might not warrant immediate notification or reaction. A change to the configuration of a device or a decrease in the load of a server can be considered a network event. For events such as these, it may be reasonable to simply log these events for future review.

Support Large Number of Devices—Managers are designed and are required to handle a significantly large number of active devices. It is not uncommon for a manager to support hundreds or even thousands of devices from a theoretical standpoint. However, as a practical matter, managers are normally not configured to poll extremely large numbers of devices due to network performance considerations.

Reporting Tools—One of the most significant requirements of a network management system is its ability to effectively produce reports. The type of reports considered essential includes performance, configuration, inventory, and fault. In many cases, the most critical area for reporting is related to performance. Network management systems can collect a large amount of performance statistics. An easy-to-use and flexible facility is required to assist with determining the general health of the network so that potential bottlenecks can be pinpointed quickly and easily. Also, the reporting software should handle inventory requirements to assist, for example, with determining device revision information to help with networking upgrades.

Easy to Use Interface—Typically, a manager has a Graphical User Interface (GUI) to ease administration functions and tasks. Presently, network management systems are undergoing a transformation with respect to interfaces. Many network management vendors are providing both native GUI support and Web-based interfaces for their products. Some vendors have taken the GUI concept to its fullest potential and many have been successful in marrying disparate network devices to share a uniform view for management and control. This has been a tremendous advantage in managing the network from a remote or help-desk standpoint. The Web model will certainly change the way network management has traditionally been done. However, it may be some time before network management products have completely migrated to a Web-enabled interface.

Configuration Management—Enterprise networks often consist of equipment that requires custom configuration information to control the functionality and to correct system operations. A network management system must provide support for device configuration changes. For example, it is not uncommon to upgrade to new releases of system software across a larger number of devices. A manager should provide a mechanism to upload the new software and ensure that the device is working correctly before attempting to upgrade the remaining devices. Should a special parameter or configuration option require modification across several devices, it would be advantageous for the manager to handle this task in a logical, uniform manner. Network management systems are often criticized for their lack of sophisticated configuration management support. However, tremendous inroads are now being made to address the complex task of configuration management and support.

Network Discovery—Due to the sheer volume of devices contained in an enterprise network, it is unreasonable to manually add all the devices to a network management system. Therefore, managers provide the ability to automatically look up or "discover" an entire network or a special class of devices. The network discovery process generally takes time and can consume a significant amount of network bandwidth. Care should be exercised when conducting the discovery process, as it can adversely affect network performance. After the discovery product is complete, the devices are placed in special views, which are usually arranged by subnetwork.

Additional Applications

Often, network management systems are deployed in environments where additional services and functions are necessary to address the unique business processes and support structure within an organization. These services will extend the usefulness and capabilities of a basic network manager by providing value-added applications that are layered onto the network management system. These applications may be available from third-party providers or from the vendor of the network management system itself. In many cases, network management vendors will seek solution partners to provide specific business software that will complement and integrate with the network management system.

The level of integration from third-party products will depend on the core services of the network management system, the effort involved with integrating into the management system, and the product functionality. Depending on the management system, integration from one vendor could mean having the ability to invoke software functions from a common menu or it could mean gaining access to the database.

Some of the more popular application and services that are available include:

Trouble Ticketing—This application provides the ability to track and manage network events and failures in an automated fashion. When trouble ticketing is integrated with a network management system, certain network events or alarms can trigger the creation of a ticket that will notify the appropriate party or individual regarding the network problem. One problem with using this automated approach is the possibility of creating unwanted or invalid tickets. For example, should a building lose power momentarily and portions of the network reboot, many tickets could be generated because a large portion of the network was unavailable. Clearly, it would be sufficient for a single ticket to be generated versus tickets for all possible devices. Some trouble ticket systems have the ability to filter incoming alarms based on user-defined criteria or other conditions. As a result, a filter could be created to measure the duration of an outage and, only after establishing the period of time elapsed, generate the appropriate ticket. When used carefully, this can provide a fully automated way to dispatch key personnel when network problems occur, without the requirement of a dedicated call support center.

Policy Based Management—Policies management is a relatively new issue in network management. A policy involves establishing a resource profile or access domain for an individual user, group, or system. It might also contain user information such as access rights, privileges, email identification, and so on. In particular, policies can be used to define the network from access control lists (ACLs) to broadcast domains. A broadcast domain describes the area or number of devices a system is permitted to communicate with. Also, virtual local area networks (VLANs) and virtual private networks (VPNs) make use of policies to help define or shape the network and establish and enforce service level agreements (SLAs).

Advanced Alarm Processing—Sometimes the basic alarm handling within the core management product doesn't provide the customization or functionality needed to address specific requirements. As a result, more advanced alarm processing capabilities might be required. For example, it might be necessary for the alarm software to provide better mechanisms for alarm notification. Sometimes activating a pager is inappropriate, particularly in a lights-out, automated operation. Instead, the alarm software should be intelligent enough to make decisions about how to best resolve the issue. This can include running an external program or script, or initiating a fail-over sequence.

Network Simulation—Network simulation software is used to emulate the behavior of a real network environment. In certain situations, it is advisable to model a network design or upgrade before any changes are made to the existing network. By interfacing with a network management system, the network simulations can be more realistic and dynamic because they are based on information about the actual devices and network topology, rather than static generic information.

02

Simple Network Management Protocol

The Simple Network Management Protocol (SNMP) provides the low-level framework for many network management systems. SNMP is widely implemented and can be found in a large variety of different networking devices, software, and systems. Today, SNMP is considered the management protocol of choice for network hardware vendors, software application developers, and end-users.

Why is SNMP so popular? First, SNMP is simple to implement as compared to other network management architectures or protocols. The protocol, MIBs, and associated framework can be run on anything from low-end personal computers (PCs) to high-end mainframes, servers, and network devices such as routers and switches. An SNMP agent component doesn't need to occupy a large *footprint* in terms of memory and doesn't require significant processing power. SNMP can generally be developed very quickly on target systems, thus increasing the time-to-market for new products and enhancements. When SNMP was first introduced, other management mechanisms were available, but SNMP proved to be more flexible and easier to implement. It is true that SNMP lacks certain features found in other network management protocols (such as OSI, for example), but its simple design, extensibility, and ease of use minimize any possible drawbacks.

Second, SNMP is free and in the public domain. As a result, no single vendor can claim ownership of the protocol nor can it be copy protected by any company or individual. The only way to influence or change SNMP is via the standards process of the Internet Engineering Task Force (IETF), which can be a daunting task. The IETF is one of the standards bodies for the Internet. Vendors may choose to make proprietary changes to SNMP, but this could prove futile because they must lobby other vendors and users to support their non-standard enhancements, which defeats the purpose of having a standard in the first place.

Third, SNMP is well documented (via RFCs, articles, and textbooks) and is well understood in the industry. This provides an established foundation for continued enhancement and adoption.

Finally, SNMP can be used to control a variety of devices. It is even finding its way into non-traditional equipment such as telephone systems, environmental control equipment, and just about anything else that can be attached to a network and requires control.

SNMP Operation

SNMP defines the packet format and information exchange between a network manager and associated agents. At its core, SNMP manipulates objects within the MIB of the agent and as a result, can be used to manage a variety of tasks that are defined within the agent. The SNMP protocol and related components are described in a number of RFCs. Any SNMP-compliant agent can communicate with any network management system that supports SNMP. The management system knows what questions to ask the agent because it has a copy of the agent's MIB.

One of the reasons SNMP is considered *simple* is because it provides three general-purpose operations that can be applied to objects. These operations, or commands, are at the heart of SNMP; they are *Set, Get, and Trap*.

Set: A management system may update or change the value of an object that is contained in an agent. The set operation is a privileged command because it can be used to alter a device configuration or control its operating state.

Get: A management system may obtain or read the value of an object that is contained within an agent. The get command is the most common SNMP operation because this is the primary mechanism used to obtain management information from network devices.

Trap: An agent may send an unsolicited message to a network manager. The purpose of the trap service is to notify a network management system of a special condition or problem without the management system specifically requesting this information.

SNMP defines the relationship and message flow between manager and agent with respect to set, get, and trap messages as shown in Figure 2.1. As you can see, in most instances the SNMP manager is directing the message exchange with the agent. However, the agent has the ability to send the manager asynchronous messages via the trap operation without specifically being polled.

SNMP doesn't define any additional mechanisms to issue commands to device agents. The only actions that can be applied to MIB objects are to set or get a value. For example, there is no *reboot* command defined in SNMP. Instead, agent software can implement specific commands by associating MIB objects with the internal commands of the device. To reboot a device, the management station would set a specific reboot MIB object to 1, for example. This would signal the agent to reboot the device and reset the MIB reboot object to its previous state.

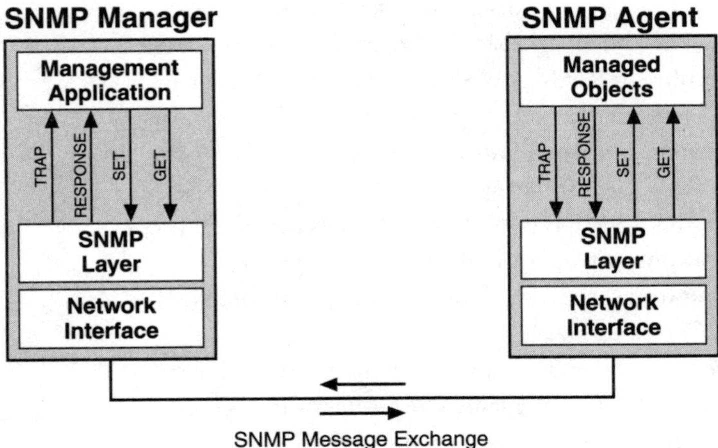

Figure 2.1 *SNMP Manager and Agent Relationship.*

Overview of SNMP Versions

SNMPv1, which accounts for the significant portion of the installed base of agents, has several fundamental problems. First, because it lacks a robust security mechanism, it can't be used to its full potential. As a result, many vendors limit the set operations on agents to minimize the potential risk of a security breach. Second, SNMPv1 doesn't handle processing large amounts of information, which also restricts the use of the SNMPv1 framework. Third, SNMPv1's relationship of network manager and agent are well defined—agents play only a single, simplistic role of accepting commands from more superior management systems. This significantly limits SNMPv1 when smart agents are needed to address specific requirements for distributed network management functions. To summarize, SNMPv1 provides:

- The basic network management framework
- Definition of the MIB-II standard
- Descriptions of the Protocol Data Units (PDUs) that include: *GetRequest*, *GetNextRequest*, *SetRequest*, *GetResponse*, and *Trap*
- Description of ASN.1 encoding language

To address some of the deficiencies in SNMPv1, a significant amount of effort has been made over the past five years to enhance SNMP. The first series of improvements came in 1993 when a set of 12 RFCs (1441-1452) was introduced, proposing added PDUs, and enhancements to the SNMP architecture and security model. This collection of RFCs was known as SNMPv2 Classic. At that time, many were expecting these improvements and planned to take advantage of the new features as soon as vendors upgraded their products.

Unfortunately, there was still much debate about SNMPv2 security and remote configuration. When it became apparent that not all the original SNMPv2 proposals were going to be widely adopted, additional work was done to define SNMP security and remote configuration management components. This led to additional proposals that included the new protocol and new MIB structure elements (documented in RFCs 1901-1908).

These proposals were more popular than SNMPv2 Classic and became known as community-base SNMPv2 or SNMPv2c. The problem with SNMPv2c is that, though it was endorsed by the IETF, it lacked security and administration.

Additional improvements to the remote management capability of SNMPv1 resulted in proposals known as SNMPv2 usec and SNMPv2*, documented in RFC 1909-1910 and 2222, respectively. The SNMPv2 usec recommends a robust security model and administrative framework. One of the problems with SNMPv2 usec is that it lacks endorsement of the IETF, which relinquishes the proposal to a non-standard. With all the proposals completed, the major functions of SNMPv2 include:

- Expanded data types such as 64 bit counters
- Improved performance and efficiency with the get-bulk PDU
- Event notification with the inform PDU
- Better error handling
- More efficient row creation and deletion

Finally, in an attempt to reach some agreement between the various remote management and security proposals, another set of

RFCs was written, which later became known as SNMPv3. These RFCs (2271-2275) have been put forth by the IETF as Proposed Standards, which means that they are available to the general public for review and discussion. SNMPv3 is SNMPv2c plus provisions for robust security and administration; it draws upon the SNMPv2c RFCs (1902-1908). At a high level, the SNMPv3 proposal attempts to:

- Put forth a security model based on DES, MD5, and other authentication protocols
- Define a view-based access control model
- Redefine some of the SNMP concepts and terms

Management Information Base (MIB)

As previously mentioned, the MIB is a storehouse of information related to the configuration and performance data contained within an agent. MIBs have an organization and common structure and may contain a large number of objects separated into groups.

Organization

MIB objects are organized in a hierarchical tree structure in which each branch has a unique name and numeric identifier. Figure 2.2 shows the standard MIB organization from the root to additional branches. The branches of the tree serve as a logical grouping of related objects. The leaves, or *nodes* as they are often called, represent individual objects. Also, sub-trees are formed and represent both additional intermediate branches and additional leaves. By using this structure, an SNMP manager (or MIB browser tool) can drill-down into the MIB in an easy, yet concise manner. A MIB browser is a piece of software that traverses a MIB tree, usually showing a graphical display of branches and leaf objects.

Objects within a MIB can be referenced by specifying each of the numeric identifiers starting with the top of the tree (or root) and proceeding to the individual leaf or object. This access method is also consistent with that of referencing files within the Unix operating system. However, one key difference is that Unix pathnames can be expressed in absolute or relative terms. MIB objects

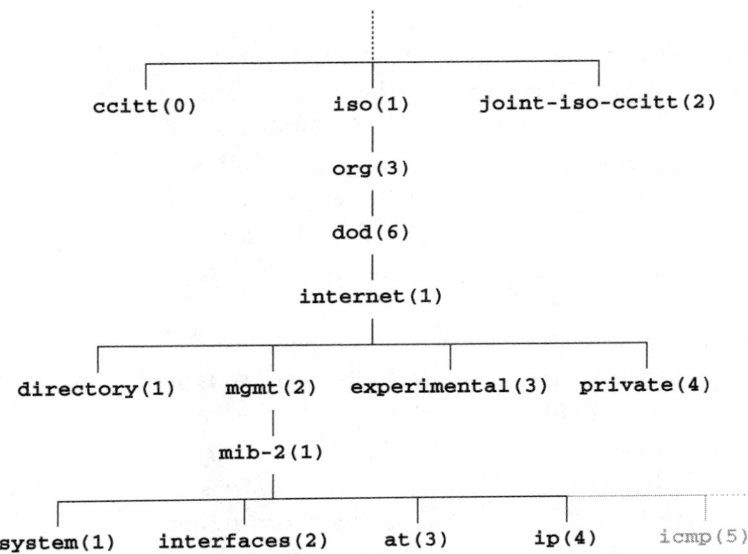

Figure 2.2 *MIB Structure and Organization.*

can only be accessed in an absolute manner; the relative format is not available. For example, Figure 2.2 shows `iso(1)` at the top-most position of the tree and `sysDescr(1)` at the leaf. The `root(.)` is implied and all branches extend from it. The common method of expressing object identifiers is to use the *dotted notation*. This notation requires that a dot separate each branch name or identifier. To access the `sysDescr(1)` object, the fully qualified identifier would be written as:

```
iso.org.dod.internet.mgmt.mib-2.system.sysDescr
```

This identifier is read from left to right. Objects can also be expressed in a short form by substituting the branch name with the numeric identifier associated with each identifier name. Thus, `iso.org.dod.internet.mgmt.mib-2.system.sysDescr` can also be expressed as `1.3.6.1.2.1.1.1`. These two expressions are functionally equivalent and reference the same MIB object. The reason to choose one form over the other is a matter of preference, although the numeric identifier is much more concise. However, many MIB browsers can display MIB objects in either format, thus making it easier to convert from one format to the other.

Object Types

Within a MIB, different object types are used to represent data structures or values contained in an agent. The objects can represent physical agent attributes, configuration information, or other data. These object types are derived from the Abstract Syntax Notation (ASN.1) standard rules. ASN.1 provides a detailed mechanism for the implementation and encoding of basic data types that are machine-independent and can be transmitted over the network in an unambiguous way.

Why is this important to SNMP or network management? Because network management must address a heterogeneous network environment, a standard way must be provided to ensure that SNMP messages can be transmitted and understood on different systems and devices. Because various computer platforms store information differently, ASN.1 provides a common format. For example, an integer on one system can be expressed with the most significant digit first, while on others it can be the least significant digit first. Also, ASN.1 data types are found in MIBs and, for us to understand network management, we must be able to read and understand MIB objects. Without a good grasp of MIBs, it will be difficult to use SNMP tools and software to manage a network effectively.

Two object data type classes are defined using ASN.1:

- Universal Types
- Application Types

The universal class consists of primitive types that can be used to build additional data types of objects within a MIB. Table 2.1 defines the available simple data types found in the universal class:

SNMP derives some application data types from the universal class type. These application types are used to further define additional types that can be used to represent specific values customized for use within the network management environment. Table 2.2 describes the application data types that are presently available in the application class.

Table 2.1 *Universal Data Types*

ASN.1 Data Type	Description
`INTEGER`	A data type representing a cardinal number where no limitation is made to the level of precision that might be required to represent an integer value
`OCTET STRING`	A data type representing zero or more octets where each octet may take any value from `0` to `255`
`NULL`	A data type meant as a placeholder, but currently not used
`OBJECT IDENTIFIER`	A data type representing an authoritatively named object that consists of a sequence of values that specify a MIB tree
`SEQUENCE` `SEQUENCE OF`	A data type used to denote an ordered list of zero or more elements that contain other ASN.1 types. `SEQUENCE OF` contains an ordered list of the same ASN.1 type

Table 2.2 *Application Data Types*

ASN.1 Data Type	Description
`IpAddress`	Represents an `OCTET STRING` that has a length of 4 bytes (32-bits) and each of the four octets relates to the four bytes of a standard IP address
`NetworkAddress`	Can represent an address from one of several network protocol address standards. Presently, it is the same as `IpAddress`

(Cont'd)

Table 2.2 *Application Data Types (Cont'd)*

ASN.1 Data Type	Description
`Counter`	A data type that represents a non-negative integer that increases until it reaches a maximum value and then resets to zero. A `counter` is an `INTEGER` that can take the value between `0` and `4294967295`
`Gauge`	A data type that represents a non-negative integer that may increase or decrease and will trigger at a maximum value. A `gauge` is like a `counter` in every other aspect
`TimeTicks`	Represents a non-negative integer that counts time in hundredths of a second since some established epoch. `TimeTicks` is like a `counter` in every other aspect
`Opaque`	A data type that provides the ability to pass arbitrary information that uses the `OCTET STRING` data type

Why include this kind of MIB detail in this book? Because the sections in the succeeding chapters will focus on using network management tools that manipulate MIB objects, it seems reasonable to present the types of objects that might be encountered. It is therefore important that the reader understand the different types of objects and why values from these objects are in a certain format or structure. Of equal importance is the access mode of MIB objects discussed below.

Accessing Objects

MIB objects are defined with access control information that specifies what kind of operation can be performed on the object. SNMP includes the following access control for MIB objects:

- Read-only
- Read-write
- Not-accessible

Read-only MIB objects are not alterable by the network management system, but values may be obtained via a *get* or *trap* operation. Why would a change to a MIB object be prohibited? The reason is very clear: certain MIB information will never change during the life of a product. For example, the MIB object `sysDescr`, which stands for *System Description*, contains vendor information for the agent. An SNMP manager should not modify this information because it would disassociate the device with the actual product vendor, thus making agent identification difficult. Also, it can adversely affect the accuracy of any software-based network inventory mechanisms. Another reason to make objects read-only is to ensure that performance information or other statistical data remain accurate rather than be altered unintentionally, which has the potential to provide incorrect information about the state of the network or device.

Read-write access is necessary when a particular object must be altered to accomplish some specific goal or be configured in a certain way. For example, it might be necessary to disable a router port due to a large number of errors detected on one of its interfaces. In this case, the network management system must set the operational status of the interface to `0`, thus shutting down the physical connection until the cause of the errors is determined.

Objects defined as *not-accessible* within the MIB usually reference object definitions or other object descriptions that are not objects themselves.

Tables

As noted above, a MIB may contain objects that represent physical characteristics or other information contained within an agent. These objects can either be in the form of discrete elements (i.e., individual objects like `sysDescr)` or, in some cases, two-dimensional tables. Tables are used to store related information that might contain several instances or copies of a MIB object. The best way to illustrate the use of a table is by examining an implementation of a table within an actual MIB.

Defined in the MIB-II standard is the `interface` group that has the object identifier defined as `1.3.6.1.2.1.2` or `iso.org.dod.internet.mgmt.mib-2.interface`. Objects within this group are used to represent physical network interfaces and related information installed within a networking device. Performance-related information is also collected and stored within this group.

For each interface within a network device, the following information is used to describe the nature of the interface and associated configuration:

- *Description:* General description of the interface
- *Type:* The type of interface such as Ethernet or Token Ring
- *Mtu:* The maximum transmission size
- *Speed:* The transmission speed of the interface
- *Physical Address:* The databank protocol or hardware address
- *Administration Status:* Shows present administrative status of the interface
- *Operational Status:* Shows actual operating status of the interface
- *Last Change:* Time when the interface became operational

Additional objects within the table are used to store the following performance monitoring information:

- Number of octets received or sent
- Number of unicast packets delivered or sent to or from high level software.
- Number of non-unicast packets delivered or sent to or from higher level software.
- Number of inbound/outbound packets discarded
- Number of inbound/outbound packets containing errors
- Number of inbound/outbound packets discarded due to bad protocol.
- Length of the output packet queue

The structure of the interface group is shown in Figure 2.3 on page 30. Tables are used to contain interface information because networking devices can contain many interfaces. For example, a router or switch device can contain literally dozens of interfaces, often representing different network protocols such as Ethernet, ATM, or FDDI. Using a table provides a straightforward and convenient way to access individual objects within a given interface definition.

The interface group includes the `ifNumber` object, which contains the total number of network interfaces within the networking device. Using the example data contained in Table 2.3 on page 31, the `ifNumber` value would be `2`. In this case, the device reports two interfaces: one defined as a pseudo-interface and the other defined as an Ethernet. It is common for networking devices to contain a pseudo-interface for internal diagnostic purposes.

The rest of the Interface group consists of a table called `ifTable`, which contains a row for each interface defined within the device. This table is indexed by `ifIndex`, which contains the value between the range of `1` and the value of `ifNumber`. The `ifIndex` object uniquely addresses each column of the table or interface.

Each row corresponds to each of the specific MIB objects contained within the `ifEntry` table. Table 2.3 shows the entire interface group in the first column and associated values taken from an actual network device in the remaining rows. Each `ifEntry` instance represents an interface defined in the table. To access the object `ifDescr` for the first interface, one would use the object identifier (OID):

```
1.3.6.1.2.1.2.2.1.1
```

or

```
iso.org.dod.internet.mgmt.mib-2.interface.ifTable.ifEntry.ifDescr
```

The objects starting from `IfInOctets` to `IfOutQLen` represent traffic counters within the agent for device interfaces and can be used to measure network and device performance.

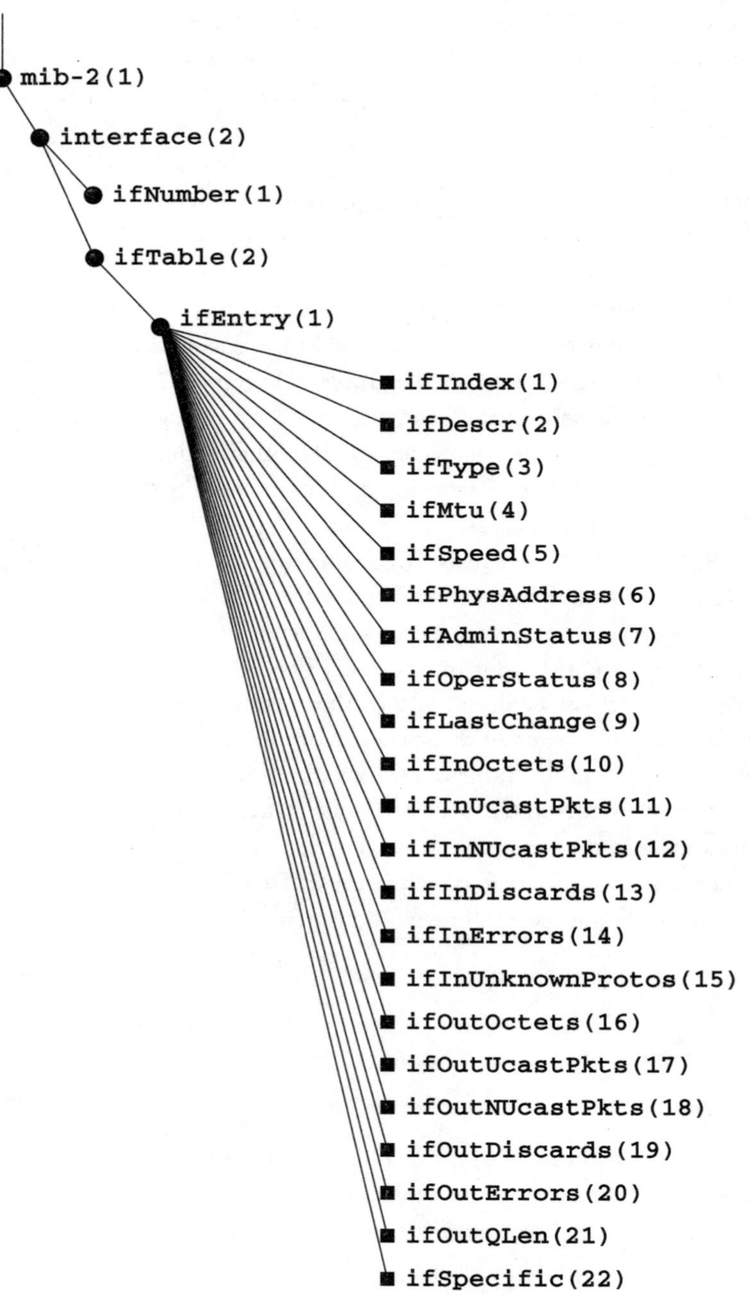

Figure 2.3 *MIB-II Interface Group Structure.*

Table 2.3 *Interface Group Instance Table*

MIB Objects	IfEntry 1.3.6.1.2.1.2.2.1	IfEntry 1.3.6.1.2.1.2.2.2
IfIndex	1	2
ifDescr	Pseudo Interface	Ethernet
ifType	1	6
ifMtu	1500	1500
IfSpeed	10000000	10000000
ifPhysAddress		0x00040010ee5d
IfAdminStatus	1	1
IfOperStatus	1	1
IfLastChange	0	0
IfInOctets	0	42617
IfInUcastPkts	445	680
IfInNUcastPkts	0	19
IfInDiscards	0	0
IfInErrors	0	5
IfInUnknownProtos	0	0
IfOutOctets	0	42600
IfOutUcastPkts	445	570
IfOutNUcastPkts	0	94
IfOutDiscards	0	0
IfOutErrors	0	87
IfOutQLen	0	0
ifSpecific	null	null

Sample MIB Object Listing

Because MIB objects are an important component of network management, some of the chapters in this book specifically describe MIB objects as they relate to system agent and management tools. Therefore, when discussing these objects, a common format has been selected as shown below.

Object Name: `agentDescr`

OID: `sunSystem.1`

Object Type: `DisplayString [255]`

Access Mode: `read-only`

Description: A description of the SNMP agent, which it uses to identify itself to other entities such as an SNMP manager. The agent assigns the string value of: `Sun Microsystems SNMP Agent`

The MIB format includes the object name, OID string, object type, access mode, and description. The object name is the name used when querying an agent for this particular object. In this example, the `agentDescr` object is a string that contains a general description of the Sun system agent. The object identifier (OID) shows which group the object is contained in and its logical position in that group. In this case, it is the first object in the system group. The `sunSystem` is a group within the Sun MIB. The object type is `DisplayString` and can be as long as `255` characters. The access mode indicates how the manager or other tool may manipulate the object. It is very common for those new to SNMP to attempt to alter `read-only` objects. The description field provides an overview of the object, its significance, and its sample value.

SNMP Communities

Often, a network management system will be deployed in a large network environment that contains a collection of many different groups of networks and devices. Thus, it is reasonable for an enterprise network to be divided into zones or communities of users in order to partition responsibility. As a result, a community name can be assigned to a class of devices that provide a security boundary that helps to implement the desired communities or zones. SNMP supports this kind of security model based on community string information, which is physically added to each device within the selected community. Some practical examples include selecting a community that represents all the Cisco backbone routers and another community that includes devices in just the sales department.

SNMP's present community-based authentication model is considered very weak and poses a significant security problem. The major reason is that SNMP doesn't provide any encryption facilities or other mechanisms to ensure that the community information is not simply copied from the network during an SNMP packet exchange. Using a packet capture tool, the entire SNMP packet could be decoded, thus revealing the community name. As a result of this limitation, many sites disable set operations to many of the agent devices. This has the unfortunate side effect of limiting SNMP usefulness because it can then only monitor object values and not alter them.

SNMP Protocol Operation

The format of an SNMP message contains three major components: a version field, a community field, and an SNMP protocol data unit (PDU) field. Unlike other TCP/IP protocols, SNMP packets are not fixed length and, instead, rely on ASN.1 formatting. This basic SNMP structure is shown in Figure 2.4.

INTEGER	OCTET STRING	SEQUENCE
Version	**Community Name**	**SNMP Protocol Data Unit**

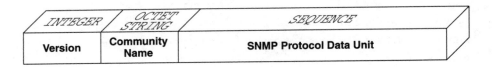

Figure 2.4 *SNMP Message Format.*

Version: This field is used to indicate which version of the SNMP protocol is being used. Presently, version 1 is the most widely implemented and supported SNMP protocol.

Community Name: The community is used as the primary security mechanism to establish authentication from a network manager to agents within SNMP. The community name or string is used as a password for which requests to access objects are permitted, based on the condition that the network manager knows the agent's password. If the agent has been configured to emit traps, an `authenticationFailure` trap is generated when a network manager queries an agent with an invalid community string.

Protocol Data Units: SNMPv1 PDUs can be one of five different types and consist of request and response components. They include:

- GetRequest
- GetNextRequest
- SetRequest
- GetResponse
- Trap

SNMPv2 defines these additional PDUs:

- GetBulkRequest
- InformRequest

Each of the GetRequest, GetNextRequest, and SetRequest components elicits a GetResponse from the responding agent that might contain valid data or an error status.

GetRequest

The GetRequest PDU is issued by an SNMP manager or application to obtain one or more MIB object(s) from an SNMP agent. Figure 2.5 on page 35 shows the packet format that contains the following fields:

PDU Type: Indicates the PDU type is a GetRequest.

Request-id: Unique identifier that permits the SNMP manager to match paired requests and responses. It also serves to aid in detecting duplicate messages that may be received when using an unreliable transport service.

Variable-Bindings: A list of requested MIB objects.

The GetRequest command is the primary way to obtain information from agents when the objects in question are known beforehand. For example, should the network manager decide to retrieve *sysDescr* and *sysUpTime* objects from an agent, the following GetRequest would be issued:

```
GetRequest (sysDescr, sysUpTime)
```

The `sysDescr` object represents a string that contains a general description of the agent and `sysUptime` reflects the amount of time an agent has been running.

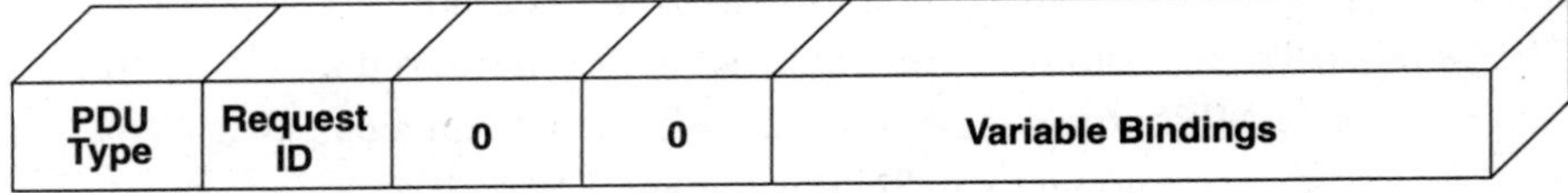

Figure 2.5 *GetRequest Message Format.*

When the agent receives the above message and no errors have occurred, it will respond with the values of the MIB objects requested via a GetResponse PDU. The GetRequest command is an atomic operation. That is, all the values requested are returned or no values are returned. When the receiving entity responds to the GetRequest, it includes the values in the GetResponse variable-binding field. If, for some reason, at least one of the values cannot be supplied, no values will be provided.

If the values requested from a manager cannot be returned by the agent, the agent will respond with an error. For example, the management system might have requested a MIB object that isn't implemented in the agent. In this case, the agent can't possibly satisfy the request and an error is returned. Also, in certain situations, returning the value of a requested object fails because it might be too large to be processed by the manager.

The *variable-binding* includes a list of objects for which values are requested. When the agent responds via the GetResponse, the variable binding includes the requested objects and associated values. Given the example above, the following GetResponse would be sent by the agent:

```
GetResponse(sysDescr="3Com Enterprise Monitor", sysUpTime=0000154477)
```

In this example, the agent is a 3Com RMON probe as indicated by the `sysDescr` field. The `sysUpTime` object contains the amount of time the device has been up and running. The value shown in the example indicates the device was running for 15 minutes and 44 seconds.

GetNextRequest

The GetNextRequest PDU is similar to the GetRequest PDU and the packet formats are identical as shown in Figure 2.5. However, the GetNextRequest PDU has one difference: It is used to retrieve objects when the structure of the MIB tree is unknown. The GetNextRequest can be a great asset when it is used to discover the exact MIB structure of an agent. Why would an agent's MIB structure be unknown to an SNMP manager? SNMP provides no direct way to determine which MIBs or MIB structure is available within an agent. Therefore, the network manager must discover the device and supported MIBs by walking the MIB tree in an automated fashion. When the GetNextRequest is sent with a particular object, the GetResponse returns the requested object's value, plus the instance of the next lexicographic object in the MIB tree. As a result, each GetNextRequest will reveal the next object within the MIB without the manager specifically requesting it. The GetNextRequest operation also provides a more efficient mechanism to retrieve objects from an agent than GetRequest because it requires fewer request/response exchanges.

SetRequest

The SetRequest is used to alter the value of a MIB object. The packet format is the same as GetRequest and GetNextRequest as shown in Figure 2.5. Unlike the GetRequest or GetNextRequest, the SetRequest is used to alter the value of a MIB object. As mentioned before, the SetRequest requires security privileges, which are presently mapped via the community string for the SNMPv1 protocol. Therefore, the agent must validate the SetRequest community string provided before the operation is permitted to succeed. The SetRequest is also atomic; either all the values can be altered or none can. If the SetRequest is successful, a GetResponse is returned and the variable-binding list contains the objects with their new values. This is how the network manager can determine that the set operation was successful. If the SetRequest was unsuccessful, an error is returned in the GetResponse.

GetResponse

Each of the SNMP operations, with the exception of the Trap, receives a GetResponse from the agent. The format of the GetResponse packet is shown in Figure 2.6 and includes the following fields:

PDU Type: Indicates the PDU type, which is GetResponse.

Request-id: Unique identifier that permits the pairing of requests and responses.

Error-status: Indicates that an exception condition occurred while processing the request.

Error-index: When an error occurred, indicates which object variable in the variable-binding list caused the error.

Variable-Bindings: A list of MIB objects that are involved in the operation.

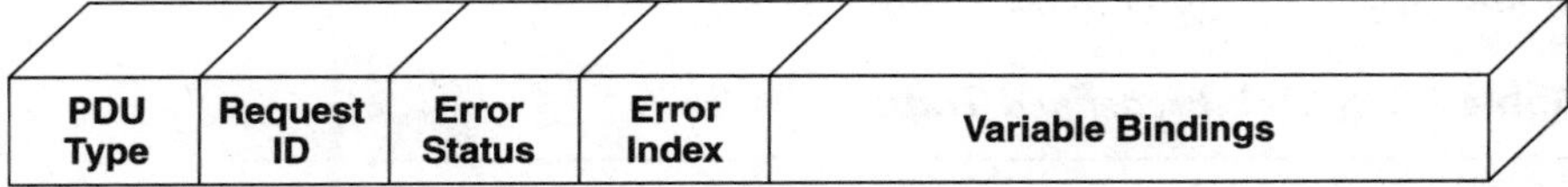

Figure 2.6 *GetResponse Message Format.*

Trap

A trap is an unsolicited message from an agent directed to a network management station that represents an asynchronous notification of some significant event or condition. The trap PDU is quite different from that of the other PDUs defined in SNMP, as shown in Figure 2.7. Unlike the other SNMP PDUs, traps do not warrant a response from the receiving network. The fields from a trap include:

PDU Type: Indicates the PDU type is a trap.

Enterprise: Contains the MIB object `sysObjectID` of the sending agent. The `sysObjectID` object includes information regarding the vendor of the agent that sent the trap.

Agent-address: Represents the IP address of the sending agent.

Generic-trap: One of the predefined trap values listed in Table 2.4.

Specific-trap: More detailed information about the trap. This is usually `zero` unless the generic-trap is an `enterpriseSpecific` trap.

Time-stamp: The amount of time between the generation of the trap and when the device was last initialized expressed in tens of milliseconds.

Variable-binding: Vendor specific information related to the trap.

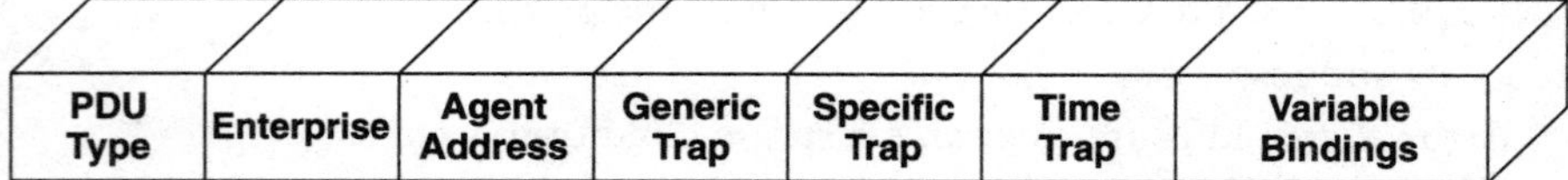

Figure 2.7 *Trap Message Format.*

Seven general trap types have been predefined and are listed in Table 2.4. The `enterpriseSpecific` trap type is provided as a mechanism for custom or proprietary traps to be defined that do not fit within the other generic trap types.

Table 2.4 *SNMP Predefined Traps*

Trap Type	**Meaning**
`ColdStart (0)`	The device is restarting or reinitializing itself such that the agent or configuration may be changed. Usually, this indicates a crash or other reboot condition
`WarmStart (1)`	The device is restarting or reinitializing itself such that no changes are made to the agent or configuration. Usually, this implies a simple refresh or reboot of the operating system environment
`LinkDown (2)`	Indicates a failure on one of the device's communications links

(Cont'd)

Table 2.4 *SNMP Predefined Traps (Cont'd)*

Trap Type	Meaning
`LinkUp (3)`	Indicates that a device's communication link is now up and running
`AuthenticationFailure (4)`	An authentication or security failure has occurred on the device. Typically, this indicates an invalid SNMP community string has been used
`EgpNeighborLoss (5)`	Indicates that external gateway protocol (EGP) neighbor, of which the device is a peer, has been labeled down and the relationship no longer is valid
`EnterpriseSpecific (6)`	Indicates that some vendor specific event has occurred. Vendors use this generic trap type to represent their own proprietary traps

GetBulkRequest

This PDU is issued by an SNMPv2 manager or application to minimize network interaction and permit the agent to return larger size packets (as compared to the GetNextRequest or GetRequest), thus improving the efficiency of obtaining a large number of objects from the agent. This uses the same PDU format as most other SNMPv1 operators. The only difference is the re-naming of the *Error-status* and *Error-index* (from the Response PDU) fields to *non-repeaters* and *max-repetitions*, respectively. These fields are defined as follows:

- *Non-repeaters:* The number of MIB objects that should be retrieved once at most.

- *Max-repetitions:* The maximum number of times other MIB objects should be retrieved.

InformRequest

The InformRequest PDU is issued by an SNMPv2 entity acting in a manager role to another SNMPv2 entity acting in the same role for the purpose of providing network management information. The major function of this PDU is to provide distributed SNMP management capabilities. Thus, an agent can implement this PDU to provide management-like services and functions. The format of this PDU is the same as the GetRequest and other related PDUs.

SNMP Response Codes

The error codes returned from an SNMPv1 agent were very limited. For example, if an SNMP manager requested the set operation on a MIB object and the agent couldn't perform the set as requested, the agent would reply with `noSuchName`. With the addition of more error codes in SNMPv2, the agent would reply with `notWritable` in this situation. The complete list of SNMP response codes is included in Table 2.5.

Table 2.5 *SNMP Response Codes*

Response Code	Description
SNMPv1	
`tooBig`	Returned by the agent if the response to a request would be too large to send
`noSuchName`	Returned by the agent in either of these two cases: 1, if a set operation is attempted for an object that is not in the MIB view or 2, if a set operation is attempted for an object that is in the MIB view, but its object is `read-only`. This code is now used for proxy compatibility

(Cont'd)

Table 2.5 *SNMP Response Codes (Cont'd)*

Response Code	**Description**
`badValue`	Returned by the agent that has detected an error in the PDU variable binding list. This code is now used for proxy compatibility
`Read-only`	Returned by the agent. This code is now used for proxy compatibility
`genError`	Returned by the agent when processing of a PDU fails for a reason other than what is listed in this table
SNMPv2	
`noAccess`	The variable is outside the defined MIB view for this operation to succeed
`notWritable`	The variable exists within the agent, but the agent is unable to modify the object
`WrongType`	The value supplied is of the wrong data type as defined by ASN.1
`WrongLength`	The value supplied is of the wrong length
`WrongEncoding`	The value supplied was not encoded correctly
`WrongValue`	The value supplied is not within the range required for the object type
`NoCreation`	The object doesn't exist and the agent is unable to create an instance of this object

(Cont'd)

Table 2.5 *SNMP Response Codes (Cont'd)*

Response Code	Description
`InconsistentName`	The object doesn't exist and the agent is unable to create an instance of this object because the name is inconsistent with the values of other related objects
`InconsistentValue`	The object provided is inconsistent with the values of the managed objects
`resourceUnavailable`	A needed resource within the agent can't be reserved to complete the request

Transmission of an SNMP Message

The following series of events occurs when a network manager formulates an SNMP message:

1. The basic PDU is constructed.
2. The PDU is passed to the security service layer if available.
3. The protocol layer formats the message, including the version and community information.
4. The entire message is now encoded using ASN.1 rules.
5. The message is passed to the transport service so that it will be delivered to the receiving entity.

The following series of events occurs when an agent device receives an SNMP message:

1. A basic check is performed to ensure the message is formatted correctly. The message is discarded if any errors are encountered.
2. The protocol version information is verified. If there is a mismatch, the message is discarded.
3. The security service attempts to verify the sending entity. If this fails, a trap is generated and the message is discarded.

4. The PDU is decoded.

5. The PDU is processed.

Connectionless Protocol

SNMP is a connectionless protocol, which means that it doesn't support the concept of establishing and controlling a dedicated connection like TELNET or FTP. SNMP transmits information between an agent and a manager by the use of requests and return responses. This removes the burden from agents of having to support additional protocols and processes associated with connection-based schemes. Therefore, SNMP provides its own mechanism to address reliability and error detection.

Master and Subagent

When deploying network management software, you commonlyhave a single agent installed on each system that will be managed. In the case of networking devices such as network routers and switches, usually only a single agent is available. In either case, the agents will communicate with one or more network managers using the standard SNMP port of `161`. For most needs, a single agent approach makes sense and is appropriate. However, there are instances when more than one agent is necessary to achieve the desired level of manageability. For example, workstation manufacturers will often provide an SNMP agent within their operating system. This particular system agent will usually support a limited number of operating system functions and parameters. If we wish to manage database services on this same system via SNMP then this will require that we install another agent to specifically monitor the database functions. This poses a problem because both agents will typically be accessed by the SNMP manager using the standard port. Further, when the agents are started by the system, the first agent will start and open the port `161` and will operate normally. However, when the second agent starts and attempts to do the same, it will get an error stating that the port is busy and it should abort operation.

Two possible approaches can be used to address this port problem. First, one of the agents can be configured to use an alternative port instead of standard `161`. This solution will work if the agent can be made to support another port when it is started by the system. Many system agents do support alternative ports, but this is by no means the rule. The major drawback to this solution is that any SNMP managers used to poll the agent must now be configured to support this new port as well. This doesn't pose a significant problem when only a small number of non-standard ports are used. However, if this solution is used on a large scale, say with many system agents all using non-standards ports across a large number of systems, the approach loses its appeal because of the administrative burden it may introduce.

The other solution might be considered more elegant, because it involves using a master agent and one or more subagents. A master agent solves the port conflict problem by becoming the keeper of the standard SNMP port and forwards all the SNMP traffic to the appropriate subagent. Subagents are normal SNMP agents, but they are registered with the master agent and are assigned non-standard ports that are used to communicate with the master agent. SNMP messages from managers are sent to the master agent, who in turn delivers the message to the correct subagent using the port it dynamically assigned to the subagent. Figure 2.8 shows a diagram of the master/subagent architecture. One major benefit of this solution it that it alleviates the administration task of modifying the SNMP managers cited as the first solution. Also, this solution can scale very well because new subagents can be added in a straightforward manner.

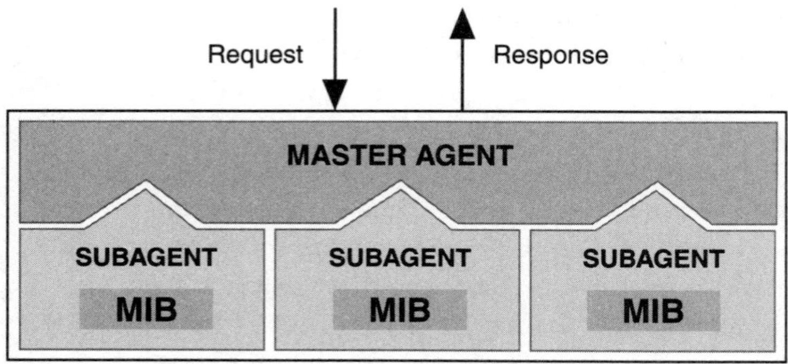

Figure 2.8 *Master/Subagent Architecture.*

On the negative side, the master agent can pose a problem because it can crash or otherwise become inoperative. This would have the adverse effect of disabling the connectivity to the subagents. Because this particular problem can be said of other software systems as well, the risk, although not zero, isn't necessarily a significant factor. Also, because the master agent is responsible for delivering the SNMP to the appropriate subagent, it takes a certain amount of processing time and overhead. This might be a factor in time-critical management functions.

Several proposals and products have been put forth in an attempt to provide a standard mechanism that supports master and subagent architectures. These include SMUX[1](RFC 1227), AgentX (RFC 2257), and vendor specific products like master agent on Solaris and the master agent on HP-UX. All of these accomplish the same purpose: permitting two or more agents to operate on the same system without port conflict problems.

1. This RFC as been promoted to historic status

03

TCP/IP Protocol Suite

As a network manager or administrator, you will be required to interact directly with the TCP/IP protocols and related services. As a result, you will need a good understanding of TCP/IP and associated protocols and applications. Many network management systems support TCP/IP as well. Today, TCP/IP is used extensively by many corporations, institutions, and other organizations to address their networking requirements. It is considered the protocol family of choice by networking manufacturers, operating system vendors, and users alike. In fact, the world's largest network, the Internet, uses TCP/IP exclusively.

If you have accessed a Web site, transferred files from an FTP server, or sent email via the Internet, you have indirectly used the TCP/IP protocols. Fundamentally, TCP/IP provides a standard way to deliver data from one system to another without the concern for operating system differences and network hardware. TCP/IP is an acronym that stands for two separate protocols: Transmission Control Protocol (TCP) and Internet Protocol (IP). However, TCP/IP generally refers to these protocols, plus a suite of related protocols. For example, the File Transfer Protocol (FTP) uses TCP/IP and provides a basic file transfer facility across devices that support TCP/IP. If the device supports TCP/IP, it is generally assumed to support FTP and a host of protocols and other services as well.

Today, the TCP/IP suite is supported on every major computer operating system available. As such, it is considered the most popular networking protocol and many of the same TCP/IP services are available on different versions of Unix. This is good news, because many of the core functions of TCP/IP and applications are the same across different versions of Unix. The operations of TCP/IP are independent of operating system or computer platform. The protocol hides the underlying operating system details and provides a common framework for establishing connectivity among systems.

Many networking devices such as routers, switches, and specialized devices implement TCP/IP protocols for local administration and control. Generally speaking, a small core set of services is available on these devices. Table 3.1 shows the list of services available on some of the most popular networking devices. As you can see, SNMP, TELNET, and FTP are the most widely implemented services.

The TCP/IP suite is built on industry standards and is documented completely in Request for Comments (RFCs). This means the protocol will remain open and standard and no single vendor can own the protocols or develop proprietary extensions. As a result, many networking hardware vendors provide support for TCP/IP in their products.

Table 3.1 *TCP/IP Protocol Support for Administration*

Device Type	TCP/IP Protocols
3Com CoreBuilder Switch	HTTP, FTP, TELNET, and SNMP
3Com RMON probe	TFTP and SNMP
Cisco 2500 Router	HTTP, FTP, TELNET, and SNMP
Lexmark Laser Printer	FTP and SNMP

TCP/IP is independent of the datalink protocol and can be used with many different networking technologies, including FDDI, Ethernet, ATM, Token Ring, Frame Relay, and SMDS. TCP/IP makes it possible to build a truly heterogeneous network consisting of products and network technologies from many different vendors and sources. In fact, the Internet, which is considered the world's largest network, consists of devices from many networking vendors that operate together. That's not to say the Internet doesn't have its share of networking issues or problems but, for the most part, many would agree that interoperability between equipment vendors isn't a major factor for the established core set of TCP/IP protocols.

From a management standpoint, many of the tools used to administer TCP/IP systems are consistent across most Unix operating system versions. These tools are described in Chapter 5, "Network Management Agents." However, one issue that can be a problem is that each Unix operating system vendor can and does implement non-protocol details differently. For example, how the IP address information is stored on each network device is not covered by any RFC standard, nor should it be. The present TCP/IP suite does provide a mechanism to dynamically assign IP addresses to devices and it also mandates that they be uniquely assigned to each device attached to the network. However, IP addresses are stored on a local system and are not a protocol matter, but rather a network management or system configuration issue, which is traditionally resolved at the operating system level. Each operating system vendor provides its own solutions of how IP address information or other operating system parameters are to be stored.

OSI Model

Networking protocols including TCP/IP can be mapped to a general network model. This model defines the relationship and services that each protocol will provide to other associated protocols, services, and applications. The most common standard network model is based on Open Standard Interconnect (OSI). The OSI model is represented by a series of layers stacked one upon another which, when viewed collectively, represent the operation of an entire network. Each layer represents a unique view of the elements that make up the network. The layers of the OSI model consist of the following:

- Application
- Presentation
- Session
- Transport
- Network
- Datalink
- Physical

Application Layer

Provides services to users including file transfer, electronic email, remote host access, and many other services.

Presentation

Used to provide a common interface for applications to the lower layers and implement common services that might include encryption, reformatting, and compression.

Session

Provides the mechanism to establish, maintain, and terminate sessions between cooperating applications.

Transport

Ensures reliable, transparent data transfer, flow control, and data error detection and recovery between two endpoints.

Network

Provides upper layer protocol transparency because different network communication methodologies may be used. This layer is responsible for establishing, maintaining, and terminating connections for different networks.

Datalink

Provides data transfer service on the physical link using frames; handles error detection, flow control, and related services.

Physical

Addresses the mechanism connectivity requirements (such as cables and connectors) and provides transmission of a bit stream that involves controlling voltage characteristics to produce the appropriate signals.

TCP/IP Protocol Architecture

The TCP/IP suite can be placed or overlaid on the OSI model to better understand TCP/IP's protocol operation and its relationship to other protocols. Figure 3.1 shows a pictorial view of where TCP/IP fits into the OSI model.

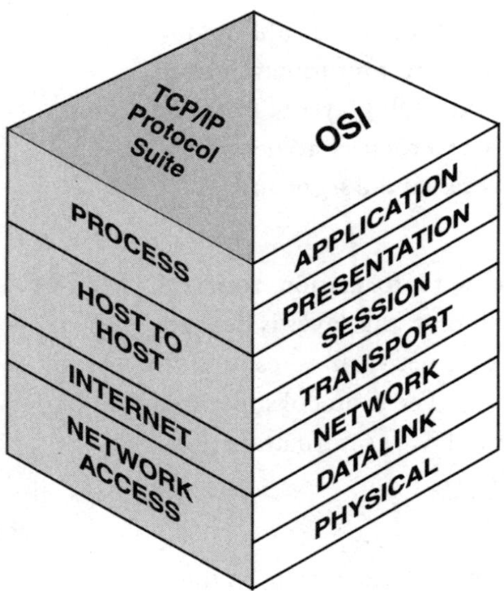

Figure 3.1 *TCP/IP over the OSI Networking Model.*

As shown in Figure 3.1, the TCP/IP model consists of four layers. Each layer maps to one or more of the OSI layers, which include:

- Process
- Host-to-host
- Internet
- Network Access

Except for network access, the other three component layers are software based and consist of programmed modules that provide the required functionality. Typically, these components are incorporated into operating systems to provide generalized access.

Process Layer

This layer provides user applications and interfaces with the host-to-host layer. Additional protocols and services are also found on this layer. The process layer maps to the presentation and application layers, which are defined within the OSI model. Applications on this layer include TELNET, FTP, SMTP, and many others.

Host-to-Host Layer

This layer is responsible for ensuring that data is reliable and that each higher-level service obtains the correct information from the sending entity. The protocol supported on this layer is TCP. The layer maps to the OSI transport layer. The term used to describe information on the host-to-host layer is called the *segment*.

Internet Layer

This layer provides an unreliable flow of information from one network to another. From an OSI standpoint, this layer is defined as the network layer. The Internet layer (or network) is responsible for routing between different IP networks. The protocol supported on this layer is IP. The term used to describe the information processed on this layer is called the *packet*.

Network Access Layer

The network access layer involves physical attachment to the network, which traditionally requires a hardware interface from the network to a computer's internal bus. This layer includes both physical and datalink layers from the OSI model. The network access component defines the network architecture and topology. Some examples include Ethernet, FDDI and Token Ring. The term used to describe the information processed on this layer is called the *frame*.

A small driver program, which is provided by the interface manufacturers, is also needed to interface the hardware to the operating system.

Process Layer Services

The TCP/IP services on the process layer include end-user tools, additional protocols, and system services. Found on different Unix platforms, TCP/IP provides a common mechanism to share files, send/receive email, access systems remotely, transfer files between systems, and accomplish other networking tasks. Although the TCP/IP protocol and application suite is large, many Unix system vendors provide a smaller subset of these services. Table 3.2 lists many of the core TCP/IP services generally available on Unix systems.

End-User Tools

The end-user tools, which are common to many Unix system implementations of TCP/IP, are applications that are generally available to normal system users. As a result, these tools do not require system root privileges for operation. For example, general users without any special consideration from an administration standpoint can invoke the TELNET and FTP commands. Some services within the TCP/IP suite refer to both end-user applications and protocols. TELNET is a good example of this because it represents both a user tool and a communication protocol.

It is interesting to note that certain organizations disable some TCP/IP services as a way of tightening security. One organization in particular did not want its users to have the ability to send or receive email on core development systems and removed the SMTP servers from those systems. Another way that organizations typically disable services is by blocking access to system ports using a firewall device or router.

Additional Protocols

The TCP/IP suite includes additional higher-level protocols that exist above the network layer and provide the necessary details to ensure that applications can communicate. For example, the file transfer protocol (FTP) defines how files and associated information are transmitted across the network. The protocol handles all the details related to user authorization, naming, and data representation among heterogeneous systems. As mentioned above, many of the associated TCP/IP applications have a corresponding protocol of the same name. This can cause some confusion because FTP represents both an end-user application and a protocol. In practice, however, this isn't a big problem because end-user applications on Unix are lower case (such as `ftp`) and protocols are generally written in upper case.

System Services

TCP/IP system services include those facilities that are provided to all users of the system and can only be controlled by the system administrator. System services might include specific system processes and special configuration files used by those processes. System network services are usually started automatically when the system is started or when the system is rebooted.

Table 3.2 *Core TCP/IP Services*

Service	**Description**
ARP/RARP	Address Resolution Protocol Reverse Address Resolution Protocol
DHCP	Dynamic Host Configuration Protocol
DNS	Domain Name Service
FINGER	Lookup Remote/Local User
FTP	File Transfer Protocol
HTTP	Hyper Text Transfer Protocol

(Cont'd)

Table 3.2 *Core TCP/IP Services (Cont'd)*

Service	Description
ICMP	Internet Control Message Protocol
LPD	Line Printer Daemon
NFS	Network File System
NIS	Network Information Services
NTP	Network Time Protocol
RDISC	Router Discovery Protocol
REXEC	Remote Execution Service
RIP	Routing Information Protocol
RLOGIN	Remote Login Service
RPC	Remote Procedure Call
RSH	Remote Shell Service
RWHO	Remote Monitoring of Users
RWALL	Remote Message Broadcast
RADIO	Radio Transmitter/Receiver
SMTP	Simple Mail Transfer Protocol
TALK	Talk to Remote/Local User
TELNET	Access to Remote System
TFTP	Trivial File Transfer Protocol
WHOIS	Remote Lookup Service

ARP—The Address Resolution Protocol provides mapping between lower-level datalink protocols (such as Ethernet and Token Ring) and high-level protocols such as IP. ARP maps datalink (i.e., hardware interface) addresses to IP addresses. The Reverse Address Resolution Protocol (RARP) is used to go the other way; it maps IP addresses to datalink protocol addresses. ARP and RARP are described fully later in this section.

DHCP—The Dynamic Host Configuration Protocol is used to provide startup (booting) information to client systems. DHCP supports IP address information, operating system configuration information, and other related information. From a network address standpoint, DHCP is an excellent way to manage IP addresses across an enterprise. For example, clients can dynamically obtain IP information while booting, thus removing the burden of your having to configure each machine.

DNS—The Domain Name System is used to map between hostnames and IP addresses. The client side provides the ability to resolve names and addresses by making requests to one or more DNS servers only. The server side component, named, listens for requests and either looks up entries in a local database or contacts another name server for resolution.

FINGER—The finger services permit the lookup of user information on either a local or a remote system. The finger service isn't a protocol, just an end-user program that uses TCP for communication with the `in.fingerd` server.

FTP—The File Transfer Protocol is used to transfer files between systems. FTP provides basic user authorization that includes using the login name and password on the remote system. The FTP interface is basic, but provides a simple way to transfer single or multiple files. The FTP server is known as `in.ftpd`. FTP supports transmission of both binary and ASCII data files.

HTTP—The Hyper Text Transfer Protocol is used to transmit Web pages and documents from a Web server to a browser.

ICMP—The Internet Control Message Protocol is a network diagnostic facility using the IP protocol. The PING tool uses the ICMP echo request/reply protocol to determine node connectivity.

LPD—The Line Printer Daemon is used to provide a printing facility for either the network or directly attached printers.

NFS—The Network File System facility provides file sharing between systems on a local network.

NIS—The Network Information Service is a directory lookup facility that provides client access to server databases. The types of information typically used within NIS include login, host, file sharing, and other system configuration information. NIS has several components.

NTP—The Network Time Protocol provides an excellent way to ensure that time and date information is synchronized between all networked Unix systems.

RDISC—The ICMP network Router Discovery Protocol is used to find routers and build a table of routes to attached networks.

REXEC—The Remote Execution Service provides execution of Unix commands on remote systems. REXEC uses a specialized authentication procedure that includes reading both the login name and password and comparing this information with the remote system. If the login information matches, the Unix command is executed. The family of remote commands includes `rsh`, `rwho`, `rlogin`, and others.

RIP— The Routing Information Protocol is used to propagate routing information between network system devices such as routers. Unix systems support RIP as well. On Solaris systems, if two or more network interfaces are installed, the system will automatically perform routing functions. The routing function is incorporated in the `in.routed` system process that is started when the system is initialized.

RLOGIN—The Remote Login Service is used to access a remote Unix system. It provides the same basic services as the Telnet program.

RPC—The Remote Procedure Call is a mechanism and protocol that permits the execution of procedures across the network in a network neutral fashion.

RSH—The Remote Shell Service provides a shell to the remote system.

RWHO—Provides a list of logged in users on a remote system. Similar to the Unix who command.

RWALL—Provides a way to write to users on a remote system. Similar to the Unix wall command.

RADIO—Radio broadcast facility.

SMTP—The Simple Mail Transfer Protocol provides the mail delivery mechanism that is used by many electronic mail packages and is the standard mailing protocol for the Internet. The `sendmail` system program implements SMTP and is responsible for mail propagation between systems.

TALK—Talk is a two-way communication facility that can be used to talk to other system users either on local or remote systems. Talk isn't a protocol, but just an end-user system utility that uses the UDP protocol.

TELNET—TELNET is the name for a protocol and end-user system utility. The TELNET utility provides a user interface to a remote Unix system. Users can log into other systems over the network and execute commands as if local to that system. Their terminal is connected via the TELNET protocol to the remote system using the `in.telnetd` server process. The TELNET protocol defines a network virtual interface that controls the flow and interpretation of a character stream between systems.

TFTP—The Trivial File Transfer Protocol is used to provide a more simplistic file transfer facility as compared to FTP. TFTP is considered a light version of FTP because it doesn't support a robust authorization mechanism or command set. TFTP is used mainly to download system configuration information or data.

WHOIS — A white pages lookup utility. The WHOIS service will search for individual users and other information from standard Internet servers.

Additional Services

Many public domain TCP/IP services and applications are also available via the Internet. Some of the resources available are improvements over the existing core set of services, while other applications provide new services and features. Many (but certainly not all) TCP/IP applications are listed in Table 3.3.

Table 3.3 *Additional TCP/IP Services*

Service	Description
ARCHIE	FTP Search Facility
GOPHER	Document Retrieval System
IRC	Internet Relay Chat Service
NNTP	Network News Transfer Protocol
WAIS	Wide Area Information Servers

ARCHIE—Archie is a database of anonymous FTP sites and their contents. Archie keeps track of the entire contents of a very large number of anonymous FTP sites and allows you to search for files on those sites using various kinds of filename searches.

GOPHER—Document retrieval system that is available via menu-driven interface (for character base devices) and the World Wide Web (WWW).

IRC—Internet Relay Chat is a way to send either public or private text messages to one or more subscribers in real time.

NNTP—The Network News Transfer Protocol provides the ability to transfer news files (also known as Usenet) between a client and server.

WAIS—Another facility to help search for indexed material and files.

Host-to-Host Layer

The host-to-host layer, or OSI network layer, is responsible for providing a robust data delivery mechanism between different network entities. The standard that provides this service is the transmission control protocol (TCP). Within a network, data can be lost or destroyed when transmission errors or network hardware failures occur. Data can also be delivered out of order and with significant delays before reaching the final destination. TCP was designed and developed to address these types of network related problems. TCP is responsible for ensuring that data arrives in the correct order and free from errors. It accomplishes these tasks by providing the following services:

Virtual Connections

TCP provides a virtual connection interface to the network that is analogous to the way phone calls are established in the telephone network. Conceptually, a user calls another machine to request data transfer. After all the details of the connection setup are complete, data transmission can be made between applications. From an application perspective, the TCP connection looks and behaves as if a dedicated hardware link has been established. However, this is only an illusion provided by the TCP streams interface.

Sequenced Data

To ensure reliable transfer, TCP keeps track of the data it transmits by assigning a sequence number to each segment. The sequence number uniquely identifies each data segment within a connection and is used to provide a positive acknowledgement to the sending entity. No acknowledgement indicates that the message should be retransmitted. The sequence number is also used to reorder any segments that might have arrived out of order. How can segments arrive out of order? Consider, for example, the network in Figure 3.2.

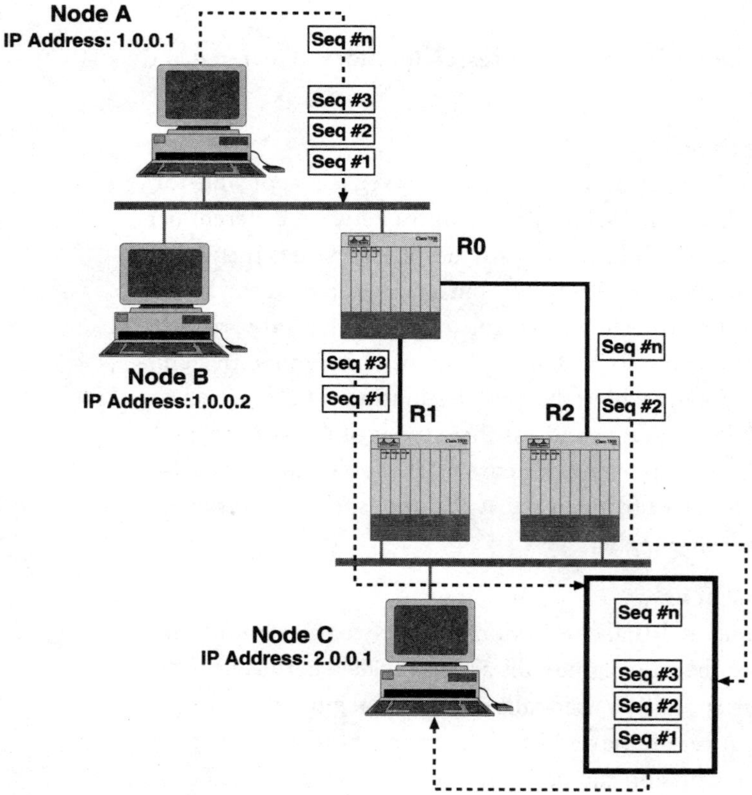

Figure 3.2 *TCP Segment Numbers in Action.*

Because more than one network path to `Node C` exists, it is possible that some TCP segments might travel via `Router R2` instead of `Router R1`. Should the path between `Node C` and `R1` become temporarily heavily loaded, for example, segments may be routed via another path. As a result, segments using the `R2` path could arrive at the destination sooner than segments using the `R1` path.

Stream Abstraction Interface

From the application layer standpoint, TCP provides a buffered byte-oriented interface between two applications or processes. The data transmitted from the source entity is exactly the same information the destination receives. For example, if the sending entity transmits the message "hello world" the destination would receive "hello world." As it turns out, this is a very useful and convenient feature for developing networking applications and services. Also, the TCP stream is buffered, which means that applications have more flexibility when it comes to processing the data from the network.

Ports, Sockets, and Connections

TCP ports are addresses that specify a network resource and are used to uniquely identify an individual application or service on the system. There are quite a few well-known address ports in use today and many of them can be found in the `/etc/services` file on Unix systems. Table 3.4 contains a partial list of some of the most commonly used TCP ports.

Table 3.4 *Common TCP Ports*

Port	Application/Service
20	FTP Data
21	FTP
23	TELNET
25	SMTP
53	DNS
119	NNTP
161	SNMP
8080	HTTP

To further understand the function of these ports, consider the services of the Unix `inetd` process. `Inetd` is called the super Internet server because it is responsible for connecting service requests from the network to the actual server program. `Inetd` knows which process to invoke because it can determine relationships between ports and services. By processing the `/etc/services` file and the `inetd.conf` configuration file, `inetd` can make the network request to the appropriate service as needed. Figure 3.3 shows the operation of `inetd` when a remote user requests a TELNET session.

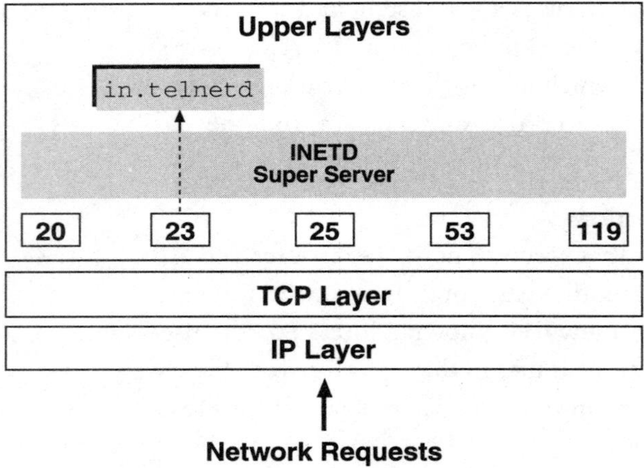

Figure 3.3 *INETD Operation with TELNET Request.*

It is important to understand that TCP uses a connection-oriented model whereby one network entity may call another to establish either a half or full duplex session. In a full duplex mode, two independent sessions are established between systems and data can flow between each system without an apparent interaction. In the half duplex mode, only a single session is made. A network entity may first establish a full duplex session and then shut down the other session if necessary. On the other hand, a service may initially establish a single half duplex session for control purposes and then start another session to carry out some specific action or task. This application behavior might seem a little strange, but the FTP service, for example, operates in this fashion.

When an FTP session begins, it first establishes a single session to the destination system. This session is used for user authentication and the command interface. When the user specifies a file transfer or executes a remote command, another session is established to service the request. After the transfer is complete, the newly created session is closed. This process is repeated for each separate transaction.

Sockets are ports that the system allocates on the user's behalf when executing network applications or other services. Because the operating system generates a unique socket number, no two simultaneously running applications on the same system will have the same socket number. On some Unix systems, the allocation of sockets begins above `1024`.

In the context of a connection, TCP uses four pieces of information to uniquely identify one session from another: source IP address, source port, destination IP address, and destination port. This is important to remember because many sessions to the same application or service can be established, even from the same host. For example, two different users can `telnet` to the same destination host without any conflicts among the ports. This is accomplished by the fact that TCP uses all four addressing elements to distinguish a unique session. Figure 3.4 shows the relationship of the TCP elements with different sessions.

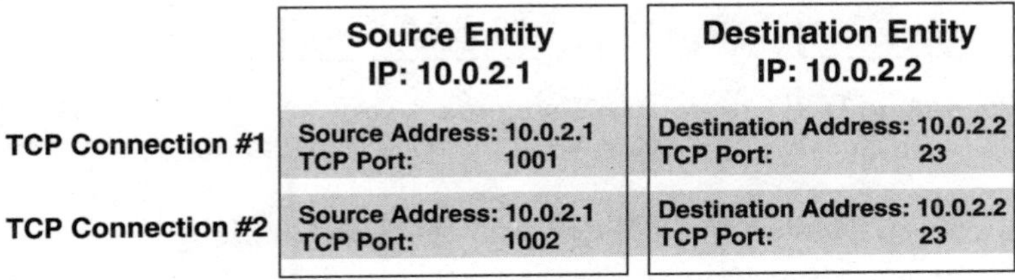

Figure 3.4 *Two TCP Sessions from Same Source/Destination.*

Positive Acknowledgement

One way TCP provides reliability is by ensuring that every message transmitted is confirmed by the receiving entity. The confirmation of TCP messages is known as positive acknowledgement and is used to ensure that the receiving entity has obtained all the segments that have been sent. When a TCP message is sent, the sending entity starts a timer. If no acknowledgement is received before the time expires, TCP assumes the message was lost or damaged in some way, preventing its delivery. As a result, TCP sends another message to replace the first and starts the timer process over again. This process continues until all segments have been acknowledged or until an internal error threshold is reached. If the sender receives no acknowledgement for outstanding segments after the internal error count has been reached, the connection will be terminated.

Establishing and Closing a TCP Connection

As previously discussed, TCP uses connections that provide a reliable, robust data transfer facility. The procedure for establishing or shutting down a connection is not a magical process. Instead, each TCP entity follows the same set of rules when creating a session or terminating one. To establish a connection, TCP uses a 3-way handshake protocol, which is outlined in Figure 3.5.

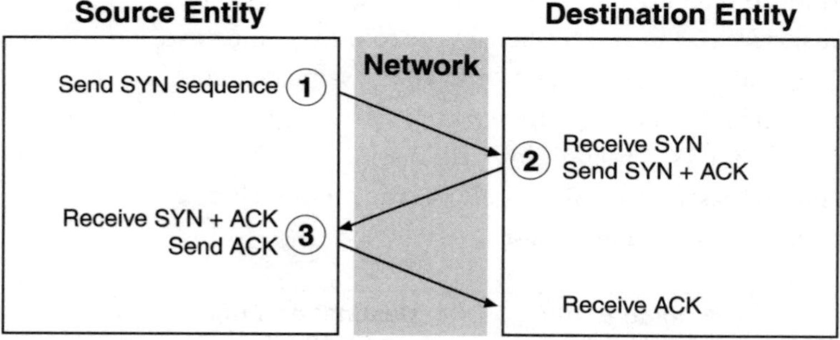

Figure 3.5 *Opening a TCP Connection Using the 3-way Handshake.*

First, the source transmits a `SYN` message segment. The `SYN` (pronounced "sin") or synchronization is a request to start a TCP session and have the `SYN` bit set in the code field. Next, the destination responds with an `ACK` segment that has both the `SYN` bit and `ACK` bits set in the code field, indicating that it has accepted the request and is continuing the handshake protocol. Finally, the source sends an `ACK` segment, which informs the destination that both entities agree that a connection has been established and that segments can now be transmitted and received.

To close an established session, TCP uses a modified 3-way handshake, which is shown in Figure 3.6. First, the source transmits a FIN or finish segment (The FIN bit is set in the code field) as a result of the application wishing to close its side of the connection. Recall that TCP views these connections as full duplex; therefore, either party may terminate their side of the connection. Once the application on the destination closes the connection, TCP emits a FIN segment to the source. Next, the source receives the FIN sequence and sends an acknowledgement.

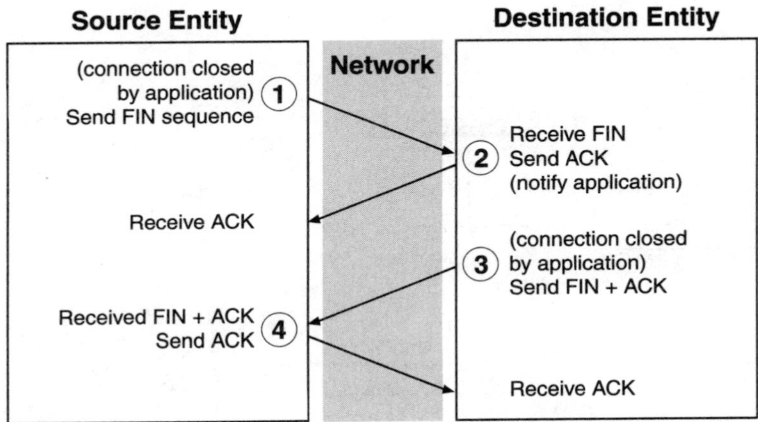

Figure 3.6 *Closing a TCP Connection.*

Please note that it takes three segments to create a TCP connection and four additional segments to shut it down. A total of seven messages are required to operate a TCP connection not including any data transfer segments.

State Machine

The operation of TCP is best described using a state machine model, which controls the basic operation of the protocol. Figure 3.7 shows the TCP state machine model. Each TCP connection goes through a series of defined states. Movement from one state to another is the result of an event or transition. The label on each transition shows what TCP receives to cause the change between states. For instance, we discussed that TCP must open a connection before data can be transferred. Normally, each TCP side of the connection starts in the CLOSED state. When a connection is desired, a transition from the CLOSED to SYN SENT state is made. At this point the client side sends a SYN packet. If the SYN packet is accepted, the remote side emits an ACK, which causes a transition from the SYN SENT to SYN RECIEVED state. Once the final ACK has been received, the ESTABLISHED state is reached and data transfer may begin. When a TCP connection has been made, it will remain in the ESTABLISHED state until either side wishes to terminate the connection or some error occurs.

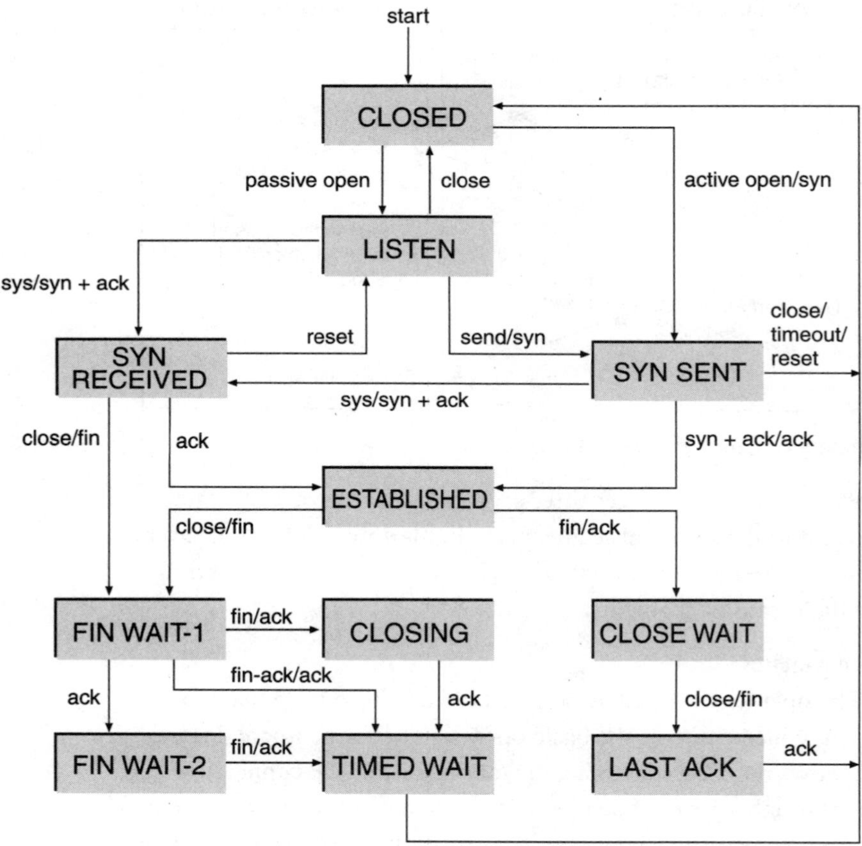

Figure 3.7 *TCP State Machine.*

When a TCP connection is terminated (either by the source or destination), the connection moves to either the CLOSED WAIT or FIN

WAIT-1 state. If the source sends a FIN segment, TCP transitions to the CLOSE WAIT state, which eventually terminates the connection. When the destination wants to close the connection, a change is made to the FIN WAIT-1 state. TCP has an elaborate mechanism to ensure that segments from previous connections do not interfere with existing ones. TCP maintains a timer, known as the maximum segment lifetime (MSL), which contains the maximum time an old segment may remain alive within the network. As a result, TCP moves to the TIMED WAIT state after closing the connection. It remains within this state for twice the MSL. After this, if any segments arrive for the connection, they are rejected.

TCP Sequence Format

TCP defines a sequence format, which includes all the necessary information to ensure that segments get to the correct destination and also contains additional control information. Figure 3.8 shows the TCP segment format.

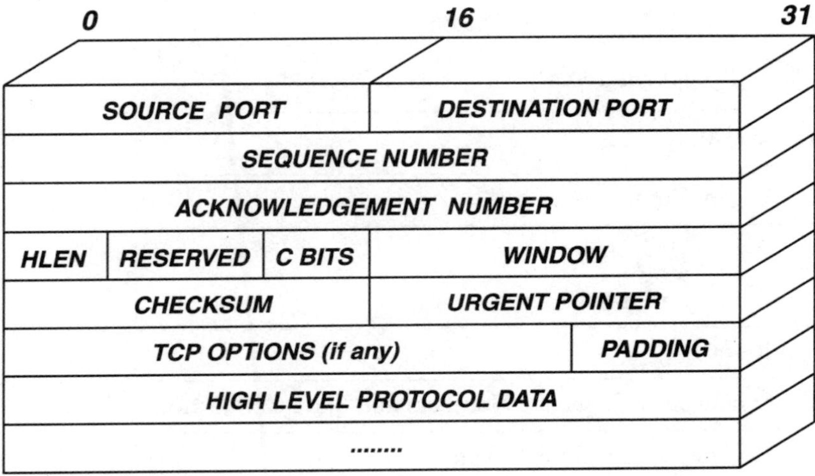

Figure 3.8 *TCP Segment Format.*

The TCP segment fields include:

Source Port: The protocol (or service) that sent this segment.

Destination Port: The protocol (or service) that will receive this segment.

Sequence Number: The position in the byte stream of the sender

Acknowledgment Number: The number of the byte that the source expects to receive in the next segment

Hlen: Integer that specifies the length of the segment header

Code Bits: Details on the purpose and content of the segment

Window: Specification of how much data TCP is willing to accept

Checksum: Integer that is used to verify the TCP header and data integrity

Urgent Pointer: Field for indicating that this segment should be processed right away

Options: Details for negotiating the maximum segment size

Data: High-level protocols or application specific information

Code Bits

These bits indicate the type of TCP segment and how it should be processed. Table 3.5 shows established codes and their associated meanings. These codes are analogous to the type field in the Ethernet frame, which means that TCP segments are self-identifying.

Table 3.5 *TCP Segment Types*

Codes	Meaning
URG	Urgent Pointer
ACK	Acknowledgement
PSH	Request a Push
RST	Reset
SYN	Synchronize Sequence Numbers and Start Connection
FIN	Reached End of Byte Stream

Window

TCP has an elaborate mechanism to handle data buffering, flow control, and retransmission of unacknowledged segments. The window field is used to help TCP determine how much data it is willing to accept in the next segment. The data size of a transaction can significantly impact overall network and application performance. To understand why, assume for the moment that a TCP connection has been established between two nodes, `X` and `Y`, and that during the previous transactions, `X` has specified to `Y` a TCP window of `1024` (which is the default). Now, `Y` begins to experience high usage and also begins to run low on available resources such as memory. Many reasons can exist for this situation. At this time, `X` is still sending TCP messages to `Y`, but `Y` is having trouble acknowledging (or perhaps even processing) segments from `X` due to the size of the messages. Since `Y` is having resource problems, the next segment sent to `X` contains a smaller window size which informs `X` that it must adjust the amount of data contained in subsequent TCP messages. After `X` receives the new window size, it begins sending Y small amounts of data.

After the resource limitation has been resolved on `Y`, either by explicit action on the part of the system administrator or by the completion of the tasks which caused the resource problem in the first place, `Y` sends `X` a larger window size and resumes processing as before. Without the ability for TCP to dynamically adjust the size of segments, in the example, `Y` would begin to drop the messages it couldn't process. This, in turn, causes `X` to retransmit them, not only wasting processing cycles on `X`, but also wasting networking bandwidth due to the retransmitted messages.

Urgent Pointer

Because TCP provides a streamed interface, it is sometimes important that an application has a way to send an out-of-band or an urgent message to the other end of the connection without having to wait for the previous messages to be processed. An example of why out-of-band is important is a user wishing to terminate a remote login session using TELNET. Often, terminals provide interrupts or control signals, which can be used to inform applications that they should terminate. In this case, TCP uses the URG bit to indicate that this is an out-of-band segment and sets the urgent pointer to specify the position in the segment where the urgent data ends.

Options

The `options` field is used to negotiate the TCP segment size, useful in a situation when it is possible to establish either a higher or lower maximum transfer unit (MTU). MTU values can be different on different physical networks. For example, ATM has a higher MTU than Ethernet.

Internet Layer

The Internet (or network of the OSI model) layer provides a delivery service that is unreliable and based on a connectionless transfer protocol. As previously indicated, the Internet Protocol (IP) operates on this layer, providing a best effort transfer service, and is responsible for routing packets among different IP networks. IP packets may be lost, delayed, duplicated, and delivered out of order.

Two versions of the protocol have been defined. The most widely implemented version is 4 (known as IPv4) and, due to protocol deficiencies and resource limitations of this version, enhancements were made which resulted in a new version known as IPv6. However, version 6 hasn't been widely implemented within the networking industry.

The major characteristics and services of IP (version 4) include:

- Unreliable delivery
- Connectionless protocol
- Packet travel over different paths
- Address format
- Subnetting
- Routing

Unreliable Delivery

The term unreliable indicates that IP makes no attempt at guaranteeing the delivery of a packet to its destination. This is in sharp contrast to the behavior and services of transmission control protocol, which provides a reliable transfer facility that ensures message delivery. IP, on the other hand, provides a best effort delivery facility and does not ensure packet transfer, but it doesn't capriciously discard them either. Despite the fact that IP is not reliable, it doesn't mean that data carried with IP isn't delivered correctly. IP simply uses an upper-level protocol like TCP to ensure guaranteed data delivery.

Connectionless Protocol

IP is said to be connectionless because it does not establish a connection through which to transfer packets, which is contrary to the behavior of reliable transfer protocols. Packet delivery is based on IP address information contained within the packet itself. Each IP packet is self-contained and independent of any other packet and is not part of a pre-established agreement between network entities. Since no connection information is maintained within IP, packet delivery is simplified and more efficient.

Packets over Different Paths

With IP, packets may travel different paths to reach their final destination even though each packet might carry a smaller portion of a much larger message. This behavior is observed when IP packets travel within an Internet. Also, packets might arrive out of order.

IP Addressing

IP defines the format of addresses and requires that each network entity have its own unique address. Addresses contain both a network and a node identification pair, which is expressed as a single number. With IPv4, 32-bits are used to represent an IP address and are expressed in dotted notation. Each address is written as four decimal integers separated by decimal points. Five different classes have been defined within IPv4. However, in practice, only the first three primary classes are used to define a network/node pair, shown in Figure 3.9.

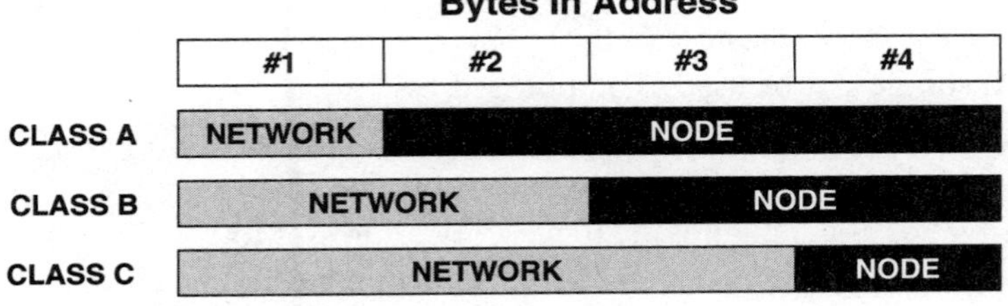

Figure 3.9 *Three Primary IP Address Classes.*

Each class specifies the format used to interpret how much of the address is used to represent the network and how much of the address is used to represent the node. The interpretations of addresses include:

Class A: The first byte is the network identification and the remaining bytes are used to specify the node. Network address range is `1-127`.

Class B: The first two bytes are the network identification and the remaining bytes are the node. Network address range is `128-191`.

Class C: The first three bytes are the network identification and the remaining byte is the node. Network address range is `192-223`.

When distinguishing the different classes, one way is to use the first byte rule. With this rule, the first byte determines to which class the address belongs. For example, using the IP address of `10.1.3.2`, `10` is the first byte of this address. The number `10` falls in the range of `1-127`, so this IP address is a Class A type and the network portion is `10` while the node portion is `1.3.2`.

IP also defines some reserved addresses that include loop-back and broadcast addresses. The loop-back network is defined as address `127` and is used as a private network for internal diagnostics and support with an IP device. This network address is reserved and is not supposed to be used as a genuine network address. In fact, the IP protocol specifications don't recommend its use on a live network. The loop-back address can be observed by issuing the Unix `ifconfig -a` command. The broadcast address defined as `255` is also considered special because it denotes a shorthand way to address all hosts within a given range. For example, given the network of `134.110.25.0`, which is a B Class network, the broadcast address of `134.110.255.255` addresses all devices within the entire `134.110` network. Because of the special meaning associated with `255`, it should not be used as a node address.

Assignment of IP addresses is accomplished through a central agency known as the network information center, or NIC. The NIC is responsible for assigning unique IP network addresses to any organization wishing to connect to the Internet. In many instances, a local Internet Service Provider (ISP) will request an IP address on your behalf or provide one of its own.

Subnetting

Subnetting is a mechanism to further divide a network into smaller subnetworks or subnets. One major motivation for implementing subnets is to distribute administration control of IP address allocation. Subnets also permit more effective use of existing addresses. With subnets, the node portion of the IP address is divided into two sections: the subnet address and node address as shown in Figure 3.10.

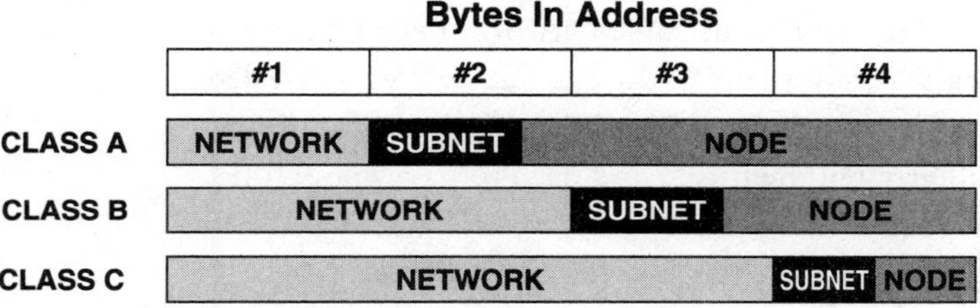

Figure 3.10 *Subnets Addressing.*

To implement subnetting, the following requirements must be met. First, a subnet address or mask must be created and incorporated within each of the device IP addresses that will participate within the subnet. This subnet mask is a special 32-bit address, which is expressed like a normal IP address using dotted decimal notation. As with a regular IP address, each of the octets within the subnet is in the range of `1` to `255`. But unlike IP addresses, the octets represent a set of masked bits that are combined with the device's IP address to yield the subnet network. In particular, determining the subnet involves combining the subnet mask and hostname with the Boolean `and` operator. Figure 3.11 shows the subnet calculation required.

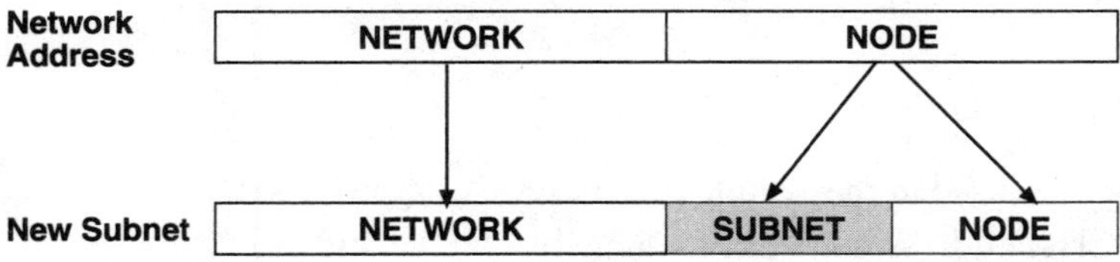

Figure 3.11 *Subnet Calculation.*

Second, each device that will participate in a subnet must use the same subnet mask address. In particular, for each interface defined on the local system, the subnet mask should be defined along with other interface parameters. For instance, under Unix the `ifconfig` command is invoked on every system interface installed in the system. The subnet mask information must be included when this system command is executed.

To further illustrate the implementation of a subnet, consider the sample network shown in Figure 3.12. In this network, we have four devices attached to the same network. Each of the devices has already received an IP address, but now we must determine what the subnet mask should be. We have determined that the network will grow in the future and need to have enough IP addresses in the subnet for approximately 200 devices. As a result, we will need to use at least 8 bits (1 octet) for the subnet.

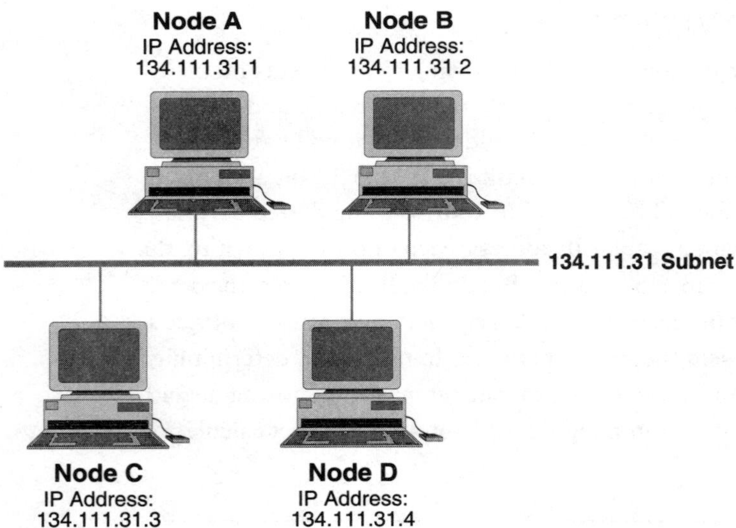

Figure 3.12 *Sample Subnet.*

The IP addresses used in the sample network are of type Class B. Recall that B Class addresses are in the range of `127-192` and the first two octets are the network address (`134.111`), while the remaining two (`31.1`, for instance) are node addresses. The only place we can take bits to use for the subnet is in the host portion of the address. We simply can't use any of the network address because that area of the address is restricted. With this in mind, we need to sub-divide the host portion into two, which is where the subnet mask comes into play. By using all ones (`1`) in the bits of the subnet fields and all zeros (`0`) in the bits of the node field, we can forge the desired subnet address by converting the IP address and subnet mask into binary:

(decimal)	(binary)	
`134.111.31.1`	`10000110 01101111 00011111.00000001`	(IP address)
`255.255.255.0`	`11111111.11111111.11111111.00000000`	(Subnet Mask)
`134.111.31.0`	`10000110 01101111 00011111.00000000`	(Subnet Address)

Applying the Boolean `and` will produce the subnet of address `134.111.31.0` or just the `31` subnet. After this subnet mask has been configured on every device within the subnet, every node, to determine the subnet address to which it belongs, will do the required `and` calculation. On many (if not all) Unix systems, this is an automatic task when the system's network services are started. To summarize, to subnet a network, include the following steps:

1. Determine the IP address class of the network you want to subnet.

2. Determine the amount of addresses you require for the subnet.

3. Determine if you can use a full octet (with at least a B Class address) for the subnet address.

4. Perform the Boolean `and` on one of the device addresses using the subnet mask.

5. Apply the subnet mask to all devices that will participate in the subnet.

The subnet mask creation in this example was relatively straightforward because a full octet was used for the subnet number. This also made the `and` calculation very simple. However, suppose we change the example, by using not a B Class address, but a C Class instead. The addresses to now assign the sample network in Figure 3.13 include `199.81.23.1` through `199.81.23.4`. With a C

Class address, the range of the first octet is `192-233`. The first three octets are the network address (`199.81.23`), while the remaining octet (`4`, in this example) is the node address. This example will complicate the subnet process a bit because we must now split the host portion and the subnet address from just one octet. However, the same procedure applies as stated above.

In order to formulate a subnet address from a Class C network address, we must borrow some number of bits to represent the subnet number. In doing so, we automatically reduce the number of IP addresses that will be free for each device within the subnet. Therefore, we need to know exactly how many devices will be installed on the subnet. To further refine our example, assume we will only need ten IP addresses for individual nodes on the subnet.

Internet Control Message Protocol

As previously discussed, IP provides a best-effort packet delivery mechanism that doesn't guarantee data delivery. IP is insulated from the low-level protocol details and makes few assumptions about the performance and reliability of the network. Data delivery is accomplished without any special coordination among other IP entities and for the most part operates quite well. However, conditions might exist beyond IP's control that make delivery difficult or impossible. For example, a remote host is temporarily removed from the network or a router becomes overloaded when a network-intensive application is started. IP needs a way to detect these types of problems.

The Internet Control Message Protocol (ICMP) provides a general error message facility for the IP protocol and related services. ICMP provides a way for IP entities that encounter errors to report them to the source that caused the problem. It is the responsibility of the source entity to correct the error. This might include, for example, reporting the error to a higher-level application. Table 3.6 lists some of the ICMP message types.

One of the most popular networking debugging utilities, `ping`, uses ICMP to determine host reachability. Ping uses the echo request and echo reply primitives that are available within ICMP to determine if a remote host is available and operating correctly on the network. The basic operation of the echo request and reply

Table 3.6 *ICMP Error Message Types*

Message Type	Meaning
Echo Request/Reply	Determine system reachability
Destination Unreachable	Can't reach desired destination
Source Quench	Stop sending data
Redirect	Detection of routing error
Time Exceeded	Stale IP packet

can be found in Figure 3.13. A user wants to determine if `Node B` is available on the network. From `Node A`, the user enters a ping command that issues an echo request to `Node B`. If `Node B` is active, it responds back to `Node A` using the echo reply. If `Node B` is not active, then `Node A` receives no response. In this case, the request from `Node A` simply times-out.

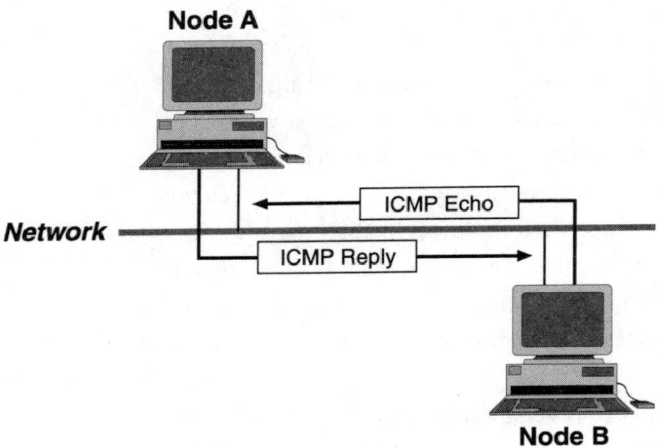

Figure 3.13 *ICMP Echo Request/Reply.*

Destination Unreachable

When a router can't deliver or forward a packet to its destination, it will emit an ICMP *destination unreachable* message to the sender. Network unreachable errors usually imply some sort of routing problem or error (i.e., incorrect route within a routing table). Destinations may be unreachable due to hardware failures that cause a system to become temporarily unavailable, or if the sender specifies a non-existent destination address. Sometimes it is impossible to know that a destination is unreachable unless the `ping` system utility is used. For example, if a user issues a TELNET request to a remote system (which happens to be connected to an Ethernet LAN) and the system has been disconnected from the network, this TELNET request will eventually time-out because Ethernet doesn't support any frame acknowledgements. As a result, no destination unreachable messages will be generated because Ethernet assumes data delivery even for a node that has been temporarily disconnected from the network.

Source Quench

The source quench within ICMP provides a way to handle congestion at the IP level. Congestion within a network can be caused by several factors. However, one primary cause is when several systems begin transmission of data that flows through a single router as shown in Figure 3.14. In this case, the router itself is overburdened by the combined traffic. Another cause of congestion is when a more powerful computer system is transmitting data to a less powerful system that cannot keep pace. If these situations go unchecked, eventually the router and under-powered system will begin to discard packets, which in turn will cause TCP to retransmit them, thus making the situation worse. In this case, the router and smaller system simply emit a source quench message, which indicates to the sender that it should stop sending data. As a result, the router and smaller system have time to process any outstanding packets.

There is no direct way to reverse the effects of the ICMP source quench message. However, any destination that receives a source quench lowers the rate at which it transmits packets to the destination. After no additional source quench messages are received, the remote system begins to gradually increase the rate of transmission.

The ICMP redirect message is used to inform routers of changes to the routing information within the network. One of the basic assumptions with TCP/IP is that routers know the routing topology within a network and this information is shared among participating routers. When a router detects a host using a non-optimal route, it emits a redirect message informing the host that a better route is available. It is up to the host to incorporate this new information within its router configuration. In some cases, this is not automatic.

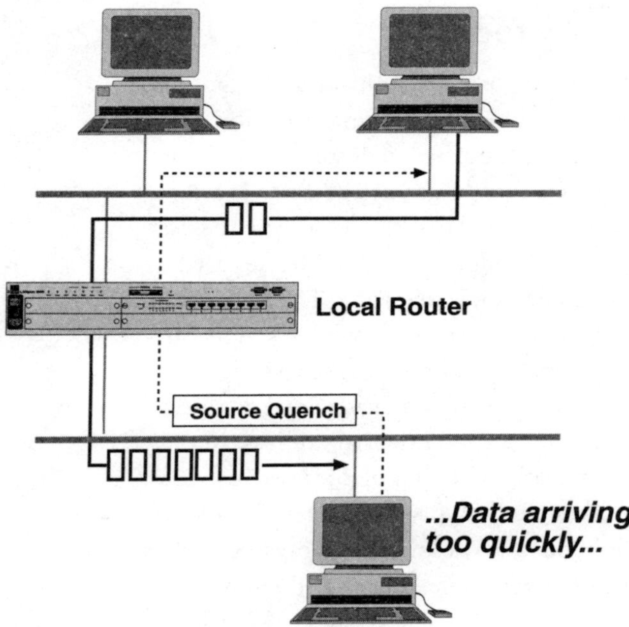

Figure 3.14 *ICMP Source Quench Redirect.*

Redirect messages do not provide a common mechanism for distributing routing information because they are limited to interaction between hosts and routers. Instead, routing protocols such as RIP are used to propagate routing information within a network.

Time Exceeded

Each IP packet contains a time-to-live field, which is used to control how long a packet may exist within the network. When a router processes the packet, it decrements this field before forwarding it. Whenever a router discards a packet because its time-to-live field is zero or because some other time-out occurred with the packet, the router emits an ICMP *time exceeded* message back to the source of the packet. This is the primary mechanism used to detect routing loops or excessively long routes within a network. The `traceroute` command, for example, uses the time-to-live field to trace the path an IP packet may take between two points and also measures the amount of time required to traverse each router en route to the destination.

Address Resolution Protocol

As we previously discussed, IP imposes a certain structure and format on the addresses used by networking devices. In version 4 of IP, the address uses 32-bits and is expressed in dotted decimal notation. In version 6, the address is even larger, at 128-bits. As with any high-level network protocol such as IP, the requirement exists for a mechanism to translate these addresses into addresses used by such protocols as Ethernet, FDDI, or Token Ring. These datalink protocols have their own addressing structure, which is quite different from IP addresses. For example, Ethernet uses 48-bit addresses and is expressed using the colon hexadecimal notation. Thus, `8:0:20:4:cf:2c` represents a valid Ethernet address. In this case, this address doesn't fit neatly with that of addresses used by IP. This is true for many other datalink protocols as well. This creates a dilemma because without a way to map IP addresses to physical interfaces, communication between nodes would not be possible.

It is desirable and very necessary that a simple, flexible, and yet powerful way to map between IP and datalink addresses be available. The Address Resolution Protocol, or ARP, has been proven to provide a very elegant and robust way to solve the address mapping problem. In particular, ARP was designed to handle address resolution of any network layer protocol to datalink protocol, not just between IP and Ethernet, for example.

The basic operation of ARP is simple: When `Node A` wants to determine the physical address for `Node B`, `Node A` will send a special broadcast message requesting `Node B`*'s* address to all devices on the network, as shown in Figure 3.15a. All hosts receive the message, including `Node B` and `Node C`, but only `Node B` will respond with the correct physical address shown in Figure 3.15b.

The term *broadcast* in the above example indicates a locally directed packet to all network devices on a particular LAN segment. Certain datalink protocols such as Ethernet provide the facility to transmit broadcast packets to all attached stations using a special destination address. ARP assumes that the details of getting messages to each station will be handled directly by the datalink protocol.

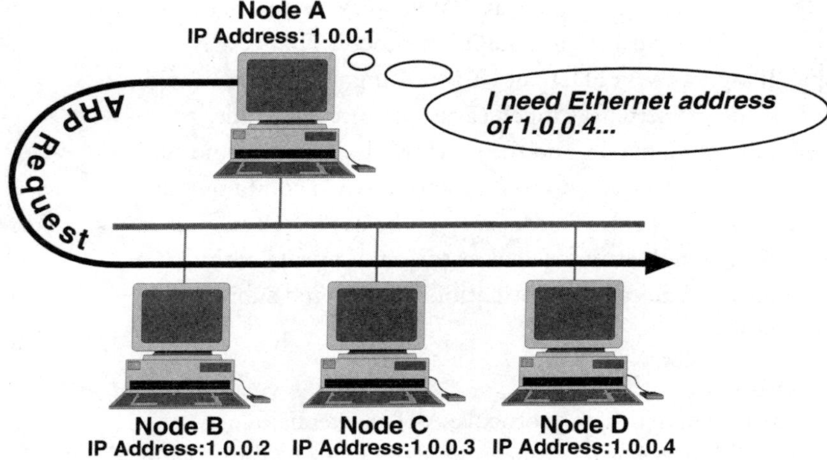

Figure 3.15a *ARP Request.*

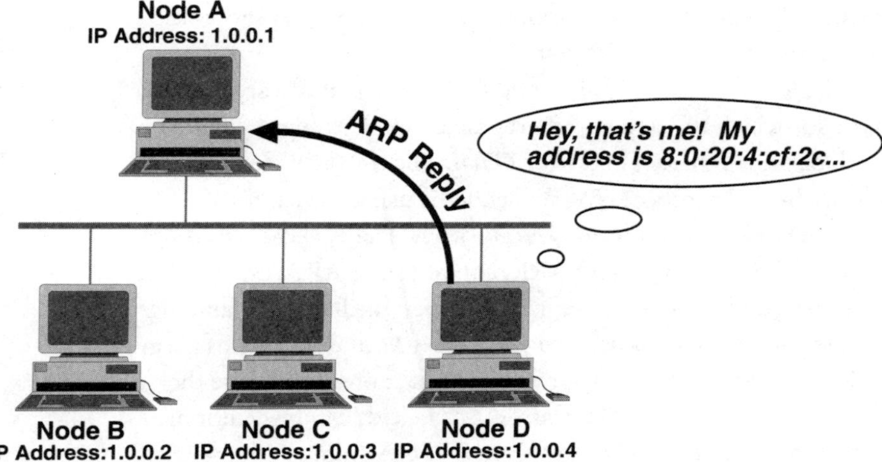

Figure 3.15b *ARP Reply.*

As you can see, the ARP protocol is very simple. Yet, despite its simplicity, it has a few profound advantages. First, ARP is dynamic in nature, which obviates the need to statically track and store IP to physical addresses. This dynamic resolution behavior frees the network manager from constantly maintaining and ensuring correct information every time a device is added or removed from the network. With today's networks, it would be impossible to accomplish such a task given the size and growth rate of many internets. Second, ARP is a standard and is available on every device that supports TCP/IP, regardless of datalink protocol. That is why, for example, IP operates on FDDI and Token Ring. This makes building heterogeneous networks much easier because ARP hides the datalink addressing details and the network designer need not be concerned about physical address resolution when combining different datalink protocols. Third, ARP can be used in IP subnets to provide a very simple way for devices to communicate within a routed Internet. Additional information on ARP and subnets are provided below.

Packet Format

Unlike other networking protocols, ARP packet fields are not all fixed-format, but rather rely on certain fixed fields near the beginning of the packet to specify the lengths of the remaining fields. To make the ARP useful for other datalink protocols, the length of the fields will depend on the type of network. Figure 3.16 shows the standard ARP message format.

The `HARDWARE TYPE` field is used to define the hardware interface type for which the sender requires an answer. Standard values include `1` for Ethernet and `2` for FDDI. The `PROTOCOL` field specifies the high-level protocol type the sender is using, which for IP, is `0800` in hexadecimal (decimal is `2048`). The Field `OPERATIONS` is used to note if the message is an ARP request (`1`), or ARP response (`2`). The `HLEN` and `PLEN` fields are used to define the hardware and high-level protocol address field lengths. The `HLEN` and `PLEN` fields permit ARP to work with any arbitrary datalink protocol because the sizes of the `HARDWARE TYPE` and `PROTOCOL` fields can be determined by inspecting the ARP packet directly. The sending entity will supply, if available, both the `SENDER HA` and `SENDER IP` field information when responding to the ARP request.

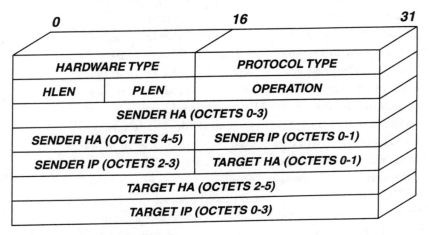

0		16 31
HARDWARE TYPE		PROTOCOL TYPE
HLEN	PLEN	OPERATION
SENDER HA (OCTETS 0-3)		
SENDER HA (OCTETS 4-5)		SENDER IP (OCTETS 0-1)
SENDER IP (OCTETS 2-3)		TARGET HA (OCTETS 0-1)
TARGET HA (OCTETS 2-5)		
TARGET IP (OCTETS 0-3)		

Figure 3.16 *ARP Message Format.*

ARP Cache

At first glance, the ARP service may seem inefficient since it will send a broadcast packet each time a device wishes to communicate with another. However, ARP implementations include the use of an ARP cache to temporarily store address bindings from previous ARP requests. In fact, before an ARP request is made, the high-level software scans the ARP cache to see if the required datalink address mapping already exists in the cache. If it does, the existing binding is used, otherwise the ARP request is sent. As a result of the cache, network traffic is reduced because ARP requests are only made when devices are not in the cache. Also, application performance is improved because the sender's ARP request can be satisfied by using the cache instead of transmitting a packet on the network. Finally, the cache provides the administrator with a way to view connectivity between the high-level protocols and the network hardware. As we will see later in this book, inspecting the ARP cache can be a powerful way to troubleshoot network and system problems.

One interesting question regarding the ARP cache: when should the bindings be discarded from the cache? The answer is not simple. If we presume to keep the ARP cache populated with entries forever (or until the system is restarted), the possibility exists that the cache will contain invalid information. Consider, for example, `Node X` and `Node Y` are communicating when `Node Y`'s network interface card (NIC) fails and is subsequently replaced. The new NIC will contain a new datalink address, unless the administrator has changed it after installation. As a result, `Node X` can't talk to `Node Y` any longer because `Node X`'s cache contains an invalid binding to `Node Y`'s datalink address. On the other hand, we can take the approach that binding in the ARP cache should expire in a relatively short period of time, say 30 seconds. Unfortunately, this will adversely affect network performance because more network broadcasts will be needed because the ARP cache will be very small. However, it will address the problem of the incorrect bindings for NIC that have recently been replaced because the old entry would have been purged before the new NIC was operational.

Perhaps the best solution to this problem can be described by taking *the middle of the road* approach. That is to say, the binding expiration shouldn't be too small to be ineffective, but also not too long to address changes in the network. In general, most Unix systems will delete ARP entries in approximately 20 minutes. Some versions of Unix also permit the administrator to change the ARP cache timeout to suite their individual network requirements.

Datalink Address Format

As indicated, datalink addresses are expressed in 48-bits (6 bytes) and are separated by colons. This colon notation is used as the primary method to represent these hardware addresses. Many Unix tools, for example, use this format. Datalink protocol addresses for FDDI, Ethernet, and Token Ring contain a vendor code identification number and serial number. This information can be used in node identification for inventory purposes. The IEEE registry authority assigns the vendor portion to any organization that produces networking hardware and has requested a vendor code. These codes are also referred to as organization unique identifiers (OUI). The first three bytes of the address represent the manufacturer or vendor of the device and the remaining three bytes represent the serial number of the unit as depicted in Figure 3.17.

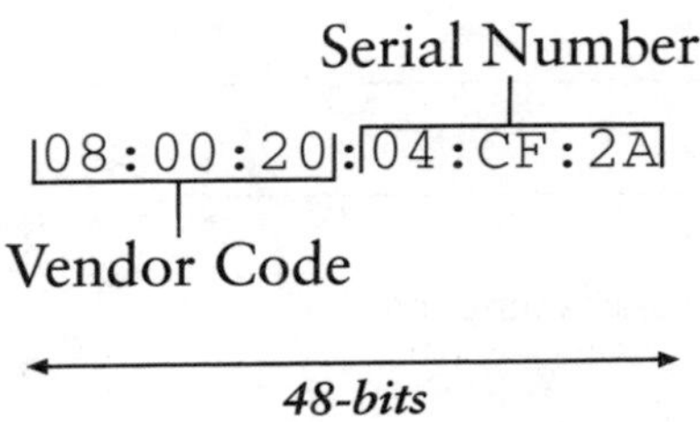

Figure 3.17 *Datalink Address Format.*

Often on a multi-homed system, the datalink addresses will be shared among all the defined interfaces. This may even be true for systems that contain different network interface types (i.e., Ethernet and FDDI).

Some of the most common vendor codes are shown in Table 3.7. Notice that more than one vendor code might be associated with the same vendor. This may be true, for example, when one company purchases another company and their entire product line has requested additional vendor codes. In this case, the vendor code of the company that was purchased now falls under the other company. This is why the table below contains multiple entries for both 3Com and Cisco. Having a few of these under your belt can be very handy during network debugging to help identify the type of device and vendor to which a particular packet belongs.

Table 3.7 *Sample Vendor Codes*

Vendor Code	Vendor
00:20:AF 00-80-3E 00-C0-D4 (many more)	3Com Corporation (Formerly Synernetics, Inc.) (Formerly AXON, Inc.)
08-00-2B AA-00-00 AA-00-03 AA-00-04	Digital Equipment Corporation (DEC)

(Cont'd)

Table 3.7 *Sample Vendor Codes (Cont'd)*

Vendor Code	Vendor
00:00:0C 00-E0-B0 00-E0-F7 00-E0-F9 00-E0-FE 00-06-7C 00-06-C1 00-10-07 (many more)	Cisco Systems, Inc. (Includes a large list of former companies)
00-00-81 00-00-A2 00-80-E3	Bay Network, Inc. (Formerly Coral Networks)
00-E0-B1	Packet Engines, Inc.
08:00:5A	IBM Corporation
08:00:20	Sun Microsystems, Inc.
08-00-09	HP Corporation
00-10-E3	Compaq Corporation

04

System Utilities and Tools

This chapter provides a detailed overview of the following Unix utilities and tools:

ARP

IFCONFIG

NETSTAT

PING

SNOOP

FPING

TRACEROUTE

This collection of tools is considered the core set that a Unix or network administrator would use to solve a variety of system- and network-related problems. Many of the tools and utilities listed in this chapter are available on most Unix systems. However, some of the tools are only available within the public domain and, as a result, must be installed separately from the operating system. In these cases, a section entitled "Software Availability" has been added for those tools to which these special circumstances apply.

ARP Tool

General Description

The `arp` command is used to display and manipulate the address table on a local Unix system. The address resolution table, also known as the ARP cache, contains a complete list of all datalink protocols to IP address mappings for the local network. Recall from the previous chapter that the ARP protocol is a dynamic facility that maps datalink addresses, such as Ethernet to IP addresses, and whenever the system wants to transmit a message, it must first know the low level (i.e., datalink) address for each node on the network.

This command provides the ability to view and modify the ARP cache. To modify the ARP table, the super-user must invoke the command. Note that the terms *ARP table* and *cache* can be used interchangeably and that binding also refers to an ARP entry. With the `arp` command, the following can be accomplished:

- Display the ARP Cache
- Delete an ARP Entry
- Add an ARP Entry

The `arp` command provides a small number of command line options listed in Table 4.1 and fully described later.

Table 4.1 *ARP Command Line Options*

Option	Description
`-a`	Displays the current ARP cache
`-d`	Deletes an ARP entry
`-f`	Used to load a file that contains entries to place in the cache
`-s`	Creates an ARP entry

Displaying the ARP Cache

To display the contents of the ARP table, use the `arp -a` command. When the table is displayed, it includes the device, IP address, network mask, flags, and physical address for each entry. A sample is shown below.

```
# arp -a
Net to Media Table
Device   IP Address               Mask            Flags   Phys Addr
------ -------------------- --------------- ----- ---------------
le0    224.0.0.1            255.255.255.255       01:00:5e:00:00:01
le1    224.0.0.1            255.255.255.255       01:00:5e:00:00:01
le1    durer                255.255.255.255       00:60:08:26:be:5e
le1    rembrandt            255.255.255.255       08:00:20:82:be:05
le1    rubens               255.255.255.255 U
le1    monet-a              255.255.255.255 SP    08:00:20:04:cf:2c
le0    monet-b              255.255.255.255 SP    08:00:20:04:cf:2c
le1    224.0.0.0            240.0.0.0       SM    01:00:5e:00:00:00
le0    224.0.0.0            240.0.0.0       SM    01:00:5e:00:00:00
```

The `Device` field corresponds to the network interface that is attached to the local network, for which the ARP entry was obtained. In the example above, two separate interfaces are shown with their own listings. In practice, most systems only contain a single interface. The `le` stands for Lance Ethernet, which is the name of hardware device driver under Solaris. Because this particular system contains two network interfaces, they are numbered `le0` and `le1`.

The `IP Address` field shows either an IP address or hostname that corresponds to the ARP entry. This is the address that is used to search the ARP table to determine if the desired entry exists.

When an IP address is displayed, this indicates that the IP address couldn't be correctly resolved to a hostname.

The `Mask` field is used to determine which part of the addresses should be examined. The `Flags` field provides additional details and options regarding the ARP entry. Table 4.2 shows the available flags and their associated meaning.

Table 4.2 *ARP Entry Flags*

ARP Flag	Meaning
`S`	Static ARP entry
`P`	Publish this ARP entry
`M`	Mapped ARP entry (Multicast Only)
`U`	Unresolved

The `Phys Addr` (physical address) field contains the low-level address for each node on the local network and is expressed in 6 hexadecimal numbers in colon notation.

ARP entries that are marked S are static and have been defined outside the normal ARP protocol (e.g., manually entered with the `arp -s` command). Each interface on the local system has a static ARP entry because the interface is local to the system and doesn't need the ARP protocol to obtain this information. Certain special purpose interfaces or addresses are also statically defined. Static entries are also used to support networked systems that don't support the ARP protocol. Therefore, the address binding must be manually entered in the ARP table. One problem with this approach is that if the IP address of any of these systems is changed as a result of moving it to a new network, the ARP information must be manually updated to effect the change.

Entries that contain the P flag will be transmitted over the network if a node makes an ARP request. Typically, the system interfaces will be published so that other local devices can build their own ARP tables. Only the IP addresses associated with genuine interfaces are advertised with ARP. It is interesting to note that ARP information obtained from other network devices is not normally published by third-party systems. It is usually the responsibility of each device to respond to ARP requests with its own ARP information. There is one special case when a system will respond to ARP requests on behalf of others. This is known as *proxy ARP* and is described below.

Mapped ARP entries include a timer, which controls how long the entry will remain in the ARP cache. By default, most systems hold the entry for approximately 20 minutes before removing it.

The `U` flag indicates that an ARP request is still pending and the mapping is presently unresolved. In the ARP example above, the system `rubens` is lacking a physical address because the ARP request hasn't obtained a reply. This is known as an *incomplete* ARP entry.

In the above example, some entries do not have corresponding physical interfaces. For example, the addresses `224.0.0.0` and `224.0.0.1` are pseudo addresses that are defined by the system for its own use. These addresses represent the multicast address facility, which is used to support real-time video/audio applications.

Deleting an ARP Cache

It might become necessary to delete one or more entries from the ARP table. For example, should a hardware failure result in the replacement of a network interface card, the network hardware address of the system will change. In this case, the existing ARP entry doesn't reflect that the low level address has changed. As a result, messages sent to this host will not be picked up because the hardware address is not recognized.

To address this problem, the `-d` option is used to delete an ARP entry, as shown below. Because removing ARP bindings can cause network problems, only the super-user is permitted to remove them. The `arp` command expects the `-d` option to be used with a valid host or IP address entry. In the example, the host `durer` is removed from the ARP table and the `arp` command displays the deleted entry:

```
# arp -d durer
durer (10.0.2.126) deleted
```

If the ARP table were now displayed, the `durer` entry would not be listed.

If a non-root user attempts to remove this host from the table, the error message would be displayed as depicted below:

```
$ arp -d rembrandt
SIOCDARP: Not owner error
```

Adding an ARP Cache Entry

Several situations may warrant manually adding entries to the ARP table. One such situation occurs when communication with a device is needed but the device, for some reason, doesn't support ARP or the implementation is non-functional. This might be the case with a very old system that is still in service. Another such situation occurs when a hardware address changes and the table must be manually updated to ensure connectivity. A third occurs when it is necessary to support proxy ARP services.

To add an ARP entry, use the `-s` option followed by the host name (or address) and the associated physical datalink address. For example, let's say we would like to add a system called `bruegel` to the ARP table. The format of the physical datalink is represented as `x:x:x:x:x:x`, where each `x` is a hexadecimal number between `0` and `FF`. To illustrate the example, the following command would be used:

```
# arp -s bruegel 08:00:20:82:be:05
```

If no error message is displayed, it can be assumed that the command was successful.

If you want to list a single entry instead of all the entries in the table, just specify the hostname or IP address as the second argument to the `arp` command. For example, to list the ARP information for `bruegel`, use the following command:

```
# arp bruegel
bruegel (10.0.2.101) at 8:0:20:82:be:5 permanent
```

Please note that this ARP binding is labeled as permanent, which indicates that the ARP information was defined statically and will not time-out. If the `arp -a` command is issued again, we will see the `S` flag option for the `bruegel` binding:

```
# arp -a
Net to Media Table
Device   IP Address                    Mask          Flags   Phys Addr
------ -------------------- --------------- ----- ---------------
le0    224.0.0.1            255.255.255.255       01:00:5e:00:00:01
le1    224.0.0.1            255.255.255.255       01:00:5e:00:00:01
le0    10.0.2.75            255.255.255.255       00:60:08:26:be:5e
le0    bruegel              255.255.255.255 S     08:00:20:82:be:05
le0    monet-b              255.255.255.255 SP    08:00:20:04:cf:2c
le1    monet-a              255.255.255.255 SP    08:00:20:04:cf:2c
le1    224.0.0.0            240.0.0.0       SM    01:00:5e:00:00:00
le0    224.0.0.0            240.0.0.0       SM    01:00:5e:00:00:00
```

The ARP entry is set up as permanent unless the temp option is specified on the command line. Permanent indicates that the mapping will not expire the way normal ARP mappings do. Unfortunately, permanent bindings are not saved across reboots.

To understand why modifying the ARP table is restricted to the super-user, consider that when static ARP entries are defined, no direct linkage exists between this information and the actual devices attached to the network. For example, the `bruegel` entry was added manually, but no mechanism is available to ARP to ensure that the physical address is indeed correct. The `arp` command assumes the information provided is accurate and that the device is actually attached to the network. Therefore, if normal users had the ability to modify the ARP table, more errors would likely be introduced which would lead to loss of network connectivity. Should the physical address field of a critical network resource (like a server) be incorrectly changed, all communication between the local system and the critical system would stop.

Proxy ARP Services

The `arp` command can be used to support proxy ARP services. Proxy ARP is a way to respond to ARP requests on behalf of another network device. Typically, this configuration is used to support devices behind a router or a specialized configuration, such as those required for remote dial-up access strategies.

Loading ARP Bindings Using a File

The `arp` command also supports the ability to add bindings that are defined within a regular file instead of specifying the information on the command line. This method is used, for example, to load in a list of ARP entries together. It is not uncommon, for example, for a series of ARP bindings to be loaded during normal system startup procedures—especially if the system doesn't support distributed database lookup schemes such as NIS. The format of a file used for this purpose includes the following fields:

```
hostname datalink address [ temp ] [ pub ] [ trail ]
```

Using a text editor, you can create a list of ARP bindings using the format above and save it to a text file—for example `/etc/arp-list`. A sample file listing is shown below.

```
bruegel 08:00:20:82:be:05 temp
rubens 08:00:20:81:ce:01 temp
rembrandt 08:00:20:86:fe:02
cezanne 08:00:20:81:bb:01
michelangelo 08:00:20:84:ee:02
```

Notice that both `bruegel` and `rubens` contain the `temp` keyword, which indicates that these entries will be deleted from the ARP table after they expire. In practice, the temp option is not commonly used because it might be undesirable for these bindings to expire and be removed from the cache. The `pub` keyword is used to publish the ARP binding to the network. The `trail` option is primarily used to indicate that trailer encapsulation is supported by the host. However, trailers have not been widely implemented and are obsolete on Sun systems; this option, for all practical purposes, can be ignored.

After the file contains the desired entries, use the `-f` option of the `arp` command to load the contents of the file into the ARP table as shown below:

```
# arp -f /etc/arp-list
```

Should you wish to load this table automatically, edit one of the system startup files (`/etc/init.d/inetsvc`, for example) and include (see listing 4.1) the following entry:

Listing 4.1 *ARP Startup Script*

```
#
# Load custom ARP table
#
echo -n "Loading local arp table..."
if [ -f /etc/arp-list ]; then
   /usr/sbin/arp -f /etc/arp-list
   echo "done."
else
   echo "failed"
fi
```

IFCONFIG Tool

General Description

The `ifconfig` command is short for interface configuration and is used to configure local network interfaces. This command is normally invoked during system startup to set up each interface with a pre-defined configuration. The `ifconfig` command can also be used to change the network interface after the system has been booted. This command provides the following:

- Lists the configuration of each defined network interface
- Disables/enables any defined network interface
- Modifies network interface configuration parameters

Two versions of `ifconfig` are available. The difference lies in their behavior with respect to name service (or host resolution) functions. The name service is responsible for mapping hostnames to IP addresses and back again. The first version of `ifconfig`, found in `/sbin`, uses a fixed configuration when resolving hostnames and cannot be altered. In contrast, the second version of `ifconfig`, found in `/usr/sbin`, provides name services based on the `/etc/nsswitch.conf` configuration file. Using this file, it is possible to alter the ordering for hostname resolution. By default, Solaris uses the first version of `ifconfig` during the first phase of network initialization and the second version when the network is fully operational. The first form is used during network initialization because the interface information must be derived from the local system. After all, the network cannot be used until the network interfaces are defined. This is a classical *chicken or egg* timing problem. After the system has booted to the point that the network is available, however, the second form of `ifconfig` can be used to set additional parameters that may be derived externally by the local system.

The `ifconfig` command provides a large number of options that are used to configure one or more interfaces on the command line. Table 4.3 lists these options, which are used as modifiers for the configuration commands.

Table 4.3 `Ifconfig` *Modifier Options*

Option	Description
`-a`	Applies to all interfaces presently installed on the system
`-ad`	Applies to all interfaces that are marked *down* on the system
`-adD`	Same as `-ad`, but applies to non-DHCP interfaces
`-au`	Applies to all interfaces that are *up* on the system
`-auD`	Same as `-au`, but applies to non-DHCP interfaces

Listing Available Interfaces

To display all system interfaces, use the `ifconfig -a` command as shown below:

```
# /usr/sbin/ifconfig -a
lo0: flags=849<UP,LOOPBACK,RUNNING,MULTICAST> mtu 8232
        inet 127.0.0.1 netmask ff000000
le0: flags=863<UP,BROADCAST,NOTRAILERS,RUNNING,MULTICAST> mtu 1500
        inet 10.0.2.126 netmask ffffff00 broadcast 10.0.2.255
        ether 8:0:20:4:cf:2c
le1: flags=863<UP,BROADCAST,NOTRAILERS,RUNNING,MULTICAST> mtu 1500
        inet 199.81.146.200 netmask ffffff00 broadcast 199.81.146.255
        ether 8:0:20:4:cf:2c
hme0: flags=863<DOWN,BROADCAST,NOTRAILERS,RUNNING,MULTICAST> mtu 1500
        inet 199.82.24.34 netmask ffffff00 broadcast 199.82.24.255
        ether 8:0:20:4:cf:2c
```

The `-a` option indicates that `ifconfig` should display all interfaces installed within the system regardless of their present configuration or operational state.

The display example above indicates that four interfaces are defined. The first, `lo0`, is the loop-back interface, primarily used for internal communication and diagnostics. The loop-back interface can be used to determine if the TCP/IP software is operating correctly on a local level. For instance, it is possible to `ping` the loop-back address to determine valid responses. The second and third (`le0` and `le1`) represent the physical hardware interfaces for 10 Mb/s Ethernet using the Lance Ethernet driver. The Lance device is used with Sun Microsystems computers. The final (`hme0`) represents the Fast Ethernet 100 Mb/s interface that is available on Sun systems.

Each interface contains a flags portion (surrounded by <> characters in the display) and several keyword configuration parameters, which must be specified when the interfaces are configured. The flag field is used to indicate the present state and special operating characteristics of the interface. The following options are supported within the flag field:

- Current Administrative State
- Supports Broadcast Traffic
- Present Operating State
- Supports Multicast Traffic

Controlling Administration State

With `ifconfig` it is possible to disable an active interface or enable a disabled interface. In the disabled state, no packets will be permitted across an interface. This is equivalent to disconnecting the interface from the network. When an interface is disabled, it is considered down from an administrative standpoint. To place an interface in the down state, invoke the `ifconfig` command with the appropriate interface and the `down` keyword option as shown below:

```
# ifconfig le0 down
```

We can use the `ifconfig` command with the interface name instead of the `-a` option to list an individual interface. The command below displays the configuration of the interface we shut down with the previous command.

```
# ifconfig le0
le0: flags=862<BROADCAST,NOTRAILERS,RUNNING,MULTICAST> mtu 1500
        inet 199.81.146.200 netmask ffffff00 broadcast 199.81.146.255
        ether 8:0:20:4:cf:2c
```

Notice the keyword `up` is now missing. This is how `ifconfig` indicates that an interface has been disabled and is not available for use. To enable this interface, we simply use the `up` command option:

```
# ifconfig le0 up
```

When the interface is up, it indicates that it is available on the network and is receiving network information. Without the indication of the `up` flag, the interface is operational, but no information is flowing to or from the network.

Modifying Interface Parameters

Two methods can be used to modify network interface parameters. First, using `ifconfig` directly, changes can be made on the command line and will take effect immediately. The second approach involves modifying the system startup and/or system files that `ifconfig` uses to configure the interface. This approach ensures that interface changes are made permanently and won't disappear across system reboots and is described in more detail below. Sometimes both approaches are used. Often, a configuration change must be implemented quickly before the system can be conveniently rebooted. As a result, `ifconfig` is used to make the immediate change; the system configuration files are also changed so that the network modifications will be permanent. Normally, when a new interface is installed on a system, this configuration may be handled by the installation procedure. However, if network interface information must be changed prior to the installation, the `ifconfig` tool must be used.

Using `ifconfig`, the following information can be changed for an interface:

- IP Address
- Network Mask
- Broadcast Address
- Datalink Address
- MTU

The IP address is specified in the normal dotted decimal notation and represents the unique address for the host on the network to which the system is attached. The network mask (netmask) subnet specifies the mask used to calculate the network and host portions of the IP address. The broadcast address is used to specify the IP address to which broadcast packets should be directed. The datalink address represents the unique low-level hardware address used in the networking protocol, such as Ethernet or FDDI, and is associated with the hardware itself. The maximum transmission unit (MTU) denotes the maximum message size that the interface can handle. The standard message size for Ethernet is 1500; FDDI is 4096; Token Ring is 2048. The MTU is rarely modified and, when it is, generally can't be configured to support higher values than what was just listed; only lower values may be used.

Let's suppose that the IP address of a system must be changed because the system is moved to a different subnet. In this case, the netmask and broadcast information remains the same. The move to the new network involves changing the IP address of the interface only. The old IP address is `128.197.9.10` and the new IP address is `128.197.10.1`. The following command would be used to change the network information on the fly:

```
# ifconfig le0 128.197.10.1
```

To make this change permanent, we are required to modify the `/etc/hosts` file. This file contain the mapping between hostname and associated IP address. On system startup, the IP address is derived from the file and applied to the interface. The netmask and broadcast information is the same; we can use the existing values. The hostname could also be specified on the command line instead of the IP address. Thus,

```
# ifconfig le0 fred
```

accomplishes the same result assuming that `fred` has been assigned the IP address of `128.197.10.1.` either in the `/etc/hosts` file or the NIS hosts database.

As you can see, changing the IP address for an interface is relatively straightforward. However, changing other interface characteristics requires a bit more work. To extend our example from above, let us now assume that we must change the netmask and broadcast information. To change the interface on the fly, we would use:

```
# ifconfig le0 128.197.10.1 netmask 255.255.0.0 broadcast
128.197.255.255
```

In the example above, the netmask and broadcast keywords must be used to identify the information that follows each keyword. The netmask contains 1s in the bit positions of the 32-bit address that are to be used for the network and subnet (if applicable) parts, and 0s for the host portion. The netmask/subnet portion must occupy at least as many bits as is standard for the particular network class. If no subnets are defined, the standard netmask is used. As described in Chapter 2, "TCP/IP Protocol Suite," the use of subnets mandates that additional bits are reserved from what is normally the host portion of the address to identify the subnet. A netmask can be specified in any of the following four ways:

- Dotted Decimal Notation
- Hexadecimal Notation
- With a plus sign
- With a pseudo network name

The dotted decimal notation is expressed in four single numbers separated by dots (e.g., 255.255.255.0). The hexadecimal format includes using the 0x prefix followed by a single value. The hexadecimal value for 255.255.255.0 is 0xffffff00.

If the plus sign is used, as in the following example, the network mask is obtained from the /etc/netmasks database or, if NIS is running, from the netmask map. The ifconfig command searches for the netmask information using the network number as the key.

```
# ifconfig le0 128.197.10.1 netmask +
```

The netmask will be assigned the value 255.255.255.0 because that is the value found in the 128.197 entry contained within the /etc/netmasks file, as shown here:

```
128.197.10.0 255.255.255.0
```

If NIS is operating, individual systems might not contain a current copy of the netmasks file. As a result, the following command can be used to examine active netmasks:

```
# ypcat netmasks
```

Alternatively, a pseudo network mask name can be defined and used. This information is derived from the /etc/netmasks file. However, this method isn't popular because most vendors recommend and support better approaches.

The broadcast address can be specified in one of two ways. First, it can be specified on the command line in the normal dotted decimal notation with all bits set to 1 (or each octet set to 255) following the network portion of the address. Second, a plus sign can be used to indicate that the broadcast address should be derived from a combination of the network and netmask fields. The command below shows an assignment of the broadcast address using the plus sign.

```
# ifconfig le0 200.100.1.1 netmask 0xffffff00 broadcast +
```

In this example, the resulting broadcast address is 200.200.100.255.

Special Configurations Parameters

Additional parameters are supported by the `ifconfig` command. These include:

- ARP
- Plumb
- Reverse ARP
- Private
- Trailers

The `arp` keyword is used to specify that the interface should support an ARP style IP address resolution. When an interface is created with `ifconfig`, the default is to support ARP. To disable ARP on an interface, use the `-arp` keyword.

The `plumb` keyword is used to initialize the interface to support logical interfaces and point-to-point (PPP) links. Logical interfaces are described in more detail below.

The `ifconfig` command can also be used to support reverse ARP (RARP) for a network interface. The `auto-revarp` keyword command obtains an IP address using RARP. A RARP server must be available on the network to respond to these requests.

The `private` keyword command is used to squelch advertisements of one or more interfaces from a routing perspective. The default is to advertise the interface available for routing.

The `trailers` keyword enables the use of datalink level encapsulation of frames that could improve network performance. However, because this type of encapsulation is non-standard, its use is limited and is no longer supported on certain Unix operating systems.

Logical Interfaces

On Solaris, the `ifconfig` command can be used to create and configure logical (pseudo) interfaces. These interfaces behave like physical interfaces and can be used to assign multiple IP addresses to the same system. From a configuration standpoint, logical interfaces are configured independently but share the same physical address and interface characteristics as the real physical interface.

To create a logical interface, the interface must first be initialized with the `plumb` command as shown below:

```
# ifconfig le0 plumb
```

After this has been done, additional `ifconfig` commands can be used to configure one or more pseudo interfaces. To configure a pseudo interface, combine the physical interface with a logical interface number reference number separated by a colon. For example, to configure the first logical interface for `le0`, use the following command:

```
# ifconfig le0:1 128.191.2.1 netmask 0xffffff00 broadcast +
```

When a logical interface is first created, it is marked `down` by default. Therefore, use the `up` keyword to permit communications as shown below:

```
# ifconfig le0:1 up
```

Logical interfaces can also be displayed just like the physical ones using the `ifconfig -a` command. The sample below shows two logical interfaces defined from the physical interfaces `le0` and `le1`, respectively.

```
lo0: flags=849<UP,LOOPBACK,RUNNING,MULTICAST> mtu 8232
        inet 127.0.0.1 netmask ff000000
le0: flags=863<UP,BROADCAST,NOTRAILERS,RUNNING,MULTICAST> mtu 1500
        inet 200.100.1.1 netmask ffffff00 broadcast 200.100.1.255
        ether 8:0:20:4:cf:2c
le0:1: flags=843<UP,BROADCAST,RUNNING,MULTICAST> mtu 1500
        inet 128.191.2.1 netmask ffffff00 broadcast 128.191.2.255
le1: flags=863<UP,BROADCAST,NOTRAILERS,RUNNING,MULTICAST> mtu 1500
        inet 10.0.2.126 netmask ffffff00 broadcast 10.0.2.255
        ether 8:0:20:4:cf:2c
le1:1: flags=843<UP,BROADCAST,RUNNING,MULTICAST> mtu 1500
        inet 10.0.2.240 netmask ffffff00 broadcast 10.0.2.255
```

To remove a logical interface, use the `unplumb` keyword command.

Ensuring Interface Changes are Permanent

As previously implied, interface changes made with `ifconfig` on the command line will not persist across system reboots. As a result, if you want modifications to the datalink address or operational status of a network interface to be permanent, a startup file will need to be modified. If other interface parameters will be changed, usually this is accomplished via changes to one or more system configuration files.

The Solaris operating system uses a three-phased approach to starting network services during system startup. The file `/etc/init.d/init` is executed first. This script is responsible for establishing just enough networking function to continue booting the system and mounting local file systems. Next, the file `/etc/init.d/inetinit` is invoked. It starts many of the required networking services for normal system operations. The final phase, which uses the `/etc/init.d/inetsvc` file, initializes the system interfaces if the NIS environment is used.

Any of the startup files can be used to make local changes to the network configuration. However, as a general rule, these types of changes are made in the files that control the final stage of network initialization. The major reason for taking this approach is to ensure that any modifications have the least possible impact if something is wrong with the new configuration. To demonstrate how to include custom configuration information into the system, assume we need to do the following:

- Change the datalink address of the `le1` interface.
- Configure two logical interfaces with different IP addresses for the `le1` interface.

The `ifconfig` command used to change the datalink address is shown below.

```
ifconfig le1 ether <datalink address>
```

`<datalink address>` is the node address you want to use, as specified in the format previously discussed.

When configuring the logical interfaces, use the following commands:

```
ifconfig le1:1 <hostA> netmask + broadcast + up
ifconfig le1:2 <hostB> netmask + broadcast + up
```

The hostnames `<hostA>` and `<hostB>` should be defined in the local `/etc/hosts` file or in the NIS hosts database. The above commands should be placed at the end of the `/etc/inetsvc` file. Rebooting the system will cause their automatic execution at system startup.

As a general rule, exercise care when changing the datalink address of any interface. Why? If a host interface is given a datalink address that is already in use by another local device, it will cause problems because any sending nodes will get duplicate replies. Also, any network requests from the duplicate device will confuse other nodes because it is possible that the original node is already defined in the other device ARP cache.

The datalink address should not be changed on the fly, but instead be modified during the rebooting process. The datalink address can't be changed using `ifconfig` while the network is active. Alternatively, you can bring down the interface using the `down` keyword and then change the datalink. Before doing this, ensure that you have another interface to use while the first interface is down or that you are directly attached to the console of the system. If the system only contains a single interface and it is marked down using the command line, then you will have cut off your only access to the system. Only a reboot can restore the network interface to its original state.

DHCP Support

Starting with Solaris 2.6, Dynamic Host Configuration Protocol support has been included within the operating system and can be configured using the `ifconfig` command. The `auto-dhcp` keyword is used to indicate that DHCP should be used for an interface to automatically acquire IP address information over the network. Why use DHCP? DHCP is a very good way to handle IP address allocation within a growing network environment where network host identifiers are modified or added on a frequent basis.

With DHCP, one or more servers must be defined that contain a master list of IP address information that can be given to client systems. Conceptually, when a client system starts up, it makes a request via a broadcast for an IP address. The server receives the request, checks its local database for an available address, performs any defined security checks, and sends a reply back to the client using its datalink address. The client uses the obtained information to define its local interface and continues the boot process.

Routing Implications

The `private` keyword can be used to indicate that the interface should not be advertised from a network routing standpoint. This has the effect of hiding the interface from the routing process that may be active on the system. Normally, routing functions are limited on those systems that contain at least two network interfaces. When two or more interfaces are found, routing functions are automatically activated.

When routing is active on the system and an interface is established with a route, the `metric` keyword can be used to alter the routing hop count for that interface.

NETSTAT Tool

General Description

The `netstat` (network status) command provides a wealth of information regarding the present status of network connections, routing information, and other important network-related information. This tool is strictly for monitoring and is one of the most popular debugging aids available on Unix. Different command line options control the display behavior of `netstat`. As such, the functionality of `netstat` can be divided into a number of categories, including:

- Active Network Sessions
- Interface Information and Statistics
- Routing Table Information
- Network Data Structures
- Miscellaneous Display Options

Displaying Active Sessions

One of the significant services provided by `netstat` is the ability to view active connections between systems. Any presently active TCP connection between the local host and any other system can be monitored. Also, any stream sockets that have been created will be displayed as well. To display the currently established connections, issue the `netstat` command without any command line arguments:

```
# netstat
TCP
   Local Address        Remote Address    Swind Send-Q Rwind Recv-Q  State
-------------------- -------------------- ----- ------ ----- ------ -------
monet.telnet         rembrandt.1036        7682      0  8760      0 ESTABLISHED
monet.telnet         rembrandt.1040        8689      0  8760      0 ESTABLISHED
Active UNIX domain sockets
Address  Type          Vnode     Conn  Local Addr      Remote Addr
f5d66120 stream-ord f593b430       0 /tmp/.X11-unix/X0
f5d66320 stream-ord        0       0
```

As indicated, the output of the above command includes two types of connections. The first is TCP and includes information regarding the local and remote addresses, statistical information, and connection status. The local and remote addresses are displayed to include hostname and port information in the format:

```
host.port
```

where `host` can either be an assigned hostname from `/etc/hosts` (or from another host resolution mechanism such as NIS or DNS) or a valid IP address. The `port` represents either a reserved port as defined in `/etc/services` or a socket allocated by the system. The `netstat` tool follows the convention of displaying both the `host` and `port` information separated by a single dot. The local address is the source and the remote address is the destination. Recall that TCP uses four elements to make up a connection and uses a state machine model as part of TCP's overall transport mechanism. As a result, `monet.telnet` and `rembrandt.1036` are considered one connection and, from the `State` field, we can see that this connection is in the `ESTABLISHED` state.

The second type of connection includes the Unix streams socket interfaces. Since these connections are mainly used for inter-process communication among system programs and applications, their use and function won't be addressed.

Recall that TCP uses a state machine to control each of the defined states and we can use the `netstat` command to track and display the state of each TCP connection. Table 4.4 shows the most common states and includes a general description of each.

Table 4.4 *TCP States shown with* `Netstat`

State	Description
ESTABLISHED	The connection is operational
LISTEN	A service or application is waiting for a client connection
SYN_SENT	Local system wants to open a remote connection
SYN_RCVD	Remote system wants to open a connection
FIN_WAIT_1	Local system is in the process of closing a connection
FIN_WAIT_2	Local system is in the process of closing a connection
CLOSE_WAIT	Remote system wants to close a connection
LAST_ACK	Final step to CLOSE_WAIT
TIMED_WAIT	Final step to FIN_WAIT_1 or FIN_WAIT_2

The above `netstat` command only displays established connections. Sometimes it is helpful to list all services that are available and active on a system. This can be accomplished by using `netstat` with the `-a` option as shown below. Please note that the following output has been reduced to make it more readable. Executing this command on most server systems will produce a larger number of service entries than what has been listed here.

```
# netstat -a
UDP
   Local Address         Remote Address      State
-------------------- -------------------- -------
      *.route                                 Idle
      *.*                                     Unbound
      *.sunrpc                                Idle
      *.name                                  Idle
      *.biff                                  Idle
```

```
      *.talk                                Idle
      *.time                                Idle
      *.echo                                Idle
      *.discard                             Idle
      *.daytime                             Idle
      *.chargen                             Idle
      *.lockd                               Idle
      *.syslog                              Idle
      *.161                                 Idle
TCP
   Local Address        Remote Address    Swind Send-Q Rwind Recv-Q  State
-------------------- -------------------- ----- ------ ----- ------ -------
      *.*                  *.*                0      0     0      0 IDLE
      *.sunrpc             *.*                0      0     0      0 LISTEN
      *.*                  *.*                0      0     0      0 IDLE
      *.ftp                *.*                0      0     0      0 LISTEN
      *.telnet             *.*                0      0     0      0 LISTEN
      *.shell              *.*                0      0     0      0 LISTEN
      *.login              *.*                0      0     0      0 LISTEN
      *.exec               *.*                0      0     0      0 LISTEN
      *.finger             *.*                0      0     0      0 LISTEN
      *.time               *.*                0      0     0      0 LISTEN
monet.telnet         rembrandt.1036        8724      0  8760      0 ESTABLISHED
      *.smtp               *.*                0      0     0      0 LISTEN
localhost.80               *.*                0      0     0      0 LISTEN
monet.80                   *.*                0      0     0      0 LISTEN
monet.telnet         rembrandt.1040        8689      0  8760      0 ESTABLISHED
```

The `-a` option provides a list of both UDP and TCP services regardless of their connection states. This is useful because it is not always obvious which transport protocol a particular service uses.

Under the TCP heading, not only are the two TCP connections displayed from the previous example, but additional services are included as well. Any services listed in the `LISTEN` state are waiting for incoming connections and are usually considered server-based resources. When a service is waiting for requests from the network, it is free to access connections from any remote address. That is why a `*.*` is listed under the remote address field. Servers also generally place a `*` in the local host portion to further indicate that the server is free to establish a connection should a client request be made. When a request from a client is sent to a server, the server makes a copy of itself to handle the request and continues listening for additional client requests. This is why when this occurs, netstat displays multiple instances of the same service as shown below:

```
# netstat -a | grep ftp

      *.ftp                 *.*                   0      0      0       0 LISTEN
  monet.ftp             rembrandt.1041         8719      0   8760       0 ESTABLISHED
```

In the output above, the ftp server is still listening for incoming connection requests while an ftp session is established to rembrandt.

Under the UDP heading, only a local address and state field have been displayed; the remote address is left blank. This is because UDP is a connectionless protocol and therefore doesn't require remote address information. Also, notice that no statistical information is available for UDP. Another indication that UDP is fundamentally different by design is that it does not need this type of information.

Despite the rather large amount of information provided with the -a option, netstat can be used to provide a quick check to ensure that the correct services are running on a given system. By scanning the output of netstat, the network administrator can easily notice any services that shouldn't be running. For example, many organizations consider the finger facility to be a security risk because it can provide user account information to anyone requesting it. Once detected, finger can be disabled by modifying the /etc/inetd.conf network configuration file.

Displaying Interface Information

The netstat command can be used to obtain details on the network interface configuration and rudimentary packet counts as well. The -i command line option is used to obtain a list of each defined interface on the system, one per line as shown below. Also, the -n option is used to display IP addresses rather than hostnames.

```
# netstat -in
Name  Mtu  Net/Dest      Address       Ipkts  Ierrs Opkts  Oerrs Collis Queue
lo0   8232 127.0.0.0     127.0.0.1     117    0     117    0     0      0
le0   1500 128.197.0.0   128.197.2.1   0      0     0      220   0      0
le1   1500 10.0.0.0      10.0.2.126    180    0     177    1     0      0
```

As you can see, `netstat` displays some of the same information the `ifconfig` command provides, plus some basic statistics regarding operating characteristics of each interface—specifically, the name of the interface, the maximum transfer unit (MTU), the network or destination address, and the address of the interface. Also, a count of the total number of input packets, input error packets, output packets, number of collisions, and packets remaining in the queue are displayed. The `Net/Dest` field shows just the address of the network to which this interface is attached. Normally, this information is derived from the interface address, but it can also be specified in the `/etc/networks` file or through NIS. The Address field is the IP address of the interface, which, again, is specified in the `/etc/hosts` file or with NIS.

The `Ipkts` and `Opkts` fields represent the reception and transmission of valid traffic across the interface, respectively. The `Ierrs` field indicates any input error packets that have occurred on the interface; this includes, for example, any runt packets (those that are smaller than the standard size) and other errors. The `Oerrs` field indicates problems with the transmission of packets on the interface. In the output above, note that the interface `le0` reports a number of output packet errors. In this case, these errors are being generated because the interface is not physically attached to a network, yet the system is attempting to send out traffic. This is also the reason that the `Ipkts` and `Opkts` fields are zero; this indicates that no traffic has been sent or received across this interface.

The `Collis` field indicates the number of collisions that have occurred as recorded by the local system. A collision is when two or more devices attempt to transmit packets at nearly the same time. After this happens, a jam signal is sent to inform all devices that a collision has occurred and that any transmission should stop briefly and then, after randomly determined intervals of time, be tried again. This is known as *back-off* and is the mechanism used by devices to resume normal operations. Collisions only occur on broadcast network technologies such as Ethernet. When the `Collis` field is non-zero, it indicates that the interface has recorded collisions for which it was directly involved. It is important to note that this field does not represent all collisions that have occurred on the network.

The `Queue` field represents packets that are waiting to be processed by the system. In practice, this field provides no useful information.

The packet totals displayed from `netstat` closely match the values obtained directly from the SNMP agent `mibiisa`. The `mibiisa` is an agent that supports MIB objects and is available on Solaris systems. The table below lists the corresponding MIB objects supported by `mibiisa` that map to the `netstat` packet count fields. See Chapter 5, "Using SNMP Agents," for more details regarding `mibiisa` and the MIB objects listed in Table 4.5.

Table 4.5 *MIB Objects that Map to* `netstat` *Output*

Netstat Field	MIB Objects
`Ipkts`	IfInUcastPkts + ifInNUcastPkts
`Ierrs`	IfInErrors
`Opkts`	IfOutUcastPkts + ifOutNUcastPkts
`Oerrs`	IfOutErrors
`Collis`	IfInErrors - ifInUNcastPkts

If the system has a large number of interfaces and you are only interested in a particular one, use the `-I` command line option to specify the one you want. For example, to display only the `le1` interface, use the following command:

```
# netstat -I le1
Name  Mtu  Net/Dest        Address          Ipkts  Ierrs Opkts  Oerrs Collis Queue
le1   1500 monet           monet            8389   16    7095   1     0      0
```

If the dynamic host configuration protocol (DHCP) is used on the system, the `-D` option may be used to obtain interface information. This option lists all interfaces that use DHCP to obtain IP address information. Also, the `-d` option can be used to show the state of all interfaces that have been configured with DHCP.

Display Routing Information

The routing table is used by the system to determine the path to use to send IP packets to particular hosts or networks. Normally, systems are configured with a default router so that routing decisions are straightforward and simple. However, there may be instances when a machine has more than one interface, each attached to a different IP network. In this case, the system might also be forwarding IP packets (routing) between these networks. As a result, the routing function becomes a bit more complex. As part of the overall routing system, a routing table is defined that can be displayed as the need arises. One of the primary ways to examine this table is with the `-r` option as shown below:

```
# netstat -r
Routing Table:
  Destination              Gateway              Flags  Ref    Use    Interface
-------------------- ------------------- ----- ----- ------ ---------
128.197.0.0          durer                  U          2       0  le0
10.0.0.0             monet                  U          3       5  le1
224.0.0.0            monet                  U          3       0  le1
default              10.0.2.1               UG         0       0
localhost            localhost              UH         0       6  lo0
```

The routing table includes a destination network, the gateway (or router), some status flags, a reference count, a usage count, and the interface the route is associated with. The `destination` field specifies the network for which the route has been established. The `gateway` field shows the IP address or hostname of the router that can forward packets to the IP address listed in the `Destination` column.

The `Flags` field displays status information regarding the route. The `U` flag indicates that the route is up and active. The `H` flag shows that the route entry refers to a host system, not an actual router. With Unix, there is always a route to the local system, which is used internally by the networking software. The `G` flag indicates that the route is via an external gateway or router. In this case, a default route has been set to `10.0.2.1`. When a system contains a single interface, a default route can be used as a shorthand method to specify the only way out of the local network. Without the default entry, every network for which the system must connect will require a separate routing entry.

The `Ref` field represents the total number of routes sharing the same datalink address. The `Use` field shows the number of packets transmitted since the interface became active.

Additional detailed information regarding internal routes, external routes, and multicast routes can be displayed using the -a and the -g options. The -a option provides a complete list of all the routes defined on the system but, from a management standpoint, this additional information isn't very useful. The -g option displays routing information that is related to the routing groups and interfaces that have been defined on the system for multicast purposes. Again, from a network management perspective, this isn't used very often. Should routing problems occur, the basic netstat command with the -r option provides most, if not all, of the needed information.

The SNMP agent, mibiisa, or another MIB-II capable agent, can also be used to gather a significant amount of information for debugging purposes. By directly reviewing the ipRouteTable MIB group, routing information comparable to the netstat output may be obtained.

Display Protocol Statistics

The netstat command can be used to display protocol statistics. The -s option, by itself, will display all the protocols including udp, ip, udp, icmp, and igmp. Because this list can be rather long, you will probably prefer to use the -P option followed by one of the protocols just mentioned. Then, only that protocol will be displayed. For instance, to display just the IP protocol, use the following command:

```
# netstat -s -P ip
IP      ipForwarding        =     1     ipDefaultTTL        =   255
        ipInReceives        = 10401     ipInHdrErrors       =     0
        ipInAddrErrors      =     0     ipInCksumErrs       =   122
        ipForwDatagrams     =     0     ipForwProhibits     =     0
        ipInUnknownProtos   =   132     ipInDiscards        =     0
        ipInDelivers        = 18827     ipOutRequests       = 10080
        ipOutDiscards       =     0     ipOutNoRoutes       =     0
        ipReasmTimeout      =    60     ipReasmReqds        =     0
        ipReasmOKs          =     0     ipReasmFails        =     0
        ipReasmDuplicates   =     0     ipReasmPartDups     =     0
        ipFragOKs           =     0     ipFragFails         =     0
        ipFragCreates       =     0     ipRoutingDiscards   =     0
        tcpInErrs           =     0     udpNoPorts          =     3
        udpInCksumErrs      =     0     udpInOverflows      =     0
        rawipInOverflows    =     0
```

If you want statistics on all the protocols to be listed, invoke `netstat` without the `-P` option. Many of the object counters displayed with this option are also available with the `mibiisa` agent. However, the remaining objects, not found in that section, are described below:

```
udpInOverflows
rawipInOverflows
```

The `udpInOverflow` is a counter that represents UDP packets that have been received and caused a buffer to overflow. The `rawipInOverflow` represents the same statistic, but for the IP protocol.

Miscellaneous Netstat Options

Some additional options are available with the `netstat` command; these include the `-f` option, which is used to designate which protocol family should be displayed when using the `-g` and `-s` options. The next, the `-m` option, provides a display of stream count statistics. These totals can be used to monitor resource limitations on the system. The final option is the `-p` option, which displays the ARP table in the same format as the `arp -a` command previously discussed.

PING Tool

General Description

The `ping` command provides two basic services. First, it can be used to determine whether a basic level of connectivity is available between one or more end points. The `ping` tool can be used to determine if a remote device is reachable from the local system and help debug connectivity among systems. Second, it can provide rudimentary network performance statistics, which can be used to diagnose traffic-related network problems. The name "ping" is derived from the phrase *p*acket *in*ter*n*et *g*roper.

The `ping` tool can be used in one of two ways: by specifying a valid hostname or IP address or by using command line options with a hostname or IP address. Using the first form, `ping` provides a handy way to determine that a remote device is available on the network.

Recall from Chapter 3, "TCP/IP Protocol Suite," that `ping` uses the Internet Control Message Protocol (ICMP) to emit ICMP requests and waits for valid ICMP replies. Because ICMP is a required protocol within the TCP/IP family, `ping` can generally be found on every device that supports TCP/IP. The `ping` tool is a client side application only; no additional software is needed nor required for it to function and interact directly with the remote system's protocol layer to accomplish its task.

Determine System Availability

The `ping` tool can be used to determine general availability of any TCP/IP device. For example, to determine if the host `rembrandt` is reachable, issue the following `ping` command:

```
# ping rembrandt
rembrandt is alive
```

In this case, `ping` reports that `rembrandt` is alive. This message generally means that the TCP/IP software is operational. Although "alive" indicates that the system is visible on the network, it is no guarantee that other network services, such as FTP or TELNET, are available. This is an important distinction. The `ping` tool can only be used to determine basic protocol connectivity—not the availability of higher-level applications or services. In fact, some systems will answer a ping even before they are fully booted. Keep in mind that no single piece of software is available that will determine that every TCP/IP application or service is installed and operating on a system.

If the host `rembrandt` is not reachable, `ping` will issue the following message

```
no answer from rembrandt
```

Normally, `ping` issues ICMP requests for approximately 20 seconds and, if no reply is received, generates the message shown above. The time-out value can be altered by providing an argument after the hostname. The command below will continue to issue requests for up to a minute (or until the host responds) before reporting the host's status:

```
# ping rembrandt 60
```

This is useful when a host requires additional time, perhaps because it is in the boot process, before it can respond to the request.

In is interesting to note that if the host `rembrandt` isn't on the same subnet as the host issuing the `ping`, it is possible that the host is functioning correctly, but that an intermediate device, such as a network router, is responsible for the lack of connectivity. In this case, `ping` can't determine why `rembrandt` is not reachable. To further understand this problem, consider the example network in Figure 4.1. This network picture shows several devices attached to two different networks that are interconnected via network `Router A`. When a `ping` request is issued from `Node B` `Network A` to `Node D` on `Network B`, the request is passed via `Router A`. If `Router A` should fail, the requests will never reach `Node D`. As a result, `Node D` becomes unreachable from the perspective of `Node B`.

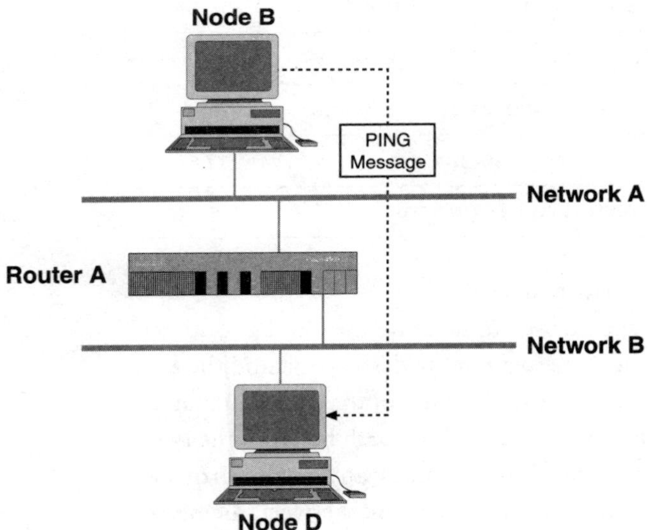

Figure 4.1 *Node Unreachable Problem.*

Because `ping` can be used to check reachability of any TCP/IP device, we can now `ping Router A` to further diagnose the problem. By probing the router closest to `Node D`, we will learn that the loss of connectivity is most likely being caused by `Router A`'s network interface to `Network B` and not `Node D`. Also, should we `ping` other devices on `Network B`, this would only confirm that all devices are unreachable and lead us to conclude that there is a problem with `Router A`. This example demonstrates that network problems can be caused by devices other than those easily identified as sender and receiver. Tools such as `ping` help to isolate the sources of routing and many other network failures or problems.

The second form of the `ping` command provides a number of options to control additional functionality. Table 4.6 provides a list of the most popular command line options available with the `ping` command.

Table 4.6 *PING Command Options*

Option	Description
`packetsize`	Modify `ping` packet size
`count`	Send only count number of packets
`-s`	Show statistics
`-n`	Show network addresses
`-I`	Modify echo requests interval
`-R`	Toggle record router options

Determining Network Performance

The `ping` command can be used to measure the amount of time required to transmit a message to a remote destination and the time required to obtain a response. This use of the `ping` command in essence measures the relative speed of the path between the two devices at a given point in time. It does not, by any means, provide a detailed analysis of the devices or connectivity between them. Rather, it provides a glimpse of the general condition of the path at the point it is measured. It could be said that network performance is like the stock market. One day it is up and the next it is down. The primary difference with respect to volatility is whether we are talking in terms of days or in terms of milliseconds. A large number of factors can cause network performance to vary.

The `ping` command provides a means of determining system response times as well, but it takes a little more work to determine if the observed performance problem is related to a slow system or a delay in the network.

The -s option is used to measure and report round time and packet loss statistics. By default, ping issues an ICMP request every second to the destination supplied on the command line and reports the status of each ICMP reply. Sample output using this option is shown below:

```
# ping -s monet
PING monet: 56 data bytes
64 bytes from monet (10.0.2.75): icmp_seq=0. time=4. ms
64 bytes from monet (10.0.2.75): icmp_seq=1. time=2. ms
64 bytes from monet (10.0.2.75): icmp_seq=2. time=1. ms
^C
---- monet PING Statistics----
3 packets transmitted, 3 packets received, 0% packet loss
round-trip (ms)  min/avg/max = 1/2/4
```

The report above provides the packet size, the hostname or IP address of the target device, a sequence number, round trip time value, and a statistical summary. The time value shows the round trip time in milliseconds (1000th of a second) for each reply received. The bottom of the report calculates the minimum, average, and maximum trip times for all replies, also displayed in milliseconds. The output continues until a ^C (control c) is issued from the keyboard or monet stops responding to the ICMP requests. The total length of the ICMP packet transmitted to monet is 64-bytes. This is the default size, which is usually sufficient. However, it might be necessary to increase the packet size to get a better measure of throughput. In this case, a large packet size may be specified after the target field. For example, the command:

```
# ping -s monet 100
```

issues the ICMP requests with a packet size of 100-bytes to the target host monet. This might be required to obtain a better picture of performance because network throughput may differ with larger packet sizes versus smaller values.

A count can be provided after the packet size argument to control how many ICMP requests are sent to the desired destination. Specifying the count in this manner is sometimes preferable when using ping within a shell script where issuing a ^C would be difficult or inconvenient. Using the count option is an ideal way to obtain a very good round trip delay average and to determine connectivity over time. Note that because the count option is expected after the packet size value, you must include both when using the count argument. Otherwise, ping will interpret the count value as the packet size. The command:

```
# ping -s steve-pc 3
PING steve-pc: 3 data bytes
11 bytes from steve-pc (10.0.2.75): icmp_seq=0.
11 bytes from steve-pc (10.0.2.75): icmp_seq=1.
11 bytes from steve-pc (10.0.2.75): icmp_seq=2.
11 bytes from steve-pc (10.0.2.75): icmp_seq=3.
11 bytes from steve-pc (10.0.2.75): icmp_seq=4.
11 bytes from steve-pc (10.0.2.75): icmp_seq=5.
11 bytes from steve-pc (10.0.2.75): icmp_seq=6.
11 bytes from steve-pc (10.0.2.75): icmp_seq=7.
^C
----steve-pc PING Statistics----
8 packets transmitted, 8 packets received, 0% packet loss
```

does not do what we probably had in mind because it interprets the value 3 as the packet size instead of the count (it indicates 11 bytes from host) The ping command adds 8 bytes of overhead for each packet sent and the 11 bytes displayed in the above command was derived from adding 3 bytes to the 8 bytes of overhead. Also, notice that the ping above must be terminated by the user because it issues more than 3 requests. If you want to issue a large number of ping requests (say 200) and increase the default packet size to 108 bytes, use the following command:

```
# ping -s monet 100 200
```

If you don't want to change the default packet size but still want to include a count value, just specify 56 bytes of data. The ping command below uses the default packet size with the specified count as shown below:

```
# ping -s monet-a 56 3
PING monet-a: 56 data bytes
64 bytes from monet-a (199.81.146.200): icmp_seq=0. time=4. ms
64 bytes from monet-a (199.81.146.200): icmp_seq=1. time=2. ms
64 bytes from monet-a (199.81.146.200): icmp_seq=2. time=1. ms
----monet-a PING Statistics----
3 packets transmitted, 3 packets received, 0% packet loss
round-trip (ms)  min/avg/max = 1/2/4
```

The `ping` tool uses a sequence number to keep track of requests and replies. Each request is given the next number in sequence and then is matched with the corresponding reply. This sequencing is used to determine packet loss if any requests do not receive an appropriate reply. Generally speaking, packet loss on a small network should be very rare and if it does occur it might indicate a network or system-related problem. However, on a large segmented network (internet with a lower case i) or on the Internet, packet loss is common and represents a normal state of affairs. Given a popular Internet site as shown below, a certain amount of packet loss is almost always observed:

```
ping -s www.whitehouse.gov 56 10
PING www.whitehouse.gov: 56 data bytes
64 bytes from www.whitehouse.gov: icmp_seq=0. time=180. ms
64 bytes from www.whitehouse.gov: icmp_seq=2. time=169. ms
64 bytes from www.whitehouse.gov: icmp_seq=3. time=191. ms
64 bytes from www.whitehouse.gov: icmp_seq=4. time=173. ms
64 bytes from www.whitehouse.gov: icmp_seq=5. time=167. ms
64 bytes from www.whitehouse.gov: icmp_seq=7. time=184. ms
64 bytes from www.whitehouse.gov: icmp_seq=8. time=268. ms
64 bytes from www.whitehouse.gov: icmp_seq=9. time=196. ms
----www.whitehouse.gov PING Statistics----
10 packets transmitted, 8 packets received, 20% packet loss
round-trip (ms)  min/avg/max = 167/191/268
```

The report above indicates that 20 percent of the packets sent to the `www.whitehouse.gov` system did not have corresponding replies —they were lost. One possible reason for this noticeable packet loss is that some of the critical Internet routers might be quite busy or even overloaded with network traffic. As a result, some of the ICMP requests might be discarded because the requests expired before they were delivered to the final destination. Also, the relative load of the target device can be a factor because these systems might not have the computing resources to answer all network requests in the time required.

Sometimes it is desirable to provide additional time for acknowledging each `ping` request instead of using the default value of 1 second. If additional time is desired between successive ICMP requests, the `-I` option can be used followed by the desired value. The interval should be long enough to provide the required amount of time for the remote system to respond. When we increase the time-out value as suggested, we will generally notice less packet loss. The command:

```
ping -s www.whitehouse.gov -I 5
```

adds a 5 second delay to each ping request, thus providing additional time before packet loss might occur.

Miscellaneous Ping Options

With the `-n` option, `ping` displays IP addresses rather than hostnames. This is useful, for example, when network problems involving DNS impact the use of `ping`. This option instructs `ping` not to invoke hostname resolution, thus permitting the tool to function while the name service is slow or temporarily disabled.

The `-R` option enables the record route option with the IP protocol. Toggling the record route informs each router along a path to place its IP address in the IP header. As a result, a list of routers that were used to reach the final destination can be obtained.

SNOOP Tool

Tool Availability

This command is available only on the Solaris operating system.

General Description

The `snoop` command is a general-purpose network traffic monitor that can be used to capture and display packets and their contents. This command can be used as *protocol analyzer*, providing one of the best ways to investigate communication problems among systems and networking devices. Most of the time network troubleshooting is centered on dealing with network configuration problems. Every now and then, however, you will be faced with a protocol-related problem and will be forced to delve into the heart of the particular protocol to resolve the problem.

The packets scanned will be displayed with information in either a short or long form depending on the command line options provided. Also, `snoop` has a very powerful filtering mechanism that can be used to search for packets that match a specific criterion.

Two primary capture modes are provided by `snoop` : promiscuous and non-promiscuous. In promiscuous mode, every packet that is transmitted on the network is captured, whether or not the packet was sent to the system `snoop` is listening from. This is the mode, for instance, that RMON probes use when monitoring network traffic. Because LAN protocols such as Ethernet are broadcast-based, every frame transmitted can be seen by any network interface attached to the LAN. Any device can read every frame transmitted if that device so chooses. When a device or interface reads every frame from the network, it is said to be in promiscuous mode. In practice, the interface must be configured for promiscuous mode and is only used on special occasions when network diagnosis is required. For this reason, only `root` may enable promiscuous mode on an interface.

With non-promiscuous mode, only broadcast frames and frames addressed to the local device will be available to the interface. The term broadcast actually refers to both normal broadcast (with all `1`s in the destination field) and multicast traffic. Under normal circumstances, the interface is in this mode.

When `snoop` is invoked without command line options, it opens the primary network interface and begins capturing frames from the local network and displaying their contents. The command

```
# snoop
Using device /dev/le (promiscuous mode)
```

when executed by root will display all network frames in the single-line, non-verbose format. The format of the output will include the source and destination hosts, the high-level network protocol, and additional protocol information as shown below:

```
rembrandt -> monet        TELNET C port=1032
rembrandt -> monet        TELNET C port=1033
    monet -> rembrandt    ICMP Echo request
rembrandt -> monet        ICMP Echo reply
```

In this example, `rembrandt`, the source host, and `monet`, the destination host, have a TELNET session established. `monet` has issued a `ping` request to `rembrandt` and `rembrandt` has responded with a reply. The `->` string indicates the direction of the communication. Note that `snoop` always orients the communication path to point to the right as in the case of the ICMP Echo request above. To indicate communication in the other direction, `snoop` reverses the hosts, not the pointer as shown with the ICMP Echo reply entry. The `snoop` command displays the high level protocols in upper case, such as TELNET and ICMP, followed by more specific information pertaining to the protocol that might include ports, additional protocols, and data.

The `snoop` tool provides a large number of command line options to control its capture modes, filter specifications, and operating characteristics. These options are grouped according to function and include:

- Operating Modes
- Display Options
- Packet Filter Options

Operating Mode Options

These options are used to control how `snoop` will capture and display network traffic. The available options are summarized in Table 4.7 and are described fully below.

Table 4.7 *Snoop Operating Mode Options*

Option	Description
`-d`	Capture using alternate network interface
`-c`	Capture specified number of packets
`-P`	Capture in non-promiscuous mode
`-o`	Save snoop output to file
`-N`	Create address-to-name file
`-i`	Read capture file instead of network interface
`-n`	Use alternative address-to-name mapping file

Normally, `snoop` will listen for traffic on the primary network interface. Usually the primary interface has the smallest numeric identifier; for example, `le0` is considered the primary. However, if you want to snoop on a different interface, use the -d option and the device name to specify the alternate interface. For example, to select the Fast Ethernet interface, use the following command:

```
# snoop -d hme0
Using device /dev/hme0(promiscuous mode)
```

Note that only the device name is used and not the directory /dev. The snoop command adds the directory information to the front of the device name when opening the interface.

By default, snoop will capture until a ^C is typed from the controlling terminal (or if placed in the background, until the process is terminated with the kill command). If you wish to specify the number of packets to be captured, use the -c option followed by the number of packets desired. To capture 10 packets from the second Ethernet interface, use the command:

```
# snoop -d le1 -c 10
Using device /dev/le (promiscuous mode)
      monet -> rembrandt      FTP-DATA R port=1047
      monet -> rembrandt      FTP-DATA R port=1047
      monet -> rembrandt      FTP-DATA R port=1047
      monet -> rembrandt      FTP-DATA R port=1047
      monet -> rembrandt      FTP-DATA R port=1047
      monet -> rembrandt      FTP-DATA R port=1047
  rembrandt -> monet          FTP-DATA C port=1047
  rembrandt -> monet          FTP-DATA C port=1047
  rembrandt -> monet          FTP-DATA C port=1047
      monet -> rembrandt      FTP-DATA R port=1047
snoop: 10 packets captured
```

In this case, snoop has captured an FTP session between monet and rembrandt. We can confirm the number of captured packets by examining the last line above. Specifying the number of packets to capture is useful when the intent is to monitor a critical network transaction that uses a fixed number of packet exchange. This option is also useful when monitoring packets within a shell script because you don't have to be concerned about stopping snoop after it has been started.

As previously indicated, snoop, by default, opens the network interface in promiscuous mode to capture all network traffic. Sometimes, it is more effective to examine packets delivered to a specified host. If we only want to capture those packets addressed to the host snoop is running on, the -P option is used to disable promiscuous mode.

```
# snoop -d le1 -P
Using device /dev/le (non promiscuous)
```

The snoop command confirms the use of the -P option by displaying the "non promiscuous" message. Why use this option? Sometimes it becomes necessary to examine all traffic that arrives normally at a particular system. With the -P option, we can see every packet that is received by the local system and nothing more. This can be used to easily detect (by monitoring the incoming packets), for example, whether a request for a particular service is reaching the system. Given a client/server environment, we can determine if requests from client systems are reaching the server (by running snoop on the server) or if a particular client is transmitting requests in the first place (by running snoop on the client).

On a very active network, and with using certain command line options, snoop can produce a large amount of output. To help manage this, the -o option can be used to redirect the captured information into a file. One reason to use a file is to inspect the network traffic in depth at a later time. When the -o option is used, snoop only displays a count of the total number of packets being saved to the file. If you want to obtain a running count of packets and not the contents of packets, use the -o option with /dev/null as the file.

To capture network traffic and save it to a file called traffic-data, use the following command:

```
# snoop -d le1 -o traffic-data
Using device /dev/le1 (promiscuous mode)
372 ^C
```

The file, traffic-data, is created in the local directory. The Unix file command reports that this file is associated with the snoop command and, as a result, can't be processed except by a program that understands the data format. It is not a human-readable text file. The command

```
# file traffic-data
traffic-data:          Snoop capture file - version 2
```

shows that traffic-data is a version 2 snoop file. If you try to view the file, it would appear to be a long series of strange characters.

To display the packets in this file, see the Display Options section below.

It might sometimes be necessary or simply convenient to use snoop at one site, capture the desired network traffic to a file, and review and inspect the output at a completely different site. The major problem in doing this is that hostname information might not map correctly when reviewing the captured packets at the new site. For instance, if we capture packets from host rembrandt from site A, and we display these packets at site B, rembrandt might not be defined. It is possible that the host rembrandt is defined at site B, but in all likelihood, the IP address information will be different from site A. In this case, only IP address information will be displayed for those packets from rembrandt.

To address this problem, snoop provides a way to create a hostname that is the same format as the /etc/host file to address mapping files. The -N option instructs snoop to build a mapping file from a previously captured snoop output file, which provides the benefit of preserving the hostname information. For example, to build a mapping file from the traffic-data file created above, issue the following command:

```
# snoop -N -i traffic-data
Creating name file traffic-data.names
```

The snoop program then creates a new file with the same name as the capture file with the string ".names" added to the end. In the above example, snoop confirms the creation of the traffic-data.names file. This example also illustrates the -i option, which directs snoop to read a capture file instead of using the network interface. Normally, when the -i option is used, snoop looks for a hostname mapping file with the same name plus the .names extension. It is possible to specify a different file name than the one with the .names extension by using the -n option along with the file name as shown below:

```
# snoop -n host-table -i traffic-data
```

Display Options

These options are used to control how `snoop` will display packets from the network. The list of the available options under this category is summarized in Table 4.8 and is described fully below.

Table 4.8 *Snoop Display Options*

Option	Description
`-S`	Display frame size
`-v`	Verbose mode
`-V`	Verbose summary mode
`-D`	Display dropped packets
`-t`	Time-stamp
`-p`	Display one or more packets from file
`-s`	Truncate packet
`-x`	Display both hexadecimal and ASCII format

Sometimes it is useful to determine the length of datalink frames. This can be helpful, for example, when investigating performance problems related to higher level applications. The `snoop` tool provides a way to obtain the size of each frame including both the header and data portion with the `-S` command line option. The sample command and output below show a file transfer session using FTP:

```
# snoop -S
Using device /dev/le (promiscuous mode)
      monet -> rembrandt    length: 1514  FTP-DATA R port=1039
      monet -> rembrandt    length: 1514  FTP-DATA R port=1039
  rembrandt -> monet        length:   60  FTP-DATA C port=1039
```

As you can see, the length field is displayed. It shows the total size of the frame in bytes. The reason the packets from `monet` to `rembrandt` are greater than 1500 bytes is because FTP is filling the packet with as much data as it can hold. Remember that Ethernet has a data capacity of 1500 bytes, not including the header portion.

So far, we have discussed using the default display capabilities of `snoop`; it displays a single line summary of the packet capture that includes source, destination, and additional protocol details. Suppose we want to obtain more specific detailed information, including the high level and datalink layer protocols. In this case, we can use the `-v` option to display the datalink protocol, plus any other protocols encapsulated within each packet. Using this option, we can decode and display any packet captured with `snoop`.

To illustrate, consider the following ARP packet exchange as displayed by `snoop` without any display options:

```
monet -> (broadcast) ARP C Who is 10.0.2.75, rembrandt
  rembrandt -> monet       ARP R 10.0.2.75, rembrandt is
0:60:8:26:be:5e
```

Now let's observe the same packet exchange (see Listing 4.2) with the `-v` option, placing `snoop` in verbose packet decode mode:

Listing 4.2 *Arp Packet Exchange*

```
ETHER:  ----- Ether Header -----
ETHER:
ETHER:  Packet 1 arrived at 21:43:15.14
ETHER:  Packet size = 42 bytes
ETHER:  Destination = ff:ff:ff:ff:ff:ff, (broadcast)
ETHER:  Source      = 8:0:20:4:cf:2c, Sun
ETHER:  Ethertype = 0806 (ARP)
ETHER:
ARP:  ----- ARP/RARP Frame -----
ARP:
ARP:  Hardware type = 1
ARP:  Protocol type = 0800 (IP)
ARP:  Length of hardware address = 6 bytes
ARP:  Length of protocol address = 4 bytes
ARP:  Opcode 1 (ARP Request)
ARP:  Sender's hardware address = 8:0:20:4:cf:2c
ARP:  Sender's protocol address = 10.0.2.126, monet
ARP:  Target hardware address = ?
ARP:  Target protocol address = 10.0.2.75, rembrandt
ARP:
ETHER:  ----- Ether Header -----
```

(Cont'd)

Listing 4.2 *Arp Packet Exchange (Cont'd)*

```
22  ETHER:
23  ETHER:  Packet 2 arrived at 21:43:15.14
24  ETHER:  Packet size = 60 bytes
25  ETHER:  Destination = 8:0:20:4:cf:2c, Sun
26  ETHER:  Source      = 0:60:8:26:be:5e,
27  ETHER:  Ethertype = 0806 (ARP)
28  ETHER:
29  ARP:  ----- ARP/RARP Frame -----
30  ARP:
31  ARP:  Hardware type = 1
32  ARP:  Protocol type = 0800 (IP)
33  ARP:  Length of hardware address = 6 bytes
34  ARP:  Length of protocol address = 4 bytes
35  ARP:  Opcode 2 (ARP Reply)
36  ARP:  Sender's hardware address = 0:60:8:26:be:5e
37  ARP:  Sender's protocol address = 10.0.2.75, rembrandt
38  ARP:  Target hardware address = 8:0:20:4:cf:2c
39  ARP:  Target protocol address = 10.0.2.126, monet
40  ARP:
```

The listing above includes only two packets! The first is the ICMP Echo request sent from `monet`, and the second is the ICMP echo reply from `rembrandt`. Each packet contains an ETHER and ARP section. The first ETHER and ARP sections represent the first packet, while the next two sections belong to the second. The ETHER, as between lines `1-8` and `21-28`, represents the datalink frame, which is formatted according to the Ethernet specification. Recall that each Ethernet frame contains a fixed-length header that includes preamble, destination, source, type, data, and checksum information. However, `snoop` only reports packet size, destination, source, type, and data fields from the Ethernet frame. The other fields are not displayed because the low-level Ethernet driver doesn't make the information available to `snoop`.

The ARP sections start on lines `9` and `29` and denote the higher-level protocols that have been encapsulated with the data portion of the Ethernet frames. As previously indicated, many higher level protocols—like TCP, IP, and IPX—can be encapsulated just like ARP. In this case, the ARP packet includes information specific to the ARP protocol—hardware type, hardware address information, ARP packet type, sender's hardware address information, and target (desired) hardware address. We can determine that the first ARP packet is a request because the `opcode` field is set to 1 and because the target hardware address is missing. This is why `snoop` places a `?` character in this hardware address field. Notice that the second ARP packet is the reply. It contains a `2` in the `opcode` field and both hardware addresses have been assigned values.

Because the verbose mode of `snoop` displays a significant amount of detail, it should be used only when inspecting a small number of packets while debugging network protocol issues or problems. This approach should be followed for two reasons. First, verbose mode displays a large number of lines per packet and, as a result, attempts to find some specific information can be difficult. The proverbial "needle in the haystack" certainly applies. Second, decoding each frame and subsequently every encapsulated protocol requires additional computing processing overhead. Using the system resources to decode packets might have an adverse effect on other system tasks and on `snoop` as well. Because `snoop` is run like any other system program, it must share the system with many competing tasks. The amount of traffic on the network will also have an effect on `snoop`, because a heavily loaded network will require more processing than a lightly loaded one. As a result, `snoop` can miss or drop packets if it is busy decoding or displaying a lot of packets.

It is important to know, particularly in a networking debugging situation, when `snoop` drops packets. If you think this might be happening, use the `-D` option to display the number of packets `snoop` drops. You might use this option, for example, when capturing a critical packet exchange between systems.

Sometimes, you will need to examine only a few protocol details and not entire packets. In this case, using the `-v` option is overkill. Luckily, `snoop` provides the `-V` option, which displays packet information between the default summary mode and the detailed decode mode provided by the `-v` option. This mode displays enough protocol details to be useful, yet doesn't inundate you with too many lines of output. A `snoop` session that contains the same ARP exchange as above is provided below:

```
# snoop -V
Using device /dev/le (promiscuous mode)
________________________________
      monet -> (broadcast)  ETHER Type=0806 (ARP), size = 42 bytes
      monet -> (broadcast)  ARP C Who is 10.0.2.75, rembrandt ?
________________________________
  rembrandt -> monet        ETHER Type=0806 (ARP), size = 60 bytes
  rembrandt -> monet        ARP R 10.0.2.75, rembrandt is 0:60:8:26:be:5e
```

As you can see, the output contains some of the information that is presented with the -v option, but without as many details. Use this mode when looking for a general overview of the types of traffic on your network, but not to debug network protocol issues or problems. For every packet, each encapsulated protocol is displayed, along with certain protocol information on a separate line. This display makes it easy to glance at the protocols contained within each packet presented.

The -x option provides a way to display a hexadecimal dump of network frames. This option is used with an offset value. The offset is used to control how much of the packet should be displayed. A value of 0 indicates that the whole packet should be shown. Consider the series of packet exchanges when the host rembrandt attempts to open an FTP session to a system called durer. The snoop command:

```
snoop -d le1 -x 0 tcp and port 21
```

will capture any FTP activity on the network. When this command is executed and an FTP session is started, the following packets will be captured:

```
  rembrandt -> durer        FTP C port=1031
         0: 0800 2004 cf2c 0010 5a28 5d7c 0800 4500     .. ..,..Z(]|..E.
        16: 002c 1b21 4000 2006 275c 0a00 024b 0a00     .,.!@. .'\...K..
        32: 0205 0407 0015 00e6 4493 0000 0000 6002     ........D.....`.
        48: 2000 1646 0000 0204 05b0 0000                 ..F........
      durer -> rembrandt    FTP R port=1031
         0: 0010 5a28 5d7c 0800 2004 cf2c 0800 4500     ..Z(]|.. ..,..E.
        16: 002c a478 4000 ff06 bf03 0a00 0205 0a00     .,.x@...........
        32: 024b 0015 0407 4a87 5083 00e6 4494 6012     .K....J.P...D.`.
        48: 27d0 735a 0000 0204 05b0                    '.sZ......
  rembrandt -> durer        FTP C port=1031
         0: 0800 2004 cf2c 0010 5a28 5d7c 0800 4500     .. ..,..Z(]|..E.
        16: 0028 1c21 4000 2006 2660 0a00 024b 0a00     .(.!@. .&`...K..
```

```
    32: 0205 0407 0015 00e6 4494 4a87 5084 5010     ........D.J.P.P.
    48: 2220 90c3 0000 0000 0000 0000               " ..........
durer -> rembrandt     FTP R port=1031 220 monet FTP server
     0: 0010 5a28 5d7c 0800 2004 cf2c 0800 4500     ..Z(]|.. ..,..E.
    16: 0051 a479 4000 ff06 bedd 0a00 0205 0a00     .Q.y@..........
    32: 024b 0015 0407 4a87 5084 00e6 4494 5018     .K....J.P...D.P.
    48: 27d0 3419 0000 3232 3020 6d6f 6e65 7420     '.4...220 monet
    64: 4654 5020 7365 7276 6572 2028 5375 6e4f     FTP server (SunO
    80: 5320 352e 3629 2072 6561 6479 2e0d 0a    S 5.6) ready...
```

As you can see, the output shows a summary line that contains the source and destination of the packet, the protocol, and port information. In this case, we see FTP with either an `R` or `C` flag, followed by the port number. The `R` indicates that the packet is a response, while the `C` means it is a request. The next part of the display shows the byte offset for the entire frame with hexadecimal and ASCII information. Most of these packets don't contain any readable information, which is why strange characters are shown on the right. The last packet, however, displays some readable characters. This packet represents part of the login procedure that is associated with the FTP application. The output below shows what is displayed to the user on the client side of the FTP connection:

```
rembrandt# ftp 10.0.2.5
Connected to 10.0.2.5.
220 monet FTP server (SunOS 5.6) ready.
Name (10.0.2.5:smaxwell):
```

Notice the FTP server string in the output above corresponds with the string contained with the last packet? With the `-x` option, it becomes very easy to search for specific patterns or other information with network packets.

Using Packet Filters

One very important aspect of network protocol debugging involves the use of packet filters. A packet filter is a predefined pattern that is compared to incoming packets and consists of a series of one or more primitives that might be combined with operators such as `and`, `or`, and `not`. When the pattern is matched, that packet is captured or displayed, or else the packet is discarded or not displayed. Packet filters are useful when searching for a particular protocol type or any other specific information available within the packet.

snoop uses two different packet filter mechanisms, depending on whether snoop is capturing from the network or displaying previously captured packets from a file. The first, known as the kernel packet filter, is installed by snoop when a filter expression is given on the command line. This filter is placed within the operating system kernel and will filter according the rules of the packet filter. Every packet is compared to the filter and when a match is found, the packet is forwarded to snoop. Otherwise, the packet is discarded. The kernel packet filter is very efficient because the processing of the filter is occurring within the kernel, not within snoop.

The second filter mechanism, known as the snoop filter, is used when the -i option is specified (i.e., when reading packets from a file). This filter is used to control which of the previously captured packets will be displayed. The snoop filter is slower than the kernel filter, but filtering is not as time critical as it is when processing packets asynchronously from the network. Figure 4.2 shows a diagram of both packet filter types.

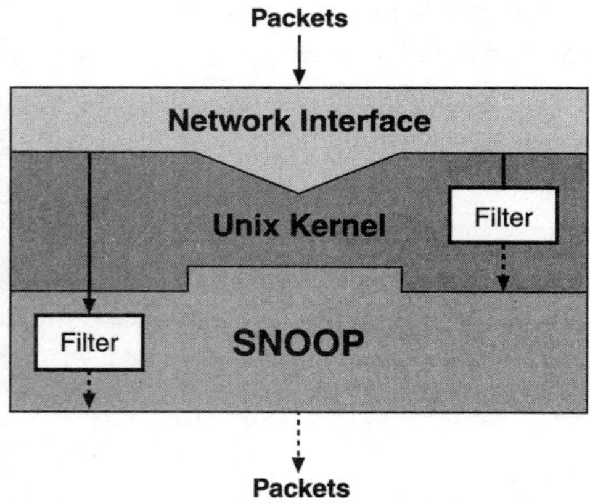

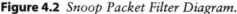

Figure 4.2 *Snoop Packet Filter Diagram.*

The snoop tool provides a large number of pre-defined expressions or primitives that can be used to build very powerful packet filters. These expressions can be divided into three groups. The first group, called address primitives, operates on packets using address information such as IP or datalink addresses; the second group, known as protocol primitives, operates on packets that use different protocols including IP, AppleTalk, and others. The final group includes Boolean and arithmetic primitives (or operators) that can be used with the first two expression types to produce compound filters. Compound filters include more than one expression type separated by reserve words such as `and`, `not`, and `or`. These filters can also include arithmetic operators such as +, -, *, and others. These expressions are evaluated to be either true or false and the result will determine what action `snoop` will take.

Address Primitives

Expressions that operate on the addressing portions of a packet are listed in Table 4.9 and are described in more detail below.

Table 4.9 *Address Related Primitives*

Primitive	Description
`gateway`	Selects packets that have been used by specified host as a gateway
`host`	Selects packets from specified host
`ipaddr` `etheraddr`	Selects packets from either IP or datalink addresses
`broadcast`	Selects broadcast packet that contains all `1s` or `FF` in either source or destination fields
`multicast`	Selects packets that are sent to multicast addresses
`net`	Selects packets that contain specified network portion used with the IP protocol
`port`	Selects packets that contain specified port addresses used with the IP protocol

The gateway primitive is used to select packets that have been forwarded by a router. This indicates that the datalink addresses of the packet (either source or destination) match that of host, but not the IP address. Normally, a router will not change the IP address information when forwarding packets, but the datalink address will match the device that forwards the packet.

The `host` primitive followed by a valid hostname can be used to select packets that are either sent to or received from the specified hostname. The `host` keyword is mainly used to avoid ambiguity that might arise if you were to specify a hostname that just happens to be the same as one of the `snoop` existing keywords. For example, when monitoring the host `gateway`, the `host` keyword must be used because the `gateway` keyword will be interpreted as a keyword, rather than as a valid hostname. Thus, the `snoop` command listed below produces an error because the gateway string is assumed to specify a local gateway.

```
# snoop gateway
snoop: hostname required:
```

The way to specify the capture of packets from a host called `gateway` would be:

```
# snoop host gateway
Using device /dev/le (promiscuous mode)
```

The `ipaddr` and `etheraddr` are used to specify actual IP addresses and datalink addresses in dotted and colon formats, respectively. For example, to capture all packets from the IP address `10.0.2.100`, the following command would be used:

```
# snoop ipaddr 10.0.2.100
```

The `ipaddr` and `etheraddr` primitives will match on either the source or destination address. Some datalink addresses begin with a letter and will cause `snoop` to misinterpret these as hostnames, rather than true addresses. To avoid this problem, prepend a zero when specifying these types of addresses.

To capture broadcast packets, use the `broadcast` primitive. A *broadcast* is a special address that designates that all devices should receive the message. Several network protocols and services such as ARP, NIS, and RIP use broadcasts to propagate certain information across the network. Using `broadcast` will result in the capture of broadcast packets from the datalink level. That is to say, any address that contains `255` or `FF` within the source or destination field will be captured. This includes datalink packets that contain broadcast (such as ARP requests) and high-level protocol broadcasts (such as an IP broadcast). This primitive could be used to capture routing data from the routing information protocol (RIP) because routers periodically broadcast routing updates.

Also, to obtain multicast traffic such as Internet radio, use the `multicast` primitive. The standard multicast address of `224.0.0.1` is used to support this type of traffic as defined by the multicast standard.

Protocol Primitives

`snoop` provides protocol primitives as a shorthand way to select specific network traffic, without requiring the low-level protocol information. For example, the `ip` primitive can be used to capture all IP traffic. Without this keyword, you would need to use the IP type of `x0800`, which is harder to remember and use. These primitives support the TCP/IP, AppleTalk, and DECnet family of protocols. A list of these protocol keywords is in Table 4.10, along with a description and associated low-level numeric values expressed in hexadecimal.

Table 4.10 *Protocol Primitives*

Primitive	Description
`apple`	AppleTalk protocol family
`arp`	Address Resolution Protocol—includes both request and reply
`ethertype`	Specifies another protocol type
`decnet`	DECnet protocol family
`ip`	Internet Protocol
`icmp`	Internet Control Message Protocol—includes both echo and reply
`rarp`	Reverse Address Resolution Protocol—includes both request and reply
`tcp`	Transmission Control Protocol
`udp`	User Datagram Protocol

To select a protocol family or type that isn't provided directly by `snoop`, use the `ethertype` primitive along with the type code for the desired protocol. For example, to monitor Novell NetWare packets (which have a type code of `0x8137`), use the command:

```
# snoop ethertype 0x8137
```

Please note, because `snoop` doesn't support the Novell protocol family directly, no packet information can be displayed beyond the datalink layer. If `snoop` finds packets that contain a Novell header, it will list the datalink information only. However, despite this disadvantage, `snoop` can still be used to identify certain packet types and provide rudimentary packet count information.

Operators

`snoop` supports several expression (or operator) types and can be combined with primitives and qualifiers to produce compound filters. These expressions include arithmetic and Boolean operators, listed in Table 4.11. Operators can be used to build powerful expressions to search for specific packets or information. Expressions can be composed of numbers, packet field selections, length primitives, and arithmetic operators. To use the value of a field in an expression within a packet, use the following syntax:

```
primitive [offset [: size] ]
```

where the word `primitive` is replaced with `ether`, `ip`, `udp`, `tcp`, or `icmp`. The `offset` is used in the base of the protocol primitive and the `size` specifies the length of the field. If not supplied, it defaults to `1`.

Packet field sections can be used in a variety of ways. Consider the following examples:

```
snoop "ether[1:4]&0xffffffff = 0xffffffff"
```

In this example, `snoop` will display all broadcast packets transmitted on the local network. This means all frames with a destination address of all 1s (255 in decimal, `0xff` in hexadecimal). The `ether[1:4]` indicates the first addressable byte of the frame (the destination address) and the 4 value specifies the length of this field. Despite the fact that Ethernet addresses are six bytes, we can examine the first four bytes to determine if it is a broadcast address.

```
snoop -V "length < 60"
```

This command will display all frames that are less than 60 bytes. For instance, ARP (Address Resolution Protocol) requests frames that are less than this number. Executing this command will display any ARP messages as shown here:

```
________________________________
        monet -> (broadcast)  ETHER Type=0806 (ARP), size = 42 bytes
        monet -> (broadcast)  ARP C Who is 10.0.3.100, cisco-swl ?
________________________________
        monet -> (broadcast)  ETHER Type=0806 (ARP), size = 42 bytes
        monet -> (broadcast)  ARP C Who is 10.0.3.100, cisco-swl ?
```

Table 4.11 *Arithmetic and Boolean Operators*

Arithmetic Operators	Boolean Operators
>	and
<	or `or ,`
>=	not or !
=	
!=	
+	
-	
*	
&	
|	
^	
%	

To display all packets that originate from a particular Sun system, for example, the command to use is:

```
snoop "ether[6:4]&0xffffffff = 0x08002004"
```

This tells `snoop` to examine the sixth byte of the frame (the source frame address) and compare it to the `0x08002004` addresses using the & (and) operator. This datalink address represents most of the address of a local system called `monet`. Recall that Ethernet addresses are six bytes in length and we needed only to use the first four bytes to uniquely identify the system desired. As a result, all packets transmitted from `monet` will be displayed. To identify another system, obtain the datalink address of the system, convert it to hexadecimal, and place it on the right-hand side of the command above.

Miscellaneous Primitives

A few additional primitives are also available from `snoop` that can't be classified as either address or protocol primitives. These include the following:

```
greater

less

length
```

The `greater` and `less` primitives are used in conjunction with other `snoop` commands to filter, based on the total length of the packet. For example, to display all packets that are greater than `56` bytes, invoke the following command:

```
# snoop greater 56
```

To display all packets that are less than `60` bytes, use the `less` primitive:

```
# snoop less 60
```

Why use the `greater` or `less` commands? The primary reason is to search for packets based on size, rather than content. Another primitive, `length`, can also be used to handle capturing packets based on their exact size. The length can be used when the need to capture packets is based on some calculation. For example, the command below will display any packet that is not equal to 56:

```
# snoop length != 56
```

Qualifiers

Three qualifiers may be used in conjunction with the primitives listed in the tables above. A qualifier can be used to further define search characteristics to pinpoint specific network traffic. These qualifiers include the following:

```
from or src

to or dst

ether
```

The `from` and `src` qualifiers are used with the `host`, `net`, `ipaddr`, `etheraddr`, `port`, or `rpc` primitives to filter, based on a specific destination address or port. The qualifiers `to` or `dst` are used to modify the same primitives mentioned above, but will result in the capture of packets going to a particular address or port. The `ether` modifier is used to resolve a name to a datalink address when used with the `host` primitive. To illustrate the use of the `host` keyword, let's suppose we want to capture traffic from a particular host only. The following `snoop` command could be used:

```
# snoop from host monet
```

Contrast the above command with the following:

```
# snoop host monet
```

In the latter example, all the traffic involving `monet`, which includes packets being sent to and received from monet, will be displayed. In the former example, only traffic from `monet` will be displayed. As you can see, this can make a big difference when attempting to isolate a network problem.

Network Management Problems

At this point, we have mainly used `snoop` in isolated but important examples. However, to further demonstrate the power of `snoop`, some common network related problems and tasks will be examined. These problems and tasks represent the kind of real world challenges that network support personnel face every day.

The snoop command will be used to accomplish the following:

- Determine who is causing IP broadcast storms
- Determine who is polling your critical devices via SNMP

To determine which systems are causing generating broadcast traffic, use the following command:

```
snoop "ip[19]&0xff = 0xff"
```

This snoop command will compare the nineteenth byte of the IP header, which is the last byte of the destination IP address that uses the broadcast address. Recall that 255 (0xff in hexadecimal) is used to represent the broadcast address. We use the 0xff mask and the and (&) symbol with this byte to test if it is equal to 255. Any value combined with the & operator with all bits enabled (i.e., 0xff) will automatically return that value. When this snoop command is run, it will display any broadcast traffic for the local network. The sample output included below shows the types of traffic that will be detected:

```
cisco-1 -> 10.0.3.255    RIP R (10 destinations)
       monet -> 10.0.3.255    ICMP Echo request
       monet -> 10.0.3.255    ICMP Echo request
       monet -> 10.0.3.255    ICMP Echo request
       monet -> 10.0.3.255    ICMP Echo request
       monet -> 10.0.3.255    ICMP Echo request
       monet -> 10.0.3.255    ICMP Echo request
       monet -> 10.0.3.255    ICMP Echo request
       monet -> 10.0.3.255    ICMP Echo request
       monet -> 10.0.3.255    ICMP Echo request
```

In this example, we see both RIP (routing information protocol) packets and a large amount of ICMP echo request. For some reason, the system monet is sending pings to the local network using the broadcast address of 10.0.3.255. RIP packets are generated by routers to advertise routing information to other routers on the network. This traffic is normal. However, the large number of echo requests may indicate abnormal activity and should be addressed.

First, we need to determine which system is responsible for sending SNMP polls to our devices. The devices in question are sending traps to the SNMP manager, but the trap doesn't include any information indicating which system is sending the polls, which is the problem. We will use `snoop` to capture `udp` packets that contain the community information being used against our devices. In order for `snoop` to display the packets we are interested in, we must compare the community string information with the data portion of the SNMP request.

Because the community string is `public` in our example, when we convert this to hexadecimal, we get `7075626c6963(p=70, u=75, b=62, l=6c, i=69, c=63)`. However, we only need to search for the first character, say "p" of this string. We can use the following `snoop` command:

```
snoop -d le0 -x 0 "ether[51]&0xff = 0x70"
```

When this command is run, we get a packet as shown in Listing 4.3 below:

Listing 4.3 *Captured SNMP Packet with "public" community string*

```
ETHER:  ----- Ether Header -----
ETHER:
ETHER:  Packet 1 arrived at 17:23:57.67
ETHER:  Packet size = 93 bytes
ETHER:  Destination = 0:0:1d:a:5d:1, Cabletron
ETHER:  Source      = 8:0:20:4:cf:2c, Sun
ETHER:  Ethertype = 0800 (IP)
ETHER:
IP:   ----- IP Header -----
IP:
IP:   Version = 4
IP:   Header length = 20 bytes
IP:   Type of service = 0x00
IP:         xxx. .... = 0 (precedence)
IP:         ...0 .... = normal delay
IP:         .... 0... = normal throughput
IP:         .... .0.. = normal reliability
IP:   Total length = 79 bytes
IP:   Identification = 4179
```

(Cont'd)

Listing 4.3 *Captured SNMP Packet with "public" community string (Cont'd)*

```
IP:   Flags = 0x4
IP:         .1.. .... = do not fragment
IP:         ..0. .... = last fragment
IP:   Fragment offset = 0 bytes
IP:   Time to live = 255 seconds/hops
IP:   Protocol = 17 (UDP)
IP:   Header checksum = 5069
IP:   Source address = 10.0.3.126, monet
IP:   Destination address = 10.0.3.100, cisco-sw1
IP:   No options
IP:
UDP:  ----- UDP Header -----
UDP:
UDP:  Source port = 32886
UDP:  Destination port = 161
UDP:  Length = 59
UDP:  Checksum = F695
UDP:

    0: 0000 1d0a 5d01 0800 2004 cf2c 0800 4500    ....]... ...,..E.
   16: 004f 1053 4000 ff11 5069 0a00 037e 0a00    .O.S@...Pi...~..
   32: 0364 8076 00a1 003b f695 3082 002f 0201    .d.v...;ö.0../..
   48: 0004 0670 7562 6c69 63a0 8200 2002 043f    ...public... ..?
   64: df74 3402 0100 0201 0030 8200 1030 8200    .t4......0...0..
   80: 0c06 082b 0601 0201 0104 0005 00        ...+.........
```

The `ether[51]` portion of the command instructs `snoop` to compare this byte in the packet to the `0x70` value we place after the equals sign. The `51` represents the fifty-first byte within the Ethernet frame that contains the community string. After the frame is displayed, we can quickly deduce the system that generated the SNMP request. If you needed to search for a different community string, you would simply convert it to hexadecimal and replace the `0x70` byte with the appropriate value

FPING Tool

Software Availability

This command is available in the public domain and is supported on HP-UX, Linux, Solaris, and most other Unix platforms.

It is available in source form only and must be compiled before you can use it. Consult the sections below for additional information.

General Description

The `fping` command is very similar to the `ping` command previously discussed in this chapter. However, this software provides a few special functions that normal `ping` does not. Like its counterpart, `fping` uses the ICMP echo Request and Reply to determine system reachability. However, unlike regular `ping`, a list of hostnames or IP addresses may be specified on the command line. Also, `fping` will process a file that contains a list of hostname or IP addresses. Instead of sending a request to a single target (like `ping` does), `fping` will send out an ICMP request to each target using a round-robin mechanism. Another important distinction is that `fping` was primarily intended to be used in script programming, not as a user command like normal `ping`. Still, when used on the command line, `fping` can effectively address some common IP address-related problems.

The command line options available with `fping` can be divided into two sections. The first controls the various display options that can be used to customize the output. The second includes operational parameters that control the way `fping` obtains reachability information from devices and processes that information.

By default, when a target replies to an ICMP request, it is noted and removed from the list of targets that should be checked. If a target does not respond within the set time or retry limit, it is considered unreachable. The `fping` command can be made to loop indefinitely (as the normal `ping`) or send a user a defined number of ICMP requests to a target.

Display Options

There is a larger number of display options available with `fping`. These options are listed in Table 4.12. Some of these options are self-evident and need no explanation beyond the description associated with that particular option. Others require additional detail and are described below.

Table 4.12 *Display Options List*

Option	Description
`-A`	Show addresses of targets rather than hostnames
`-Q`	Like the `-q` option, but shows summary results information every `n` seconds. Unfortunately, this command doesn't seem to work
`-a`	Show systems that are alive and reachable, given a list of targets on the command line
`-d`	Show hostnames of targets instead of addresses. This is the reverse of the `-A` option
`-e`	Show round trip times from when packet was sent to receipt of reply
`-q`	Quiet mode. Don't display any results, but set the exit return status
`-u`	Show systems are not alive, given a list of targets on the command line
`-v`	Displays command version information and email address to send comments and bug reports to

One of the especially useful features of `fping` is that, given a list of targets following the `-a` option, it will display the systems that are reachable. For example, consider the following command:

```
# fping -a vermeer monet rodin louvre
monet
rodin
louvre
```

The hosts `monet`, `rodin`, and `louvre` are displayed—indicating that they are alive—while `vermeer` was not displayed because it didn't respond.

Conversely, the opposite list can be displayed with the `-u` option. In this case, the hosts that don't respond are displayed:

```
# fping -u vermeer monet rodin louvre
vermeer
```

We can go a step further and place a list of targets inside a file for processing. Let's assume a file called `host-list` contains the following IP addresses:

```
10.0.2.75
10.0.2.100
10.0.2.150
10.0.2.151
10.0.2.152
10.0.2.153
10.0.2.200
10.0.2.201
```

By redirecting the input to the `host-list` file, `fping` can process a larger number of targets instead of requiring you to specify them one by one on the command line. Thus,

```
# fping < host-list
10.0.2.75 is alive
10.0.2.100 is alive
10.0.2.150 is alive
10.0.2.151 is alive
10.0.2.152 is alive
10.0.2.153 is alive
10.0.2.200 is alive
10.0.2.201 is alive
```

is a more reasonable way to handle a larger number of hosts.

If you prefer, the `-f` option can also be used instead of the file redirection above. Thus the commands

```
# fping < host-list
# fping -f host-list
```

are functionally equivalent and yield the same result. But this option is restricted to the `root` user, while any system user can use the redirection option shown in the previous example.

These two options (`-u` and `-a`) are very handy and can be used in a variety of situations. For example, let's assume you want to be notified via email when certain systems are down. A simple script, (see Listing 4.4) like that shown below, might do this for you:

Listing 4.4 *Sample FPING Script*

```
#!/usr/bin/ksh

#
# Simple script to notify user when
# systems are down
#

FILE=$1

FPINGCMD=`fping -u < $FILE`
MAIL=/bin/mailx
USER=root

if [ "$FPINGCMD" != "" ]; then
        $MAIL -s "down system(s)" -u $USER $FPINGCMD"
fi
```

This script runs the `fping` command against the hosts included in the specified file and, if any devices contained in the file can't be reached, the user `root` is sent mail. Obviously, a more robust and elaborate script could be written, but the point here is that `fping` can be used to help automate some small network management tasks.

On special occasions, it might be necessary to manipulate IP addresses directly rather than hostnames as in the previous examples. When given a list of hostnames, it would be nice to return IP addresses. The `-A` option directs `fping` to display IP address information instead of the hostname. So, in our example above, we process a file that contains a list of IP addresses. In this case, we will process a list of valid hostnames. The file `hostname-list` contains the following:

```
monet
durer
vermeer
rembrandt
lex-mark
gateway
rodin
louvre
```

By processing this file with the `-A` option, we get:

```
# fping -A < hostname-list
10.0.2.126 is alive
134.111.2.1 is alive
10.0.2.75 is alive
10.0.2.75 is alive
10.0.2.129 is alive
128.197.2.200 alive
10.0.2.200 is alive
10.0.2.101 is alive
```

The `fping` command not only provides a way to determine whether systems are operating on the network, but also can provide some amount of performance information. In particular, a few options are available that display various amounts of statistics regarding the performance from the source of the `fping` to each target. The `-e` option will show the round trip or elapsed time from the moment the packet is sent until it returns. The command

```
# fping -e rembrandt
rembrandt is alive (2.82 ms)
```

provides output very similar to what you get when you use `ping` with the `-s` option. Another useful option, `-s`, shows a more complete cumulative statistical profile of the target:

```
# fping -s rembrandt
rembrandt is alive
       1 targets
       1 alive
       0 unreachable
       0 unknown addresses
       0 timeouts (waiting for response)
       1 ICMP Echos sent
       1 ICMP Echo Replies received
       0 other ICMP received
 3.09 ms (min round trip time)
 3.09 ms (avg round trip time)
 3.09 ms (max round trip time)
        0.015 sec (elapsed real time)
```

With this option, a detailed breakdown is provided and shows the overall number of targets and the number of targets found alive (in this case `1`); other information is self explanatory, and the actual elapsed time is measured in seconds. To determine its accuracy, consider this example:

```
# date; fping -s rodin; date
Sat Oct  3 13:25:01 EDT 1998
rodin is unreachable
       1 targets
       0 alive
       1 unreachable
       0 unknown addresses
       4 timeouts (waiting for response)
       4 ICMP Echos sent
       0 ICMP Echo Replies received
       0 other ICMP received
 0.00 ms (min round trip time)
 0.00 ms (avg round trip time)
 0.00 ms (max round trip time)
        4.080 sec (elapsed real time)
Sat Oct  3 13:25:05 EDT 1998
```

Here, the `fping` is surrounded by the Unix `date` command. The `date` program is executed before the `fping` is started and after. Discounting any delays from the operating system, the elapsed time is fairly correct. The elapsed time might not be 100 percent accurate due to several factors but, for most applications, it should be sufficiently accurate. A non-reachable system was chosen for this example so that `fping` would be forced to send out additional packets and wait the maximum amount of time. This gives a larger amount of time to measure the requests without resorting to using additional options that will be necessary when the target is a live system.

Operational Options

Many operational options are available with `fping`. They are listed in Table 4.13. Some of these options are self-evident and need no explanation beyond the description associated with that particular option. Other options require additional detail and are described below.

Table 4.13 *Operational Options List*

Option	Description
`-b`	Number of bytes of data to include in the ping request
`-B`	This option followed by a value is used to determine the delay time that `fping` uses when waiting for replies. The value is used as a multiplier and must be given in floating point format
`-c`	Determines the number of requests sent to each target
`-C`	Similar to `-c`, but per-target statistics are displayed in a format that is easier to parse
`-f`	Obtain list of targets from specified file. This is restricted to the root user. Regular users should use file redirection instead of this option
`-l`	Send an indefinite amount of requests to target. Can be stopped by `^C` (control-c)
`-p`	Set the amount of time in milliseconds that `fping` will wait between successive packets for a target. This is only meaningful with `-l`, `-c` , or `-C` options
`-r`	The number of attempts that will be made at pinging a specified target. The default value is 3
`-t`	The amount of time to wait for the first response to the initial packet request. The default is 500 milliseconds

The `fping` command sends a number of requests to a target, waiting longer for a reply with each successive request. The value used is determined by a wait factor, which uses a multiplier for each request that doesn't receive a reply. The value of 1.5 is the default multiplier factor. To change this value, use the -B option followed by a floating-point value. For example, using the default we observe the following:

```
# fping -s rembrandt
rembrandt is unreachable
       1 targets
       0 alive
       1 unreachable
       0 unknown addresses
       4 timeouts (waiting for response)
       4 ICMP Echos sent
       0 ICMP Echo Replies received
       0 other ICMP received
 0.00 ms (min round trip time)
 0.00 ms (avg round trip time)
 0.00 ms (max round trip time)
        4.077 sec (elapsed real time)
```

By using the -B option, the delay factor can be doubled for each packet sent. As a result, we see a significant amount of time used for each of the packet requests:

```
# fping -B 3.0 -s rembrandt
rembrandt is unreachable
       1 targets
       0 alive
       1 unreachable
       0 unknown addresses
       4 timeouts (waiting for response)
       4 ICMP Echos sent
       0 ICMP Echo Replies received
       0 other ICMP received
 0.00 ms (min round trip time)
 0.00 ms (avg round trip time)
 0.00 ms (max round trip time)
       20.037 sec (elapsed real time)
```

Notice that the elapsed time has increased to approximately 20 seconds because the delay factor is multiplied by each packet sent.

To control the number of requests fping sends to each target, use the -c option. By default, 4 attempts are made before giving up on the specified system. This option can be used to change this number as shown in the following example:

```
# fping -c 5 monet
monet : [0], 84 bytes, 3.55 ms (3.55 avg, 0% loss)
monet : [1], 84 bytes, 2.53 ms (3.04 avg, 0% loss)
monet : [2], 84 bytes, 1.63 ms (2.57 avg, 0% loss)
monet : [3], 84 bytes, 1.99 ms (2.42 avg, 0% loss)
monet : [4], 84 bytes, 1.64 ms (2.26 avg, 0% loss)
monet : xmt/rcv/%loss = 5/5/0%, min/avg/max = 1.63/2.26/3.55
```

FPING Program Information

The `fping` program is in the public domain, and as such it must be retrieved and subsequently installed. It is provided in source form only. The procedures for building the program and installing the binary have been provided below.

Conditions of Use

The following statement appears in the software documentation:

```
/*
 * Redistribution and use in source and binary forms are permitted
 * provided that the above copyright notice and this paragraph are
 * duplicated in all such forms and that any documentation,
 * advertising materials, and other materials related to such
 * distribution and use acknowledge that the software was developed
 * by Stanford University. The name of the University may not be used
 * to endorse or promote products derived from this software without
 * specific prior written permission.
 * THIS SOFTWARE IS PROVIDED "AS IS" AND WITHOUT ANY EXPRESS OR
 * IMPLIED WARRANTIES, INCLUDING, WITHOUT LIMITATION, THE
 * IMPLIED WARRANTIES OF MERCHANTIBILITY AND FITNESS FOR A PARTICULAR
 * PURPOSE.
 */
```

Author:

```
Roland J. Schemers III - Stanford University
schemers@Stanford.EDU
```

Obtaining from the Internet

The FPING package may be obtained from several FTP sites on the Internet:

```
ftp://ftp.stanford.edu/pub/packages/fping/fping-2.2b1.tar.gz
ftp://sesame.hensa.ac.uk/ftp/mirrors/ftp.kernel.org/pub/software/admi
n/mon/fping-2.2b1.tar.gz
ftp://www.wooten.net/ftp/pub/unix/att/tcputils/fping.tar.z
```

Installation Procedure

The installation procedures for this package include the following:

1. Obtain the FPING package from one of the sites above or from the CD-ROM available with this book.
2. Uncompress the GNU archive:

   ```
   gunzip fping-2.2b1.tar.gz
   ```

3. Untar the archive into the directory you will be using:

   ```
   tar xvf fping-2.2b1.tar
   ```

4. Normally, the untarring will create a new directory named fping-2.2b1plus the software version number. Change to this directory:

   ```
   cd fping-2.2b1
   ```

5. Next, run the `configure` command from this directory:

   ```
   ./configure
   [lots of output]
   ```

   After several pages of output, the `configure` program will ask a small number of questions.

   ```
   [questions here]
   ```

6. If no errors were encountered, run the `make` command:

   ```
   make
   [lots of output]
   ```

7. After the `make` has completed and no serious errors were displayed, install the package by running:

   ```
   make install
   [lots of output]
   ```

If you encounter a problem during the installation, consult the `READ.ME` file, which can be found on the top-level directory of the FPING distributions.

TRACEROUTE Tool

Software Availability

This command is standard on Solaris 2.7 and is available in the public domain for HPUX, Linux, previous versions of Solaris, and other Unix platforms. The source is also available and can be compiled on many other Unix platforms as well.

General Description

The `traceroute` command is used to examine and record the path to a specified network destination. Within a traditional IP network, one or more routers are used to provide connectivity between different IP networks. IP routers come in all kinds of shapes and sizes from a simple multi-home Unix system with two interfaces to an industrial-strength Cisco router series that contains a large number of interfaces. In each of these cases, the routing function is primarily the same; it forwards IP packets from one interface to another based on established routing information. The `traceroute` command uses the time-to-Live (TTL) field contained with an IP packet and attempts to obtain an ICMP `TIME_EXCEEDED` message. Coupled with an attempt to attach to the destination at an unreachable port, it will cause a systematic response from every router along the path to the ultimate destination. It accomplishes this task by sending out requests (or probes) with a TTL of `1` and increases it by `1` until it either reaches the desired host or it exceeds the maximum TTL value. By default, the TTL is set to `30` hops, but this can be changed using a command line option.

This command has a large number of command line options, but the only required argument is either a hostname or IP address of the destination. For example, to display the IP path between the local system running `traceroute` and the destination system called `vermeer`, issue the following command:

```
# traceroute vermeer
```

Figures 4.3a and 4.3b show a sample network that consists of one router and two network nodes. When the above `traceroute` command is executed on `monet`, the following output will be displayed:

```
monet# traceroute vermeer
traceroute to vermeer (128.197.2.200), 30 hops max, 40 byte packets
 1  router-1 (10.0.2.129)  4.256 ms *  2.899 ms
 2  vermeer (128.197.2.200)  7.340 ms  7.433 ms  7.526 ms
```

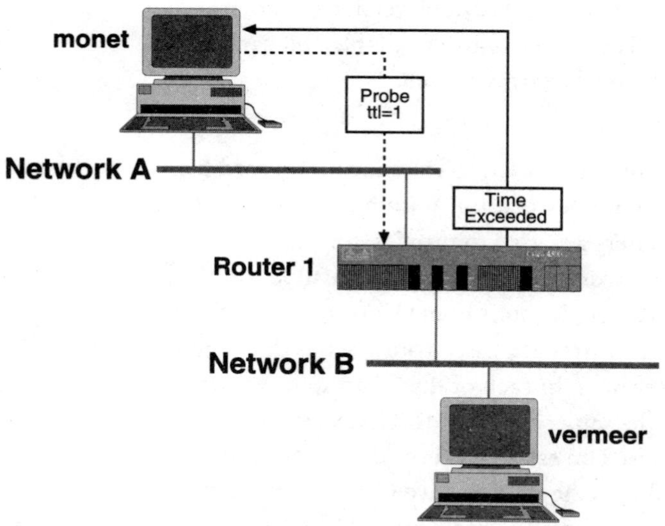

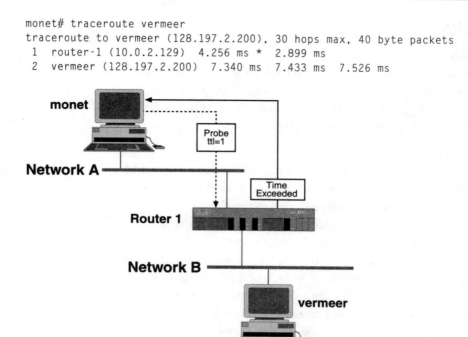

Figure 4.3a *Traceroute with 1 Hop.*

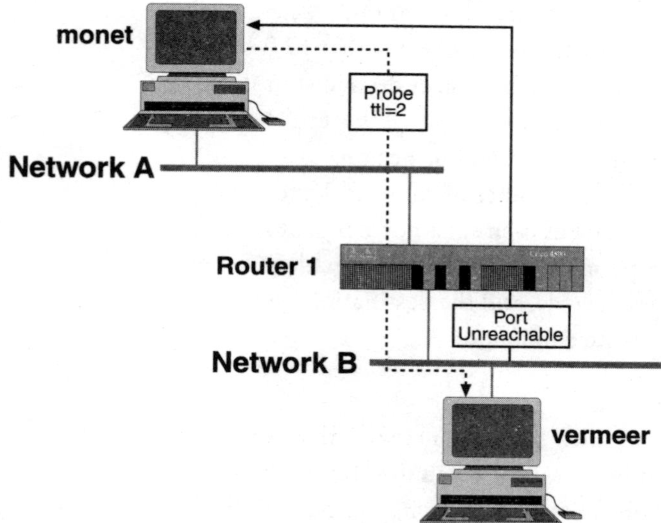

Figure 4.3b *Traceroute with 2 Hops.*

By default, `traceroute` sends a total of three probes, each with a different TTL value, to every hop. The first line of the output includes the destination along with the IP address, the default number of hops `traceroute` uses, and the size of the packets being sent. The second line (with a `1`) displays the first hop encountered by `tracerouter` (Figure 4.3a). Because `vermeer` is on a different physical network than `monet`, a router must be used to reach this system. Because the default router in this example is `router-1`, the first packet is sent there. The first packet sent is an ICMP request packet with the TTL field set to 1. With IP, any packet that reaches the router decrements the TTL by 1, which makes it zero. When a router gets a packet and the TTL is zero, it is supposed to discard the packet and notify the sender. This forces the router to respond with a `TIME_EXCEEDED` message back to `monet`. After this happens, `traceroute` measures the amount of time between when it sent the packet and when it obtained the reply. This is known as the *round trip time* or *RTT* and is displayed in milliseconds (1000th of a second) as shown after the hostname and IP address information. This implies that the RTT of the first series of probe packets took `4.25` milliseconds (or .004 seconds) and the third series was `2.89` milliseconds (or .028 seconds).

The second line details the second routing hop and shows that `traceroute` reached the destination system `vermeer` with slower RTT times than the first (see Figure 4.3b). When the second probe was sent, the router decremented the TTL, and then passed this packet to the `vermeer`. Because the `traceroute` is attempting to access an unused port, `vermeer` responds with the `PORT UNREACHABLE` error. In fact, as a general rule on large (and sometimes small) internets, performance between systems and networks will and can vary a significant amount even from one moment to the next.

There is no restriction on what constitutes a destination; it can be any kind of device that ranges from a simple host system to an Internet router. The only requirement is that it must support IP.

Reading Traceroute Output

Due to variations and problems with router devices along certain paths, the general fluctuations of network routes can lead to unpredictable and strange `traceroute` output. As a result, certain codes might appear after the timing information is displayed. These codes and their associated meanings are included in Table 4.14.

Table 4.14 *Traceroute Display Codes*

Code	Meaning
*	Indicates no response to probe packets
!	The TTL in the received packet is set to 1
!H	Destination host is unreachable
!N	Destination network is unreachable
!P	Destination protocol is unreachable
!S	The source route option has failed. In practice, this shouldn't happen and if it does, it indicates a bug or problem with the router that generated the error
!F	Fragmentation was needed for a probe packet. In practice, this shouldn't happen and if it does, it indicates a bug or problem with the router that generated the error
!X	The path is blocked due to communication being administration disabled. In other words, the path is shutdown or blocked from a software standpoint
!N>	Indicates an ICMP error code where N is that number

Some of these display codes can come in handy when debugging network problems. For example, if a destination (like www.whitehouse.gov) is not reachable by the system that is running the traceroute command, executing

```
monet# traceroute www.whitehouse.gov
```

will produce

```
traceroute to www.whitehouse.gov (198.137.240.91), 30 hops max, 40 byte packets
 1  monet (10.0.2.126)  4.281 ms !N *  1.896 ms !N
```

In this example, the network 198.137.240 can't be reached from the local system and traceroute displays the error string !N to indicate this problem. In this particular case, monet can't send any packets to 198.137.240 because no route to that network exists. The * means that the particular probe packet never received a response and the * is used as a timeout indicator. Also, to further verify these results, use the ping command with the same destination. Thus,

```
monet# ping www.whitehouse.gov
```

will show the same, except the error is a little more descriptive:

```
ICMP Net Unreachable from gateway monet (10.0.2.126)
 for icmp from monet (10.0.2.126) to www.whitehouse.gov
```

In the same way, both !H and !P error codes are also used to debug general network problems, but in these two cases, !H reports when a host is unreachable and the !P reports when the protocol is unreachable. The host unreachable message will be displayed, for example, when the network is also unreachable.

Given the fact that at any point in time, the performance or RTT between networks and systems can change significantly, a trace to the Web site of the Louvre Museum first reveals:

```
# traceroute 198.137.240.91
traceroute to 198.137.240.91 (198.137.240.91), 30 hops max, 40 byte
packets
 1  10.0.2.76 (10.0.2.76)  19.906 ms  9.801 ms  8.174 ms
 2  199.70.195.38 (199.70.195.38)  197.460 ms  188.000 ms  181.029 ms
 3  12.77.194.1 (12.77.194.1)  166.802 ms  184.713 ms  185.857 ms
 4  12.127.12.205 (12.127.12.205)  245.026 ms  270.253 ms  266.718 ms
 5  12.127.15.145 (12.127.15.145)  215.191 ms  211.920 ms  208.979 ms
 6  192.205.31.165 (192.205.31.165)  217.875 ms  232.610 ms  222.274 ms
 7  204.6.117.65 (204.6.117.65)  266.797 ms  239.000 ms  215.671 ms
 8  38.1.4.69 (38.1.4.69)  235.431 ms  225.447 ms  301.119 ms
 9  38.1.25.5 (38.1.25.5)  235.369 ms  236.134 ms  263.557 ms
10  38.1.25.5 (38.1.25.5)  252.172 ms  238.984 ms  263.013 ms
11  38.146.148.45 (38.146.148.45)  241.956 ms  248.091 ms  243.300 ms
12  198.137.240.33 (198.137.240.33)  249.361 ms  228.717 ms  252.927 ms
13  198.137.240.91 (198.137.240.91)  238.799 ms  259.967 ms  236.384 ms
```

When the trace was repeated later, it shows:

```
# traceroute 198.137.240.91
traceroute to 198.137.240.91 (198.137.240.91), 30 hops max, 40 byte
packets
 1  10.0.2.76 (10.0.2.76)  7.619 ms  5.863 ms  6.206 ms
 2  199.70.195.42 (199.70.195.42)  177.685 ms  177.691 ms  177.842 ms
 3  12.77.242.129 (12.77.242.129)  170.712 ms  177.096 ms  173.517 ms
 4  12.127.12.205 (12.127.12.205)  260.239 ms  248.072 ms  252.829 ms
 5  12.127.15.145 (12.127.15.145)  219.767 ms  215.645 ms  232.399 ms
 6  192.205.31.165 (192.205.31.165)  232.259 ms  225.243 ms  219.236 ms
 7  204.6.117.65 (204.6.117.65)  228.997 ms  218.067 ms  219.365 ms
 8  38.1.4.69 (38.1.4.69)  445.758 ms  232.797 ms  276.249 ms
 9  38.1.25.5 (38.1.25.5)  245.674 ms  443.611 ms  577.309 ms
10  38.1.25.5 (38.1.25.5)  432.994 ms  222.527 ms  242.844 ms
11  38.146.148.45 (38.146.148.45)  257.668 ms  249.923 ms  263.074 ms
12  198.137.240.33 (198.137.240.33)  276.658 ms  242.361 ms *
13  198.137.240.91 (198.137.240.91)  248.266 ms  245.006 ms  251.071 ms
```

As you can see, most of the response times were very close. However, significant delays could be observed with hops 8, 9, and 10. In these cases, the RTT was almost doubled, which further indicates that performance on a large routed network (such as the Internet) will and does vary over time.

Changing Operational Characteristics

The `traceroute` command contains a number of operational parameters that can be modified to affect how it traces a path to the specified destination. Each of these parameters has an associated command line option that can be used to alter its default values. These options are listed in Table 4.15.

Table 4.15 *Traceroute Operational Options*

Option	Description
`-i`	Specify an alternate interface
`-p`	Set the alternate port to send probe packets
`-g`	Specify a router for loose source routing
`-f`	Set the initial TTL value to be used

(Cont'd)

Table 4.15 *Traceroute Operational Options (Cont'd)*

Option	Description
`-s`	Use the specified address as the source address in transmitting probe packets
`-q`	Set the number of probe queries
`-m`	Set the maximum hops
`-d`	Enable debug flag (SO_DEBUG)
`-F`	Don't fragment
`-t`	Set the type of service (TOS) flag
`-w`	Set the wait time for probe packets
`-x`	Don't calculate checksums

When `traceroute` is executed on a system that is multi-homed (i.e., a system that contains more than one network interface), it selects the first interface it encounters. Unfortunately, this might not be what you want because the destination you are after can only be accessed from another interface. To address this issue, the -i option can be used to force `traceroute` to send probe packets using the interface specified with this option. Thus the command

```
traceoute -i hem0
traceroute: Warning: Multiple interfaces found; using 10.0.2.126 @
hme0
```

will cause `traceroute` to use the Fast Ethernet interface instead of the FDDI interface that it would normally use.

In certain situations, the default TTL value of `30` is not enough to reach a destination that might contain a larger number of routes. When this occurs, `traceroute` will never reach the destination. In this situation, use the `-m` option to increase the hop count.

When doing a `traceroute` to certain devices, it might sometimes fail, despite the fact that the path to the device is operational. Further, using the `ping` command against the device indicates that it is working correctly as well. Why? Before we answer this question, let's look at an example:

```
monet# traceroute -m 5 128.197.2.200
traceroute to 128.197.2.200 (128.197.2.200), 5 hops max, 40 byte
packets
 1  rodin (10.0.2.129)  10.193 ms *  2.158 ms
 2  * * *
 3  * * *
 4  * * *
 5  * * *
```

This `traceroute` produces no response to the probe packets. Note the use of the `-m` option to keep the number of probe packets small.

The answer to this problem lies in the fact that, by default, `traceroute` sends probe packets based on the UDP protocol. It is most likely that the destination in question does not support this protocol directly or can't handle the UDP designation port used. From a TCP/IP standpoint, not all devices are required to support UDP and if they do support UDP, they do not necessarily support the port number used by `traceroute`.

When `traceroute` sends out probe packets, it uses, by default, the UDP port of 33434 and assumes that this port isn't being used by any other application or network service. It uses this high port number in hopes that the destination will respond with a port unreachable message, thus terminating the route tracing. On the other hand, if that port is being used, it will cause problems for `traceroute`. If this happens, use the `-p` option followed by another port number and `traceroute` will use that port instead of the default.

For example:

```
monet# traceroute -p 10 -m 5 128.197.2.200
traceroute to 128.197.2.200 (128.197.2.200), 5 hops max, 40 byte
packets
 1  rodin (10.0.2.129)  10.193 ms *  2.158 ms
 2  * * *
 3  * * *
 4  * * *
 5  * * *
```

If this still doesn't do the trick, attempt to use the -I option, which will instruct traceroute to use the ICMP protocol when sending probe packets instead of UDP. So the command

```
monet# traceroute -m 5 -I 128.197.2.200
```

with the -I option produces the correct results:

```
traceroute to 128.197.2.200 (128.197.2.200), 5 hops max, 40 byte
packets
 1  rodin (10.0.2.129)  4.412 ms *  2.235 ms
 2  vermeer (128.197.2.200)  6.875 ms  6.955 ms  6.935 ms
```

As you can see, this took a bit of trial and error to obtain the desired result. However, this is not a contrived example; rather, vermeer represents an actual device: a laser printer. The real point here is that, when tracing to a particular destination, there can be many reasons why traceroute fails to reach a destination and they might not mean that the device is down or disconnected from the network.

Display Options

Two options are available to modify the output of traceroute. The first, -v, will display, for each hop, the size and destination of the response packets. The following shows an example:

```
traceroute -v vermeer
# traceroute -i le1 -v rembrandt
traceroute to rembrandt (10.0.2.75), 30 hops max, 40 byte packets
 1  rembrandt (10.0.2.75) 56 bytes to 10.0.2.1  3.450 ms  2.085 ms
2.094 ms
```

The second, -n, is used to display addresses in numerical form rather than using the symbolic name. This removes the added task from traceroute to have to resolve each router's hostname.

05

Networking Management Agents

This chapter provides a detailed overview of the Solstice Enterprise Agents (SEA) and University of California at Davis (UCD) SNMP system agent. The Solstice Enterprise Agents actually contain two agents: a master and a subagent. Because the term Solstice also refers to Sun's network management framework and mix of products, the terms *master agent* and *subagent* will be used to describe these agents from Sun. The SEA package also includes support for the Desktop Management Interface (DMI). However, this chapter only focuses on the

SNMP portion and not on the DMI services or functionality. Included is an overview of how to use, obtain, install, and configure the master, subagent, and UCD agent. A description of the MIB groups and objects supported with each of the agents is presented as well.

Software Availability

The Sun SNMP agent and master agent are available only on the Solaris platform. They are shipped standard on the present version of Solaris, but can be installed on previous releases as well. The UCD SNMP agent is available on Solaris, HP-UX, Linux, and several other Unix platforms. The Sun agents are available from the Sun Web site in binary form only; the UCD agent is also available from the Internet in source or binary form. Consult the end of this chapter on specific download information and installation instructions for these tools.

Overview of Agents

All the agents listed above provide some of the same fundamental services; namely the retrieval and setting of MIB objects. Each of the agents supports the standard SNMP basic operations, including `get-request`, `getnext-request`, `set-request`, `get-reply`, and `trap`. Additionally, each of the agents provides some specialized functions such as support for disk or memory management. Table 5.1 outlines the functionality of each agent and can be used as a quick reference guide when choosing an agent. Selecting which agent to use depends on the environment and the types of problems you are attempting to solve. It might, for example, be necessary to use all three agents because each provides services that are required.

The functionality of each of the agents can be summarized into several categories that include:

- MIB-II Support—Indicates that the agent supports either most of or the entire standard MIB-II set of objects.
- Process Management—Indicates that additional MIB objects are available to manage Unix processes. Basic operations include listing and controlling these processes via the agent.

- Remote Configuration—Indicates the capability for the agent to manipulate its own configuration file via the SNMP protocol. For example, the agent can be made to dynamically alter a predefined action when the monitored object reaches a critical threshold.
- Extended MIB Support—The agent supports additional MIB objects, which provides more information beyond the MIB-II standard. This might either include proprietary vendor-specific MIBs or standard MIBs such as the RIP-MIB.
- Flexible Configuration Files—This implies that the agent provides a flexible set of configuration options and keywords, primarily used to control the operating state and behavior of the agent.
- Performance Objects—The agent supports additional MIB objects, which can be used to provide additional performance information or statistical data.
- Customizable Actions—The agent can execute external scripts or programs as directed by the agent. Usually, these actions are a direct result of some specific condition or event that the agent has detected.
- Memory/Disk Management—The agent provides additional MIB objects that can be used to provide additional memory or disk information or statistical data.
- Master Agent Support—The agent provides the capability for subagents to register to receive SNMP messages. The master agent is responsible for handling outside communication on behalf of the subagents. The master agent uses the SNMP port `161`, while the subagents communicate with the master agent on another predefined port.
- Extensible—The agent can be extended to support additional functionality and support new features such as executing external Unix shell script or other commands. This might also imply that the agent provides a development environment that

includes interfaces that facilitate adding new features by recompiling (or linking) various components of the package.

- SNMPv2/v3—The agent supports some of or the entire SNMPv2 and SNMPv3 protocol specifications.

Table 5.1 *Functional Overview of Agents*

Category	Sun Master	Agent Sun	UCD
MIB-II Objects		✓	✓
Process Management Objects	✓	✓	✓
Remote Configuration			✓
Additional System Objects		✓	
Flexible Configuration		✓	✓
Additional Performance Objects		✓	✓
Customizable Actions			✓
Memory Management Objects			✓
Disk Management Objects			✓
Master Agent	✓		
Subagent Management	✓		
Extensible Capabilities			✓
SNMP v2/v3			✓ (partial v3)

Sun's Master Agent

Sun provides a standard SNMP network management master agent that can be used as a basis for an enterprise management strategy. Sun provides an agent called `snmpdx`, which is used to provide a master/subagent facility for one or more subagents. Recall from Chapter 2, "Simple Network Management Protocol," that the main purpose and role of a master agent is to permit many SNMP agents to coexist. Because each SNMP agent must listen for requests on the well-known SNMP port `161`, a mechanism must be provided so that all agents can share this port without conflict. Without special arbitration, the first agent to use the port would obtain an exclusive lock on the port and all other agents would be denied access. With the `snmpdx` agent, many subagents can be installed on the same system without the traditional port contention problem. Also, this master agent supports a collection of MIB objects that describe each of the subagents that have been configured with the master agent.

Sun's SNMP Agent

Sun provides a standard SNMP network management system agent. This agent, known as `mibiisa`, supports SNMPv1 and provides read/write access to both MIB-II and Sun enterprise-specific objects. The agent supports the standard basic operations associated with SNMPv1. This agent works under Sun's master/slave agent architecture, which means that it can operate in conjunction with a master agent or in standalone mode. This agent provides the ability to manage Sun workstations and servers from an operational and performance standpoint. It supports the standard MIB-II object groups and some additional groups defined by Sun. Taken together, this agent can be used to monitor some of the more critical network management problems that face network and system managers alike.

The advantages of using this agent include integration into the operating system and support by the vendor. As a result of the agent being shipped with Solaris, installation is a snap because the agent component can very easily be loaded with the operating system software. On older versions of the operating system that don't already have the agent, it is possible to install in a straightforward manner by using Sun's `pkgadd` utility. Additionally, because the agent was developed by Sun, it will be supported should problems arise that require technical assistance. Finally, vendor support ensures that users can expect enhancements and new functionality to be included in future releases of the agent. This is important because SNMP will continue to change to meet the growing requirements of network and system managers.

UCD's SNMP Agent

The UCD agent, known as `snmpd`, provides a comprehensive list of SNMP-related services. This agent supports SNMPv1 and SNMPv2 network management protocols. This means it supports not only the basic SNMP operations, but also those associated with SNMPv2, such as `get-bulk`, `get-inform`, and several others. It supports MIB-II, the UCD MIB, and several other MIBs as well. The agent provides the capability to remotely execute Unix commands that have been configured based on certain events or conditions. The agent can be used to monitor both system memory and process information.

The advantages of using the UCD packet are significant. First, the software provides a very complete set of tools and features available within the public domain. The package includes user SNMP tools, plus a fully functional SNMP agent. Many SNMP packages are available on the Internet, but most don't compare to the stability, robustness, and features found within the UCD package. Next, despite the fact that the UCD software is public domain, it seems to have a loyal following and has seen continuous improvement over the years, even surpassing some well-established commercial products in terms of SNMP protocol support or features. The UCD tools are supported on a large number of computer platforms and operating systems. Finally, the UCD is free, which means it can be deployed across the network enterprise without concern for licensing issues. This makes the UCD agent very attractive to budget-constrained institutions and other organizations.

Agent MIBs

Each of the agents described in this section implement either standard or private (or both) MIBs. Because both the Sun and UCD agents use private MIBs, access to these objects is at the enterprise branch level. Figure 5.1 shows the path from root to each of the vendor's private branches.

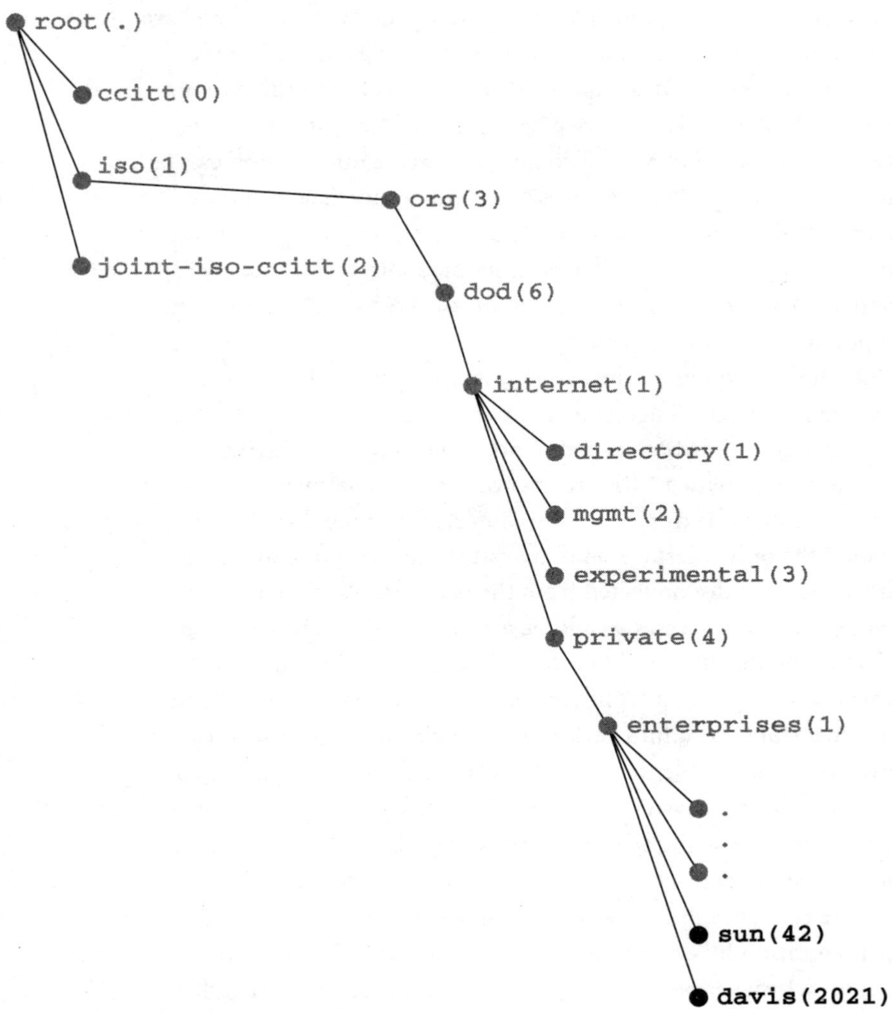

Figure 5.1 *Sun/UCD Agent MIB Branches.*

Security Considerations

The capabilities of these agents are very powerful and can have a profound impact on network management. Because these agents provide access to critical portions of the system, care should be taken when configuring and using them. For example, the configuration file for the Sun Agent provides the ability to set community strings for both read and write access to the MIB. Many network management systems and agents (including the ones listed here) are configured with the standard community strings of `public` and `private` by default. It would be important to change these to nonstandard passwords when deploying these agents at a local site. Despite the fact that SNMP community string information can be obtained via a packet capture device and decoded, community names still should be unique and hard-to-guess. In a large installation it might be necessary to use a set of community strings for a collection of devices either geographically co-located or for certain types like Cisco or Bay routers.

Failure to configure the agents correctly can be disastrous. For example, with the Sun agent, a network interface can be disabled with a simple SNMP `set` command if the community string is `public`. Someone with a MIB browser or `snmpset` command tool could easily disable one or more system interfaces. If the disabled interface is the only interface on that system, the system would effectively become disconnected from the network. As a result, all network-related processes would be affected by this action. In some environments, this would be considered an outage and would carry some significant consequences. To restore the system to its original state, the administrator must login to the system console if available and enable the interface using the `ifconfig` command. Alternately, if no system console exists, the system must be rebooted by power cycling the system; this step also adds to the possibility of system loss.

The rule of thumb here is to be careful when setting up the agent configuration files and don't use the standard SNMP community names whenever possible. As you will see, an access control list (ACL) can be created with the Sun and UCD agents to add further protection.

Sun's Master Agent

Master Agent Configuration/Configuring a Subagent

Before a subagent can be used, it must be registered with the master agent. This is accomplished by updating a small number of configuration files that are located in the `/etc/snmp/conf` directory. When the master agent starts, it parses any registration and resource files located in this directory. The master agent also ensures that messages from the network flow to the correct subagent and messages emitted from the subagents are also forwarded correctly. To register with the `snmpdx` master agent, the following files must contain entries for the subagent:

```
agent.reg
agent.rsrc
```

The `agent` prefix represents the name of the subagent that will be configured under the master agent. The `agent.reg` file is used to register the subagent with the master agent. The registration file consists of a keyword (or token) followed by a single value separated by a new line. Comments are permitted in these files by using the hash character (#). A single collection of keywords and values are enclosed in brackets and constitute a subagent entry. The keywords that can be used in the registration file include `name`, `subtrees`, `timeout`, and `watch-dog-time`.

The `name` keyword is simply a label for naming the subagent internally. The `subtrees` keyword is used to specify the MIB tree that the subagent supports when queried by another SNMP entity. The `timeout` keyword is used to control how much time the master should wait for the subagent to process an SNMP request. The `timeout` value is expressed in microseconds. The `watch-dog-time` keyword is used by the master agent to determine if the subagent is still functioning by periodically checking the status of the subagent. To further illustrate, consider the registration file (see Listing 5.1) that is used by the `mibiisa` subagent:

Listing 5.1 *Agent Registration File*

```
agents =
{
        {
                name = "snmpd"
                subtrees = { mib-2, sun }
                timeout = 2000000
                watch-dog-time = 86400
        }
}
```

In this case, the name of the `mibiisa` subagent is `snmpd`, which is used internally to the master agent. The `subtrees` values denote two macros that are shorthand for specific OID strings. The `mib-2` is defined as `1.3.6.1.2.1` and `sun` is `1.3.6.1.4.1.42`. The `timeout` value in the above example is 2 seconds (or 2,000,000 microseconds.); the `watch-dog-time` value is expressed in seconds.

The resource file, `agent.rsrc`, is also needed when configuring a subagent to work with a master agent. This file is primarily used to indicate the registration file and the subagent program name. The resource file for the `mibiisa` subagent is listed below. This file shares the same format as the registration file, with keywords followed by values. The resource file requires a `registration_file`, `policy`, `type`, and `command` keyword and associated values. The `registration_file` token is used to assign the subagent registration file that the master agent will use. The `policy` token is used to indicate how the master agent should execute the subagent. The `command` token represents the subagent program that the master agent will start after it completes parsing both the registration and resource files for each of the subagents. The SNMP port can also be specified in this file by using the `port` keyword. However, the subagent can also let the master agent assign a port to use by using the `$PORT` string. In the example below, the `mibissa` subagent uses the `$PORT` string instead of statically assigning a port.

Listing 5.2 *Agent Resource File*

```
resource =
{
        {
                registration_file = "/etc/snmp/conf/mibiisa.reg"
                policy = "spawn"
                type = "legacy"
                command = "/usr/lib/snmp/mibiisa -p $PORT"
        }
}
```

Also, the master agent requires the following files:

```
snmpdx.acl
snmpdx.reg
snmpdx.rsrc
```

The `snmpdx.acl` file can be used to specify the community string information that the master agent will use to control access to its MIB. The control mechanism is primarily used for the master agent MIB objects, not any of the subagent MIBs. This is an important distinction because the subagents (for example, the `mibiisa` agent) rely on the `snmpd.conf` file for this purpose, not the `snmpdx.acl` file. The `snmpdx.reg` is the master agent registration file that serves the same purpose as the subagent file. The `snmpdx.rsrc` file is used to specify some timing parameters for the master agent. All these files are located in the `/etc/snmp/conf` directory.

Command Line Options

The `snmpdx` agent supports several command line options, which are listed in Table 5.2 and are described in following section.

Table 5.2 *Master Agent Command Line Options*

Option	Description
`-a`	Specifies the path of the access control file used by the agent
`-c`	Changes the path to search for the agent configuration file
`-d`	Activates debugging level
`-h`	Prints online help
`-i`	Specifies the path of another status file that is used by an agent
`-m`	Instructs the agent to forward SNMP messages based on specified mode
`-o`	Used to specify the path of the enterprise OID mapping file
`-p`	Used to specify port instead of the default of `161`
`-r`	Specifies the path of the resource file
`-y`	Invokes recovery of the subagents

The -a option is used to specify the path and filename for the access control file. The agent uses this file to control access to the MIB by external entities. The default file is /etc/snmp/conf/snmpdx.acl. The -i option is used to give another full path for the master agent status file. This is the file used by the master agent for recovery after a crash. It contains the Unix process id, port number, resource name, and agent name of each subagent defined. The default location and name of the status file is /var/snmp/snmpdx.st.

The -c option is used to change the default configuration path from /etc/snmp/conf. The master agent searches for the agent configuration, resource file, and OID mapping files in this location. The -o command line option is used to change the default location and name of the enterprise-name OID file. The master agent uses this file to map vendor names to enterprise numbers. This file is, by default, /etc/snmp/conf/enterprises.oid. Trap processing by the master agent requires this information to determine vendor-specific information. The -r option controls which resource file is used by the master agent. This file contains agent configuration information and the default path; the file name is /etc/snmp/conf/snmpdx.rsrc. Because the master agent is started at system boot time, these options should be changed in the /etc/init.d/init.snmpdx system startup file so that they may be permanent. However, it is recommended that any changes to the startup file be tested before the startup file is executed on a system reboot.

Why change the location of the files? Well, in some sites, the standard practice is to use a special file system location that has been previously set up and is commonly available across every system on the network. Further, this area might be archived more regularly than other file systems and, as a result, used to store all configuration files for third-party tools. Using this area can be more beneficial than the default local for this reason. Also, if you want to test new configurations that may exist in other locations and with different file names, these options can help as well.

The -h option is useful because it can be used to display the help summary of the master agent. Running the snmpdx master agent command with the help option will display the available command line options and their associated arguments as shown below:

```
# /usr/lib/snmp/snmpdx -h
Usage: snmpdx [-h]
        [-h]
        [-n relay_agent_name (default relay-agent)]
        [-p port (default 161)]
        [-r resource-file (default /etc/snmp/conf/snmpdx.rsrc)]
        [-a access-control-file (default /etc/snmp/conf/snmpdx.acl)]
        [-c config-dir (default /etc/snmp/conf)]
        [-i pid-file (default /var/snmp/snmpdx.st)]
        [-o enterprise-oid-file (default /etc/snmp/conf/enterprises.oid)]
        [-y]
        [-m GROUP | SPLIT (default GROUP)]
        [-d trace-level (range 0..4, default 0)]
```

The master agent provides the capability for messages to be displayed by using the `-d` option. This option can be very useful when debugging agent configurations or operational problems. Four debugging levels are supported that range from 0 (no debugging) to 4 (full debugging). The fourth level of debugging includes agent configuration information, decoding each SNMP message PDU, session information, and complete packet content displayed in hexadecimal. The third level includes the agent configuration, SNMP decoding, and session information, but not the packet display. The second level includes only the agent configuration and session information and the first level agent configuration, but little session information.

The `-m` option is used to specify the mode to forward SNMP requests to each subagent. Two modes are available with the master agent. The first, `GROUP`, indicates that multiple variables can be included with each request from the master agent. The second mode, `SPLIT`, ensures that each variable in the incoming request results in one send request to each subagent. The default forwarding mode is `GROUP`.

The `-p` option is used to specify an alternative port that the master agent will use when receiving or transmitting SNMP messages. The master agent uses the default SNMP port of `161` to send and received SNMP messages. Using this option, the master agent will listen on another port specified after the `-p` argument. For example, the master agent will listen on port `200` if the command below is executed:

```
# /usr/lib/snmp/snmpdx -p 200 -y
```

Remember, if the default SNMP port is changed, any SNMP management software that will query the agent must also be configured to use this new port. Otherwise, SNMP queries made on the old port will never reach the agent and will, instead, timeout. One primary reason for using this option is to support more than one instance of the master agent on the same system. This configuration could be used during testing of a newer version of the master agent without affecting the operation of the current version.

The `-y` option is used when the master agent has crashed or restarted after one or more subagents are already running. This option is used when the master agent must recover from its previous state before the crash to determine the configuration and status of each of the defined subagents. Further, you will notice that the `-y` option is included when the `snmpdx` command `/etc/init.d/init.snmpdx` (located in the system startup file) is executed. This startup script executes the master agent as shown below:

```
/usr/lib/snmp/snmpdx -y -c /etc/snmp/conf
```

When the agent is automatically started by the system, the master agent has no way of determining its previous state, and therefore uses the recovery option by default. Any subagent not found to be running when the master agent starts is restarted automatically by the master agent.

Master Agent MIB

The `snmpdx` agent implements a collection of MIB objects that provide information of the operational state and configuration of the master agent and any configured subagents. These objects are defined in the `/var/snmp/mib/snmpdx.mib` file under Sun's enterprise number (`42`) and are referenced from the `products` group (`enterprises.sun.products`) under the `sunMasterAgent` branch. Figure 5.2 shows the hierarchy of the `sunMasterAgent` group from the standard `enterprises` branch.

Because of the large number of these objects relating to the master agent, only the most important objects have been described and listed here. For those objects not presented, consult the `/var/snmp/mib/snmpdx.mib` file for additional information.

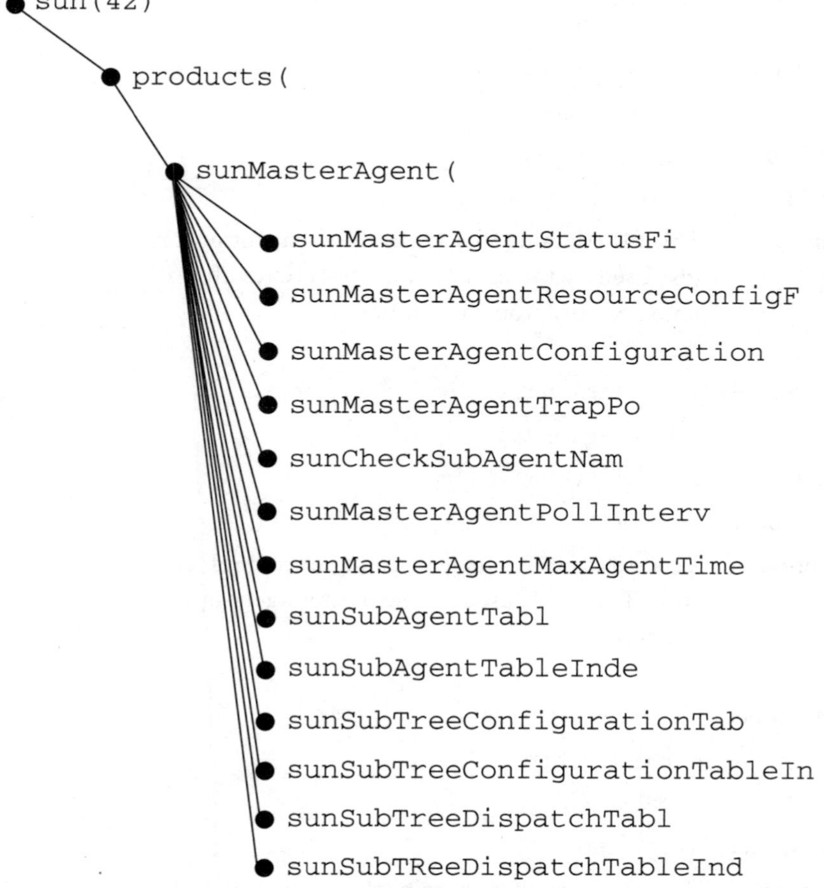

Figure 5.2 *sunMasterAgent MIB Group Tree.*

The `sunMasterAgent` group includes the following collection of MIB objects:

- Global Agent Objects
- Sub Agent Configuration Objects

Global Agent Objects

The global agent objects provide configuration information of the master agent and all registered subagents. This information is important because it might become necessary to poll the master agent directly to help debug both master agent and subagent operational issues and other problems. The objects are listed below:

Object Name: `sunMasterAgentStatusFile`
OID: `sunMasterAgent.1`
Object Type: `Display String`
Access Mode: `read-write`
Description: This file contains a list of all the subagent process ids. Used by the master agent to recover after it unexpectedly stops or is killed.

Object Name: `sunMasterAgentResourceConfigFile`
OID: `sunMasterAgent.2`
Object Type: `Display String`
Access Mode: `read-write`
Description: Used to contain subagent configuration information. This file is used by the master agent upon startup.

Object Name: `sunMasterAgentConfigurationDir`
OID: `sunMasterAgent.3`
Object Type: `Display String`
Access Mode: `read-write`
Description: The directory that contains the configuration files for the master agent.

Object Name: `sunMasterAgentTrapPort`
OID: `sunMasterAgent.4`
Object Type: `INTEGER`

Access Mode: `read-only`

Description: The port used by the master agent to receive SNMP traps from each of the subagents. These traps are then forwarded to one or more managers found in the master agent configuration file.

Object Name: `sunCheckSubAgentName`

OID: `sunMasterAgent.5`

Object Type: `Display String`

Access Mode: `read-write`

Description: Used by the subagents to check to ensure that no duplicate subagent with the same name is running.

Object Name: `sunMasterAgentPollInterval`

OID: `sunMasterAgent.6`

Object Type: `INTEGER`

Access Mode: `read-only`

Description: This variable contains the time interval when the agent will perform housekeeping activities such as determining if the resource file has changed, re-discovering each subagent, and other related tasks.

Object Name: `sunMasterAgentMaxAgentTimeOut`

OID: `sunMasterAgent.7`

Object Type: `INTEGER`

Access Mode: `read-only`

Description: This object is used to signify the maximum allowed time-out a subagent can set. This is used by the master agent to wait when sending requests to a subagent before the request is considered to have expired.

Sub Agent Configuration Objects

Additional objects within the `snmpdx.mib` file provide information on each subagent operating under the master agent. This information is available via a table and using index objects. The table (`sunSubAgentTable`) lists all the subagents that have been registered with the master agent. Each entry in this table is described as `sunSubAgentEntry` object. Access to the `sunSubAgentTable` is via the `sunSubAgentEntry` object. Figure 5.3 shows the hierarchy of the `sunSubAgentTable` group from the standard `enterprises` branch.

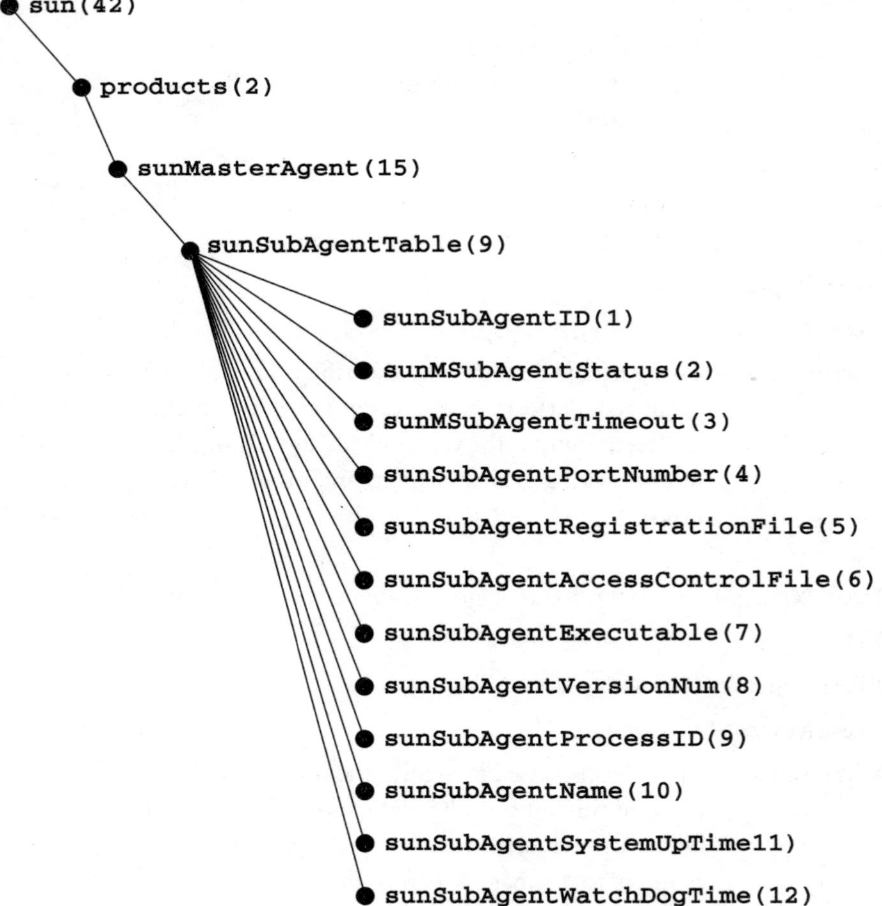

Figure 5.3 *Subagent MIB Group Tree.*

The `sunSubAgentEntry` table consists of the following subagent related objects:

Object Name: `sunSubAgentID`
OID: `sunSubAgentEntry.1`
Object Type: `INTEGER`
Access Mode: `read-only`
Description: This is the unique ID for each subagent running under the master agent.

Object Name: `sunSubAgentStatus`
OID: `sunSubAgentEntry.2`
Object Type: `INTEGER`
Access Mode: `read-write`
Description: Indicates the state of the subagent. Possible states include `init(1)`, `load(2)`, `active(3)`, `inactive(4)`, and `destroy(5)`.

Object Name: `sunSubAgentTimeout`
OID: `sunSubAgentEntry.3`
Object Type: `INTEGER`
Access Mode: `read-write`
Description: The maximum amount of time the master agent will wait for a subagent to complete a request. This value is expressed in microseconds.

Object Name: `sunSubAgentPortNumber`
OID: `sunSubAgentEntry.4`
Object Type: `INTEGER`
Access Mode: `read-write`
Description: The port number used by the subagent to listen for requests from the master agent.

Object Name: `sunSubAgentRegistrationFile`

OID: `sunSubAgentEntry.5`

Object Type: `Display String`

Access Mode: `read-write`

Description: Specifies the registration file used by the subagent. Each subagent must have its own file and contain subagent name, MIB tree information, preferred SNMP port, etc.

Object Name: `sunSubAgentAccessControlFile`

OID: `sunSubAgentEntry.6`

Object Type: `Display String`

Access Mode: `read-write`

Description: Specifies the access control file used by the subagent. This file stores SNMP community information.

Object Name: `sunSubAgentExecutable`

OID: `sunSubAgentEntry.7`

Object Type: `Display String`

Access Mode: `read-write`

Description: Contains the executable subagent program.

Object Name: `sunSubAgentVersionNum`

OID: `sunSubAgentEntry.8`

Object Type: `Display String`

Access Mode: `read-write`

Description: The version information regarding the subagent

Object Name: `sunSubAgentProcessID`

OID: `sunSubAgentEntry.9`

Object Type: `Display String`

Access Mode: `read-write`

Description: The process ID of the subagent.

Object Name: `sunSubAgentName`

OID: `sunSubAgentEntry.10`

Object Type: `Display String`

Access Mode: `read-write`

Description: The name of the subagent as specified in the registration file.

Object Name: `sunSubAgentSystemUpTime`

OID: `sunSubAgentEntry.11`

Object Type: `TimeTicks`

Access Mode: `read-write`

Description: The system up-time of the subagent.

Object Name: `sunSubAgentWatchDogTime`

OID: `sunSubAgentEntry.12`

Object Type: `INTEGER`

Access Mode: `read-write`

Description: The amount of time the master agent waits before polling the subagent to ensure that it is still operating correctly. This value is expressed in seconds.

Sun SNMP Agent

The Sun agent can provide the following services:

- Obtain network statistics
- Obtain system process information
- Obtain system memory information
- Send traps to specified systems

This system and network information will be available by polling the agent's MIB. The agent supports both MIB-II and portions of Sun's private MIB. The Sun MIB is described below. The trap definition must be done in the agent configuration file and is also described below.

Command Line Options

The `mibiisa` utility supports several command line options as outlined in Table 5.3.

Perhaps one of the most important is the `-r` option, which can be used to disable write access to the agent's MIB. Because the `mibiisa` utility implements SNMPv1, the agent doesn't provide a very robust security model. It might be necessary to limit the access to the system objects supported by the agent. Using this option, all SNMP `set-requests` will be rejected, but read access will operate without being affected.

Any attempt to alter or set a MIB object after the `-r` option has been used will cause an error. More specifically, when using a MIB browser, for example, if an attempt is made to set MIB objects that are placed in read-only mode, the authentication trap message will be generated.

Table 5.3 *Master Agent (snmpd) Command Options*

Option	Description
`-a`	Disable authentication traps
`-c`	Specify path to search for the configuration file
`-d`	Enable debugging output
`-p`	Use specified port instead of `161`
`-r`	Place the MIB in read-only mode

By default, the directory that `mibiisa` searches for the required configuration file is `/etc/snmp/conf`. To specify an alternate directory, use the `-c` option followed by the directory name. This option can be used to help test new configuration files that might reside in other directory locations. The `mibiisa` agent requires a configuration file and if it can't locate a valid configuration, it will exit with an error.

When an SNMP entity attempts to poll an agent with the incorrect community string, an authentication message is dispatched to the addresses configured in the `mibiisa` configuration file. If you would like to disable these trap messages, use the `-a` option.

To place the agent in debug mode, the `-d` option can be used when invoking the agent on the command line. Also, an optional debug level can be included that decreases levels of debugging from `3` (which is the highest) to `1` (which is the lowest).

Depending on the networking services presently running on the system, it might be necessary to use a different UDP port instead of the default of `161`. This will be a requirement if the `mibiisa` agent is running with a master agent. In this case, the agent will need to be started on a different port using the `-p` option. For example, to start the agent on port `32000`, use the following command:

```
# /usr/lib/snmp/mibiisa -p 32000
```

Configuring the Sun Agent

The `mibiisa` agent uses a configuration file called `snmpd.conf` and, by default, searches the `/etc/snmp/conf` directory for this file. This file contains configuration information that controls access to the agent's MIB and additional control information. Each entry contains a keyword followed by a string value, separated by one or more white spaces. Comments are also supported in this file by using the pound sign (#) and are ignored when processed by the agent. The keywords that can be used are outlined in Table 5.4 and are described in more detail below.

Table 5.4 *Agent Configuration Options*

Keyword	Description
`sysdescr`	System agent information
`syscontact`	System contact information
`syslocation`	Information on physical location of system

(Cont'd)

Table 5.4 *Agent Configuration Options (Cont'd)*

Keyword	Description
`trap`	Sends traps to specified hosts
`system-group-read-community`	Controls read access to MIB-II and Sun's system objects
`system-group-write-community`	Controls write access to MIB-II and Sun's system objects
`read-community`	Controls read access to the entire MIB
`write-community`	Controls write access to the entire MIB
`trap-community`	Trap community string
`kernel-file`	Symbol lookup file
`managers`	Hosts that are permitted to communicate with agent

`sysdescr`: This keyword maps to the MIB object `sysDescr` and the associated value used by the agent when responding to requests for this object. This is used to describe the system on which the agent is running (e.g. `Utltra SPARC 2` or `SPARCclassic`). Values for this object might include any string, but it should represent some information related to the type of system and perhaps operating system information as well.

`syscontact`: This keyword maps to the MIB object `sysContact` and the associated value is used by the agent when responding to requests for this object. It is used to describe the contact group or name that is responsible for the system (e.g. `Steve Maxwell x3190`).

`syslocation`: This keyword maps to the MIB object `sysLocation` and the associated value is used by the agent when responding to requests for this object. It is used to describe the physical location of the system (e.g. `Building 2, Graphics Lab 11-B`).

`trap`: This keyword is used to specify one or more hosts that should receive traps from the agent. Up to five hosts may be included with this option. Either the IP addresses or hostnames may be used. Any additional hosts beyond the maximum will be ignored. One use of this keyword is for forwarding authentication traps when an SNMP entity attempts to poll the agent with an incorrect community string. This is the primary way to determine if another party is attempting to access a device without having the proper authorization.

An authorization trap may also indicate that the community string was changed on the agent side and this change was not propagated to the manager side as well. Also, it means that a new SNMP management software package was recently installed that uses the community strings of `public` or `private`, and that these must be adjusted to the strings used at the local site.

`system-group-read-community` and `system-group-write-community`: These keywords are used to control read/write access to the agent MIB that includes the system group within only MIB-II and Sun's object groups.

`read-community` and `write-community`: These keywords are used to control read/write access to the entire MIB.

`trap-community`: This keyword specifies the community string for trap messages.

`kernel-file`: This keyword is used to specify where the agent should search for symbols.

`managers`: This keyword is used to control which hosts are permitted to communicate with the agent for either read or write access. It forms a basic access control list (ACL) for the agent. The ACL is one very good way to address some of the security flaws within the SNMP security model. However, bear in mind that this option provides a fundamental authentication mechanism, which is vulnerable to compromise. Therefore, consider the `managers` option as only part of your overall security strategy.

Sample Configuration

To further illustrate the agent configuration file options, a sample (see Listing 5.3) has been provided.

Listing 5.3 *Agent Sample File*

```
#
# System Information
#
sysdescr      SPARC Ultra 60
syscontact       Steve Maxwell
syslocation      Science Center room 22B
#
# Community Strings (system group only)
#
system-group-read-community     louvrehasart
system-group-write-community    louvrehasart
#
# Community Strings (entire MIB)
#
read-community  louvrehasart_1834
write-community louvrehasart_1824
#
# Trap Information
#
trap            rembrandt
trap-community  louvrehasart
#
# Standard Unix kernel
#
kernel-file     /vmunix
#
# Which systems are permitted to talk to this agent
#
managers        rembrandt monet
```

The system information (sysdescr, syscontact, and syslocation) should be specific to each system the agent is running on. In this example, the agent is running on a SPARC ultra 60 workstation, the contact for the system is Steve Maxwell, and the system is located in the Science Center room 22B. Note that any descriptive information could be included. Therefore, the sysdescr might not represent the actual system type the agent is running on. The system MIB objects are accessed with the read and write community string of louvrehasart. Access to the rest of the MIB for both read and write access is set to the string louvrehasart_1824. The system community string is different from the entire MIB so that you might want others to have access to system information (for inventory purposes, for example) without having access to the core of the other agent objects. All traps generated from this agent will be sent to the host `rembrandt` with a community string of `louvre-hasart`. Using the `managers` keyword as the basic ACL, the agent is permitted to access SNMP requests from the hosts `rembrandt` and `monet` and all other requests will be discarded by the agent.

Sun Agent MIB Objects

The `mibiisa` agent supports all of the objects defined within MIB-II, plus additional objects under the Sun enterprise wide vendor number (`42`). The MIB-II objects have been previously described in Chapter 3, "TCP/IP Protocol Suite." However, Sun has changed some of the attributes relating to either the return values or access modes of the standard MIB-II definitions. These changes and the additional Sun objects are described in this section.

Sun MIB Differences

The differences between `mibiisa` objects and the standard MIB-II objects include:

- Access to MIB objects has changed
- Certain MIB objects contain fixed values

Table 5.5 outlines these differences and contains a list of MIB objects, flags that indicate the object differences, the access method (either read-write or read-only), and the return value, if any. The object flags `V` and `A` refer to whether the object change is related to the value (`V`) of the object or the access mode (`A`) of the object. A check mark is placed in the column to indicate which object attribute is different from standard MIB-II definitions. For example, the access mode of the `sysName` object is read-write within MIB-II, while the Sun MIB provides only `read-only` access. As a result, a check mark is placed in column A. Most of the Sun objects in this table just return a fixed value. In many of these cases, a `1` is returned, which means that the agent doesn't support the object and is provided only for compatibility purposes.

Table 5.5 *Comparison of MIB-II and Sun MIB Objects*

MIB Object	V	A	Access within MIB-II	Access within mibiisa	Value with mibiisa
sysName		✓	read-write	read-only	
atIfIndex		✓	read-write	read-only	
ipDefaultTTL		✓	read-write	read-only	
ipRoutIfIndex	✓		read-write	read-write	(fixed)
IpRouteMetric1	✓		read-write	read-write	-1
IpRouteMetric2	✓		read-write	read-write	-1
IpRouteMetric3	✓		read-write	read-write	-1
IpRouteMetric4	✓		read-write	read-write	-1
IpRouteMetric5	✓		read-write	read-write	-1
IpRouteType	✓		read-write	read-write	(fixed)
IpRouteAge	✓		read-write	read-write	0
IpRouteMask	✓		read-write	read-write	(fixed)
icmpInDestUnreachs	✓		read-only	read-only	1
icmpInTimeExcds	✓		read-only	read-only	1
icmpInParmProbs	✓		read-only	read-only	1
icmpInSrcQuenchs	✓		read-only	read-only	1
icmpInRedirects	✓		read-only	read-only	1
icmpInEchos	✓		read-only	read-only	1
icmpInEchoReps	✓		read-only	read-only	1
icmpInTimestamps	✓		read-only	read-only	1
icmpInTimestampReps	✓		read-only	read-only	1
icmpInAddrMasks	✓		read-only	read-only	1

(Cont'd)

Table 5.5 *Comparison of MIB-II and Sun MIB Objects (Cont'd)*

MIB Object	V	A	Access within MIB-II	Access within mibiisa	Value with mibiisa
icmpInAddrMaskReps	✓		read-only	read-only	1
icmpOutDestUnreachs	✓		read-only	read-only	1
icmpOutTimeExcds	✓		read-only	read-only	1
icmpOutParmProbs	✓		read-only	read-only	1
icmpOutSrcQuenchs	✓		read-only	read-only	1
icmpOutRedirects	✓		read-only	read-only	1
icmpOutEchos	✓		read-only	read-only	1
icmpOutEchoReps	✓		read-only	read-only	1
icmpOutTimestamps	✓		read-only	read-only	1
icmpOutTimestampReps	✓		read-only	read-only	1
icmpOutAddrMasks	✓		read-only	read-only	1
icmpOutAddrMaskReps	✓		read-only	read-only	1
ifInUnknownProtos	✓		read-only	read-only	1
ipAdEntBcastAddr	✓		read-only	read-only	1
ipAdEntReasmMaxSiz	✓		read-only	read-only	65535
ipNetToMediaType	✓		read-only	read-only	Returns (3) dynamic
ipRoutingDiscards	✓		read-only	read-only	0

Sun Enterprise MIB Objects

The Sun enterprise objects supported by mibiisa include the following groups:

- sunSystem
- sunProcessTable
- sunHostPerf

The sunSystem group provides generic host information, such as agent and system information. The sunProcessTable contains information regarding the presently running system processes found on the agent's system. The sunHostPerf contains performance-related information. Each of these groups is described fully below. These groups are part of the Sun enterprise MIB, which contains additional groups. However, the agent only supports the three groups listed above. Figure 5.4 shows the hierarchical representation of all the groups under the Sun MIB from the enterprises branch.

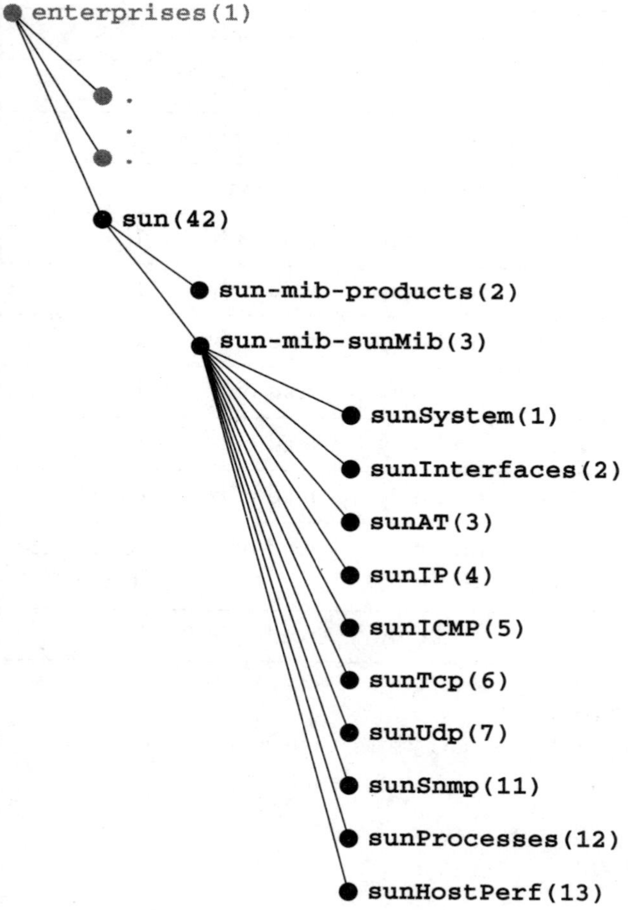

Figure 5.4 *Sun Enterprise MIB.*

The sunSystem group consists of objects that can be used to obtain system information such as the description of the system agent, the host identification string, part of the message-of-the-day file, and the system time. Figure 5.5 shows a hierarchical representation of the objects found in this group extending from the sun branch.

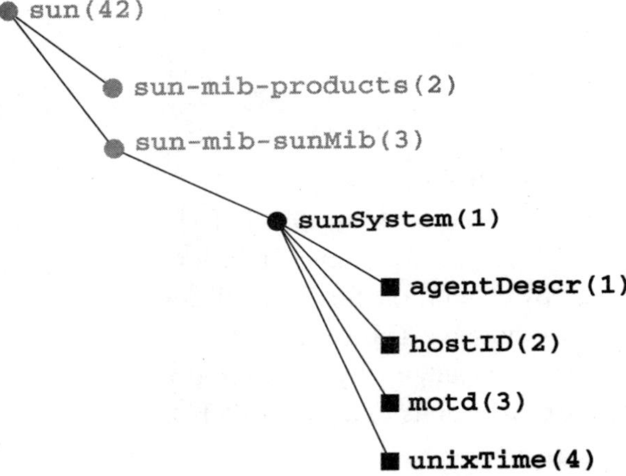

Figure 5.5 *sunSystem MIB Group Objects.*

A detailed description of these MIB objects is included below:

Object Name: agentDescr
OID: sunSystem.1
Object Type: Display String [255]
Access Mode: read-only
Description: A description of the SNMP agent, which is used to identify itself to other entities such as an SNMP manager. The agent assigns the string value of: Sun Microsystems SNMP Agent

Object Name: hostID
OID: sunSystem.2
Object Type: Display String [255]

Access Mode: `read-only`

Description: This object represents a 4-byte hardware identifier, which should be unique for every Sun system. This value is equivalent to executing the `hostid` utility on the Unix command line.

Object Name: `motd`

OID: `sunSystem.3`

Object Type: `Display String [4]`

Access Mode: `read-only`

Description: Displays the first line from the `/etc/motd` file. This is the message of the day file in which the file contents will be displayed every time a user logs into the system. By default, the first line will contain the operating system version and related information, but may contain any other information the administrator wants to make available.

Object Name: `unixTime`

OID: `sunSystem.4`

Object Type: `Counter`

Access Mode: `read-only`

Description: This displays the Unix system clock as measured in seconds from 1/1/1970.

Sun Process Table Group

The `sunProcessTable` is a table that consists of objects that can be used to obtain a list of system processes and related information. Figure 5.6 shows a hierarchical representation of these objects as related to the main `sun` branch. The `psEntry` object is the index for the `sunProcessTable` and is used to access each member, which represents a different Unix process. Because each of the objects listed below is a member of the `sunProcessTable`, the OID is represented as the index from the `psEntry` object's point of view.

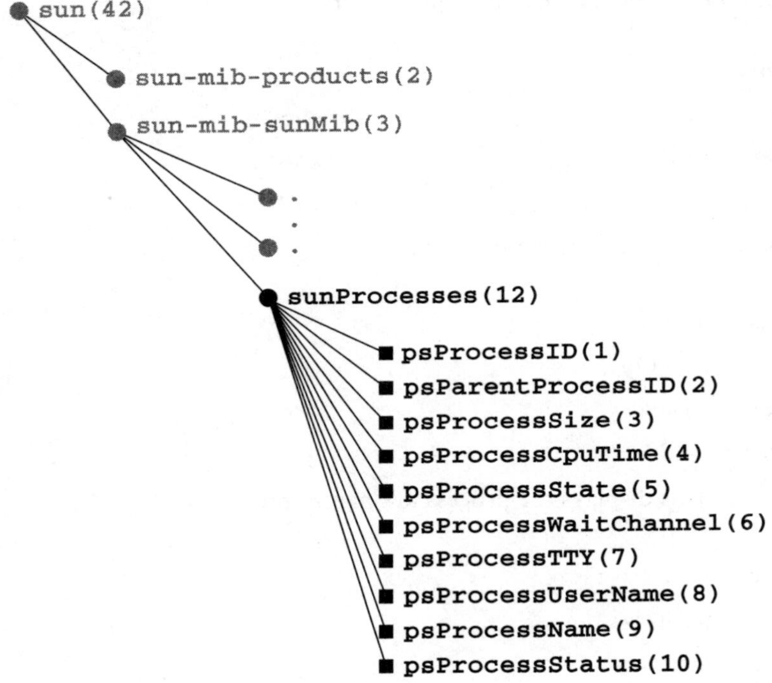

Figure 5.6 *sunProcessTable MIB Group.*

The information available within this group can also be obtained and compared to the operating system ps command. To better understand how this group of objects is used, Figure 5.7 shows the objects that correspond to the fields from the process status command.

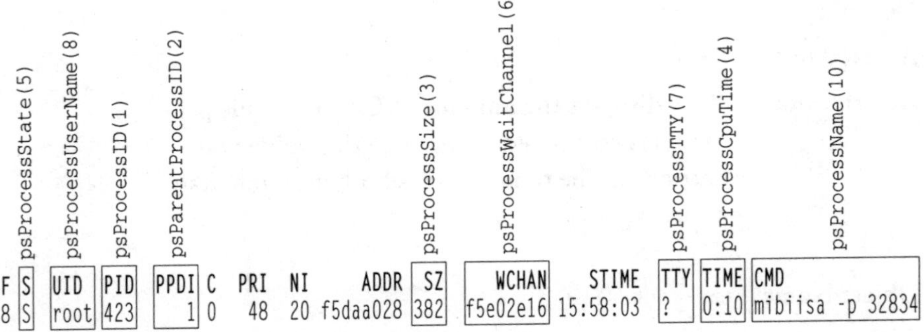

Figure 5.7 *Process Status MIB Mapping.*

The process table contains the following objects:

Object Name: `psProcessID`
OID: `psEntry.1`
Object Type: `Counter`
Access Mode: `read-only`
Description: This displays the process id.

Object Name: `psParentProcessID`
OID: `psEntry.2`
Object Type: `Counter`
Access Mode: `read-only`
Description: This displays the process id's parent process.

Object Name: `psProcessSize`
OID: `psEntry.3`
Object Type: `Counter`
Access Mode: `read-only`
Description: This displays the size of the memory the process is using. This includes stack and data segments of the program.

Object Name: `psProcessCpuTime`
OID: `psEntry.4`
Object Type: `Counter`
Access Mode: `read-only`
Description: This displays the amount of CPU time this process has consumed at the time this value was retrieved. The time includes both user and system time.

Object Name: `psProcessState`
OID: `psEntry.5`

Object Type: `Display String [4]`

Access Mode: `read-only`

Description: This displays the current running state of the process. This includes the use of the following flags:

`R` - Runnable

`T` - Stopped

`P` - In page wait

`D` - Non-interruptable wait

`S` - Sleeping (less than 20 seconds)

`I` - Idle (more than 20 seconds)

`Z` - Zombie

Object Name: `psProcessWaitChannel`

OID: `psEntry.6`

Object Type: `Display String [16]`

Access Mode: `read-only`

Description: This displays the reason the process is in wait mode.

Object Name: `psProcessTTY`

OID: `psEntry.7`

Object Type: `Display String [16]`

Access Mode: `read-only`

Description: This displays the controlling terminal of this process, if any.

Object Name: `psProcessUserName`

OID: `psEntry.8`

Object Type: `Display String [16]`

Access Mode: `read-only`

Description: This displays the name of the user associated with this process.

Object Name: psProcessUserID
OID: psEntry.9
Object Type: counter
Access Mode: read-only
Description: This displays the numeric user id associated with the psProcessUserName string.

Object Name: psProcessName
OID: psEntry.10
Object Type: Display String [64]
Access Mode: read-only
Description: This displays the name of the command string for this process.

Object Name: psProcessStatus
OID: psEntry.11
Object Type: Counter
Access Mode: read-write
Description: Object used that can be used to send a signal to this process. The signal sent to the process is the value this object has been set to.

Sun Host Performance Group

The sunHostPerf group consists of a collection of system performance-related objects that range from the total number of timeticks used by a process to the total number of network collisions. Due to the rather large number of these objects, only the most useful objects will be described. If you are looking for a complete list of available objects within this group, consult the Sun MIB file /var/snmp/mib/sun.mib for additional information.

Among the more useful objects within the sunHostPerf group are objects relating to system swap, device interrupts, and network traffic. Figure 5.8 shows a hierarchical representation of these objects as related to the main sun branch. The traffic objects are counters, which represent totals for the entire system regardless of the number of network connections and are similar to the output from the `netstat` command. For example, the `rsIfInPackets` object provides the total number of input packets from the network for all network interfaces defined on the system.

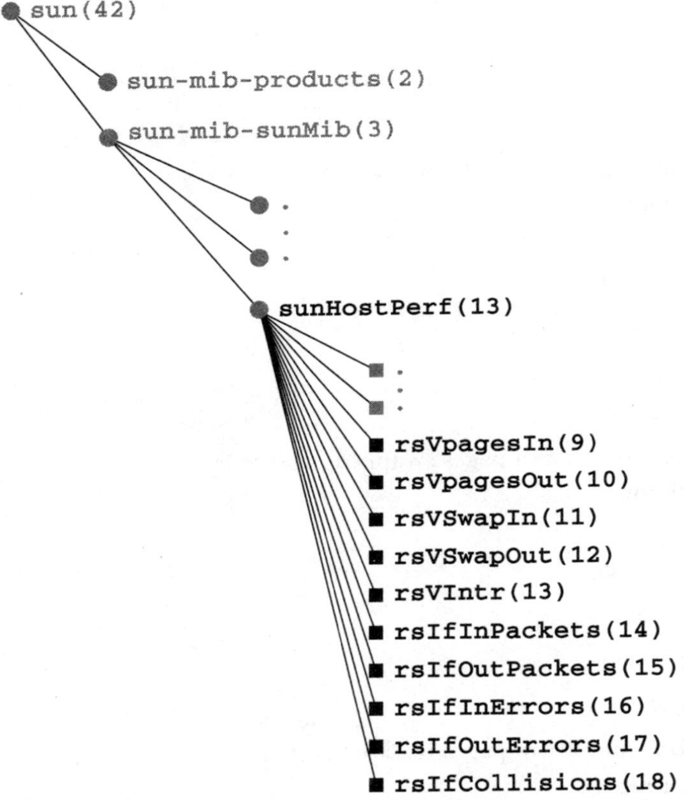

Figure 5.8 *sunHostPerf MIB Group Objects.*

The Sun host performance group includes some of the following objects:

Object Name: `rsVpagesIn`

OID: `sunHostPerf.9`

Object Type: `Counter`

Access Mode: `read-only`

Description: Total number of pages read in from disk since last reboot.

Object Name: `rsVpagesOut`

OID: `sunHostPerf.10`

Object Type: `Counter`

Access Mode: `read-only`

Description: Total number of pages written to disk since last reboot.

Object Name: `rsVSwapIn`

OID: `sunHostPerf.11`

Object Type: `Counter`

Access Mode: `read-only`

Description: Total number of pages swapped in since last reboot.

Object Name: `rsVSwapOut`

OID: `sunHostPerf.12`

Object Type: `Counter`

Access Mode: `read-only`

Description: Total number of pages read out from disk since last reboot.

Object Name: `rsVIntr`

OID: `sunHostPerf.13`

Object Type: `Counter`

Access Mode: `read-only`

Description: Total number of device interrupts since last reboot. This includes interrupts for all devices such as disk and other peripheral devices.

Object Name: rsIfInPackets

OID: sunHostPerf.14

Object Type: Counter

Access Mode: read-only

Description: Total number of input packets obtained from the network since last reboot.

Object Name: rsIfOutPackets

OID: sunHostPerf.15

Object Type: Counter

Access Mode: read-only

Description: Total number of out packets transmitted to the network since last reboot.

Object Name: rsIfInErrors

OID: sunHostPerf.16

Object Type: Counter

Access Mode: read-only

Description: Total number of input errors from the network since last reboot.

Object Name: rsIfOutErrors

OID: sunHostPerf.17

Object Type: Counter

Access Mode: read-only

Description: Total number of output errors encountered while attempting to transmit to the network since last reboot.

Object Name: rsIfCollisions

OID: sunHostPerf.18

Object Type: Counter

Access Mode: `read-only`

Description: Total number of output collisions recorded on the network since last reboot.

UCD's SNMP Agent

General Description

The UCD Agent (`snmpd`) is a very powerful, extensible, fully functional SNMP system agent and is available on a large number of Unix platforms. See the Installation section for a list of specific platforms that are supported. As previously mentioned, the agent supports the MIB-II (network statistics), SNMPv2 MIBs, SMUX MIB, Host Resource MIB, and the UCD-SNMP MIB. These MIBs by default are located in the `/usr/local/share/snmp/mibs` directory. However, the agent will still function correctly if it is unable to locate these files.

From a network management perspective, the agent can be used to monitor critical system operating parameters (such as system load average) and provide alerts when these resources reach a critical threshold. The agent can be used to:

- Monitor disk space usage
- Monitor system processes
- Monitor system load
- Invoke Unix commands and shell scripts
- Monitor agent information and status
- Provide MIB extensions
- Provide access to several MIBs

Each of these features will be explored in greater detail to include how to configure the agent to monitor these resources and how to proactively address system resource limitation problems.

Agent Configuration File

The agent requires a configuration file to operate. This file, by default, is located in the `/usr/local/share/snmp` directory. It contains one or more action directives and each line contains a single keyword with an associated number of arguments. The keyword can be divided into one of the following categories: monitor, security, extensible, and informational. The monitoring directives include those used to monitor specific resources such as disk space or system load. Security keywords are used to define various layers of security for access to the agent, which may include ACL (access control lists) and various views of the MIB objects. The extensible keywords define ways to add functionality to the agent without changing the agent software. Finally, the informational keywords are used to assign static information to MIB objects. Each of the keywords has a fixed number of required parameters and may have additional optional arguments as well. Table 5.6 lists the supported keywords and functions sorted by the category to which they belong.

Table 5.6 *UCD Agent Keywords Sorted by Category*

Category	Keyword	Description
Monitor	`proc`	Checks to make sure specified processes are running
	`disk`	Determines available disk space of specified file system
	`load`	Monitors system load average
Security	`com2sec`	Security Configuration Parameter
	`group`	Security Configuration Parameter
	`view`	Security Configuration Parameter
	`access`	Security Configuration Parameter

(Cont'd)

Table 5.6 *UCD Agent Keywords Sorted by Category (Cont'd)*

Category	Keyword	Description
Extensible	`exec`	Executes the specified command and makes the output available via the MIB
	`pass`	Passes a MIB tree to specified program that can manipulate the MIB objects
Informational	`syslocation`	Used to represent the physical location of agent device
	`syscontact`	Used to represent the contact person for agent device

Comments are supported by placing a # character at the beginning of a line.

When the agent first starts up, it reads the configuration file. If changes are made to the file after the agent has started, the agent can be instructed to re-read the configuration file in two ways. First, the MIB object `VERUPDATECONFIG` can be set to `1`. For example, using the UCD `snmpset` tool, the following command would force the agent on system `rodin` to process the configuration file:

```
# snmpset rodin public 1.3.6.1.4.1.2021.100.VERUPDATECONFIG 1
```

Second, the `-HUP` signal can be sent to the agent process by using the `kill` command. Before issuing this command, we must obtain the process id of the agent. This can be done, for example, by issuing the `ps` command. Assuming that the process id was found to be `304`, the following command is functionally equivalent to the `snmpget` command above:

```
# kill -HUP 304
```

Some of the agent keywords, when executed, are used to monitor resources that modify certain MIB objects that indicate the return status or additional information of the command. These objects are part of the agent's MIB and are accessed from the UCD (`2021`) private branch. The starting path of the MIB is:

```
iso.org.dod.internet.mgmt.enterprises.ucdavis
```

or

```
(1.3.6.1.4.1.2021).
```

Monitoring System Load

The agent provides the ability to monitor the system load average via the `load` agent command. The system load average is the average number of jobs (or programs) in the run queue. The agent provides the same basic information as the Unix `uptime` and `w` commands. The syntax of this command includes:

```
load [1 minute max] [5 minute max] [15 minute max]
```

The `load` command, followed by either 1 maximum, 5 maximum or 15 maximum, will instruct the agent to monitor the system load for these times. If the system load exceeds the maximum for 1 minute, 5 minute, or 15 minute running averages, then the agent will set the `loadaveErrorFlag` object to 1 and include a descriptive error message in the `loadaveErrMessage` object. If no maximum load command is specified, then the default value of 1 minute is used.

The `load` command is an excellent way to monitor system utilization across a large number of systems. Establishing the system load threshold can be a little tricky because different kinds of systems might need different thresholds. For example, a workstation might experience high system load because the user just started a CPU-intensive application. On the other hand, a user starting the same application on a server with a large number of users could pose a significant problem. Also, some systems might always have a higher load than other systems, but because the system is expected to be used in this manner, it might not be a problem.

For critical systems, a load average higher than 2 or 3 may indicate a severe problem that must be addressed in a timely manner. In the following example, the agent has been configured to monitor the 1-minute load average threshold of `2`:

```
load 2
```

Should this limit be reached, the agent's MIB will be updated appropriately as shown below:

```
enterprises.ucdavis.loadTable.laEntry.laErrorFlag.1 = 1
enterprises.ucdavis.loadTable.laEntry.laErrorFlag.2 = 1
enterprises.ucdavis.loadTable.laEntry.laErrorFlag.3 = 0
enterprises.ucdavis.loadTable.laEntry.laErrMessage.1 = "1 min Load
Average too high (= 2.50)"
enterprises.ucdavis.loadTable.laEntry.laErrMessage.2 = "5 min Load
Average too high (= 2.26)"
enterprises.ucdavis.loadTable.laEntry.laErrMessage.3 = ""
```

In this case, the MIB shows that both the `1` and the `5` minute load averages exceeded the `2` limit threshold. The reason the MIB shows three instances of the `laErrorFlag` and `laErrMessage` is because the load average is measured in terms of 1, 5, and 15 minute averages, thus three separate parameters.

The agent can also provide access to both the current system load averages and the parameters for the configuration of the `load` command itself. For example, the following was obtained from the agent when the load was above `2` mark:

```
enterprises.ucdavis.loadTable.laEntry.laNames.1 = "Load-1"
enterprises.ucdavis.loadTable.laEntry.laNames.2 = "Load-5"
enterprises.ucdavis.loadTable.laEntry.laNames.3 = "Load-15"
enterprises.ucdavis.loadTable.laEntry.laLoad.1 = "2.50" Hex: 32 2E 35 30
enterprises.ucdavis.loadTable.laEntry.laLoad.2 = "2.26" Hex: 32 2E 32 36
enterprises.ucdavis.loadTable.laEntry.laLoad.3 = "1.38" Hex: 31 2E 33 38
enterprises.ucdavis.loadTable.laEntry.laConfig.1 = "2.00" Hex: 32 2E 30 30
enterprises.ucdavis.loadTable.laEntry.laConfig.2 = "2.00" Hex: 32 2E 30 30
enterprises.ucdavis.loadTable.laEntry.laConfig.3 = "2.00" Hex: 32 2E 30 30
```

As you can see, the load averages for `1` and `5` minutes are above `2`. Also, the `laConfig` object is set at `2.00` for each load average threshold level. The `laNames` object is simply used as a label to describe each load average window. This information was obtained directly from the agent configuration file.

Monitoring Disk Space

The agent can be used to monitor disk space consumption of any mounted file systems with the `disk` command. The syntax of this command includes:

```
disk file-system [minimum]
```

The agent will monitor the specified file system and determine if the total disk space available is less than the minimum. If it is, the MIB object `diskErrorFlag` will be set to `1` and the MIB object `diskErrorMsg` will contain a descriptive message. If no minimum is provided, the agent uses the default value of `100K`. The minimum value is stored in the `dskMinimum` object and is set to the specified minimum from the configuration file or set to the default if no minimum value is found in the configuration file.

By way of example, consider the following agent commands:

```
disk  /
disk  /usr   1000
```

The first disk command will monitor the `root(/)` file system and compare the minimum value of 100 kilobytes (Kb), which is the default value to the total disk space available. The second command will monitor the /`usr` file system and compare the minimum value of 1,000Kb. Because the minimum is in units of Kb , we must add three zeros to the end so we get 1,000,000 or 1 megabyte (Mb). When we run the agent on a test system, we get the following when querying the agent's MIB:

```
enterprises.ucdavis.diskTable.dskEntry.dskMinimum.1 = 100000
enterprises.ucdavis.diskTable.dskEntry.dskMinimum.2 = 1000
enterprises.ucdavis.diskTable.dskEntry.dskAvail.1 = 56924
enterprises.ucdavis.diskTable.dskEntry.dskAvail.2 = 32545
enterprises.ucdavis.diskTable.dskEntry.dskErrorFlag.1 = 1
enterprises.ucdavis.diskTable.dskEntry.dskErrorFlag.2 = 0
enterprises.ucdavis.diskTable.dskEntry.dskErrorMsg.1 = "/: less than
100000 free (= 56924)"
enterprises.ucdavis.diskTable.dskEntry.dskErrorMsg.2 = ""
```

You will notice that two sets of MIB objects are defined. The first set corresponds to the root (`/`) file system, which is the first instance because it appears first in the agent configuration file. The second instance is for the `/usr` file system because it comes after the first entry.

As you can see, the `dskMinimum` objects are set accordingly; the `dskMinimum.1` instance, which maps to the `/` file system, is set to 100 Mb (100,000,000 Bytes) while the second, `diskMinimum.2`, which maps to the `/usr` file system, is set to 1 Mb (1,000,000 Bytes). The agent also stores the available disk space of each monitored file system in the `dskAvail` object, one for each file system. In this case, the `/` file system is approximately 56 Mb, while the /usr file system is approximately 32 Mb. The `dskErrorFlag.1` object for the root file system is set because the root file system is less than 100 Mb and the `dskErrorMsg.1` also contains more descriptive information. The `dskErrorMsg.2` object does not contain any information and the `dskErrorFlag.2` is not set because the `/usr` file system contains enough space to satisfy the disk space test.

The MIB also contains other information that can be used when monitoring disk space. The information is comparable to the output of the Unix `df` (disk free) command. For example, given the `df -k` command, this includes a summary of the disk space of the mounted file systems. The output below includes a partial list of the file systems reported:

```
Filesystem            kbytes    used   avail capacity  Mounted on
/dev/dsk/c0t3d0s0      82303   25286   56935    31%    /
/dev/dsk/c0t3d0s6     232141  199364   32545    86%    /usr
```

When the agent MIB is queried, we find the following:

```
enterprises.ucdavis.diskTable.dskEntry.dskPath.1 = "/" Hex: 2F
enterprises.ucdavis.diskTable.dskEntry.dskPath.2 = "/usr" Hex: 2F 75
73 72
enterprises.ucdavis.diskTable.dskEntry.dskDevice.1 =
"/dev/dsk/c0t3d0s0"
enterprises.ucdavis.diskTable.dskEntry.dskDevice.2 =
"/dev/dsk/c0t3d0s6"
enterprises.ucdavis.diskTable.dskEntry.dskTotal.1 = 82303
enterprises.ucdavis.diskTable.dskEntry.dskTotal.2 = 232141
enterprises.ucdavis.diskTable.dskEntry.dskAvail.1 = 56935
enterprises.ucdavis.diskTable.dskEntry.dskAvail.2 = 32545
enterprises.ucdavis.diskTable.dskEntry.dskUsed.1 = 25286
enterprises.ucdavis.diskTable.dskEntry.dskUsed.2 = 199364
enterprises.ucdavis.diskTable.dskEntry.dskPercent.1 = 31
enterprises.ucdavis.diskTable.dskEntry.dskPercent.2 = 86
```

Notice the MIB contains all the information that the `df` command provides. This includes the mount points, file systems, total disk space for each, available disk space, used disk space, and percent disk space used. This information can be extremely helpful, for example, because it is possible to monitor disk space usage by a percent instead of raw bytes by using the `dskPercent` objects. Also, the remaining objects can be used as an automated mechanism for inventory of system storage capacities. More information on these and other agent MIB objects are include in the *UCD MIB* section.

Monitoring System Processes

The `proc` command can be used to monitor specific services or Unix processes. The syntax includes:

```
proc process [maximum limit] [minimum limit]
```

This keyword is followed by a valid process name or command that is monitored by the agent. This directive is used to monitor a critical process or a set of processes that must be running continuously on the system. If the process is not found running on the local system by the agent, an error flag is set in the MIB object `procTable.prEntry.prErrorFlag` and a descriptive message is also placed in the MIB object `procTable.prEntry.prErrMessage`. The agent uses the Unix `/usr/bin/ps -e` command to search for running processes as specified with the `proc` command. For instance, the following can be used to ensure that the `mountd` process is alive:

```
proc mountd
```

Additionally, a maximum and minimum value can be included to further refine the number of processes that should be running. The maximum is used to indicate how many processes should be running concurrently while the minimum determines the smallest number that must be running. Because it is customary to have multiple `mountd` processes on a system, the agent can be configured to monitor the exact number. For the sake of discussion, let's assume that we have enabled the system to support four copies of `mountd`. The syntax of `proc` command is:

```
proc mountd 4 4
```

If the agent detects that either less than four or greater than four `mountd` process are running, it updates the MIB appropriately.

If no maximum and minimum values are specified, the default of zero is assumed. In practice, the use of both the maximum and minimum options can provide a flexible way to address specific monitoring requirements.

In the following example,

```
proc ntalkd 4
```

the `ntalkd` process is monitored and if more than four are running currently, the agent will update the MIB. Therefore, the maximum option provides a convenient way to ensure that only a certain number of processes are permitted to run currently. If we want to go a step further, we can automate the agent to take an action when `ntalkd` processes are found (for example, kill the process). *Because no minimum was listed, the agent will take no action when no* `ntalkd` *processes are found to be running.*

The selection of which Unix processes to monitor with the `proc` keyword is largely a matter of determining which services are critical to the operation of your environment. If the computing systems are used to support publishing software, you might care more about print spoolers and word processing applications while systems supporting online order entry software might need to have database server processes monitored.

On the other hand, one might take the approach that everything running on a system is critical and must be monitored. At first glance, this might seem like a reasonable strategy. Unfortunately, this can lead to other problems and may well be overkill in most situations. If all system processes are going to be monitored, does this include temporary processes like networking services as well? If so, which ones? Also, maintaining the configuration file for the agent of these processes can be a chore at best because it must be updated whenever new applications and software are either added or removed from the system. Performance of the agent will be affected as well. In certain situations, this might be unacceptable.

Assume we have configured the agent to monitor the `mountd` and four `ntalkd` processes. The following example shows the values of the MIB when the agent detects that none of the `mountd` or `ntalkd` processes is running:

```
enterprises.ucdavis.procTable.prEntry.prErrorFlag.1 = 1
enterprises.ucdavis.procTable.prEntry.prErrorFlag.2 = 1
enterprises.ucdavis.procTable.prEntry.prErrMessage.1 = "No mountd
process running."
enterprises.ucdavis.procTable.prEntry.prErrMessage.2 = "Too few
ntalkd running (# = 0)"
```

Extending the Agent

One of the most powerful features of the UCD agent is that it can be extended to include execution of external commands. These commands can either be shell scripts or binary programs, which are specified as part of the agent configuration. The output of these commands is captured within the MIB so that the information can be made available via SNMP get requests. Still, the agent supports the concept of passing control of part of a MIB tree to an external program. When this program is executed, it can access the specified MIB tree. This gives the agent the ability to dynamically alter MIB objects, without requiring custom agent development.

To invoke external Unix commands or shell scripts from the agent, use the `exec` keyword command. The syntax of this command includes:

```
exec label program [args]
exec MIB program [args]
```

In the first form, the `exec` command is used with a label, program, and optional arguments. The label is used as an identifier, which is useful when perusing the agent's MIB. The program is the actual Unix binary or shell script that the agent will invoke with any specified command line arguments listed in the `args` field. When the agent executes this command, the output is placed in the agent's MIB under the `extEntry` table. In the example below, the `exec` command uses the `who` command to determine the run level of the local system:

```
exec runlevel /usr/bin/who -r
```

When the agent invokes this command, the output is placed in the agent's MIB and is available for viewing. Using a `snmpwalk` tool, the following sample output was obtained from the agent:

```
enterprises.ucdavis.extTable.extEntry.extIndex.1 = 1
enterprises.ucdavis.extTable.extEntry.extNames.1 = "runlevel"
enterprises.ucdavis.extTable.extEntry.extCommand.1 = "/usr/bin/who -r"
enterprises.ucdavis.extTable.extEntry.extResult.1 = 0
enterprises.ucdavis.extTable.extEntry.extOutput.1 = "    .        run-
level 3  Dec 21 10:44     3      0  S."
enterprises.ucdavis.extTable.extEntry.extErrFix.1 = 0
```

Notice that the `extResult` object contains a `0` because the command completed successfully. Also, both the `runlevel` label and command `/usr/bin/who -r` are stored in the `extNames` and `extCommand` objects respectively.

One problem with using this version of `exec` is that only a single line of output is saved to the MIB. As a result, any output after the first line will be discarded by the agent. Luckily, the second form of the `exec` command can be used to capture output when there is more than one line.

With the second form, the `exec` command includes a MIB definition that will be used to store the `exec` command information and the complete output of the command that was executed by the agent. For example, given the command:

```
exec .1.3.6.1.4.1.2021.55 top-list /usr/local/bin/top -b
```

This will run the `top` command and assign the output to the MIB branch `.iso.org.dod.internet.private.ucdavis.55`. The `top` command is used to display the system load and system process information. Normally `top` will continuously display this information, but in this case, the command was executed with the `-b` option, which instructs `top` to display a snapshot of the system and then exit.

To examine the output of `top`, we simply do a MIB walk on the `2021.55` MIB branch. Please note for readability purposes, the `enterprises` string was dropped from the output below.

Thus the command,

```
snmpwalk monet public .iso.org.dod.internet.private.ucdavis.55
```

will give us the `top` results:

```
ucdavis.56.1.1 = 1
ucdavis.56.2.1 = "top-list"
ucdavis.56.3.1 = "/usr/local/bin/top -b"
ucdavis.56.100.1 = 0
ucdavis.56.101.1 = "last pid:   498;  load averages:  0.16,  0.15,  0.12    16:10:43."
ucdavis.56.101.2 = "36 processes:  35 sleeping, 1 on cpu."
ucdavis.56.101.3 = "." Hex: 0A
ucdavis.56.101.4 = "Memory: 24M real, 508K free, 11M swap in use, 36M swap free."
ucdavis.56.101.5 = "." Hex: 0A
ucdavis.56.101.6 = "." Hex: 0A
ucdavis.56.101.7 = "  PID USERNAME THR PRI NICE  SIZE RES STATE TIME CPU COMMAND."
```

```
ucdavis.56.101.8 = "  498 root  1  30  0 1396K 1096K cpu     0:01  6.24% top."
ucdavis.56.101.9 = "  497 root  1  50  0 1780K 1220K sleep   0:01  5.14% snmpwalk."
ucdavis.56.101.10 = " 412 root  1  58  0 1024K  780K sleep   0:00  0.04% csh."
ucdavis.56.101.11 = " 193 root  7  51  0 1924K 1132K sleep   0:00  0.02% nscd."
ucdavis.56.101.12 = " 402 root  1  58  0 2472K 1720K sleep   0:07  0.02% snmpd."
ucdavis.56.101.13 = " 108 root  1  58  0 1360K  480K sleep   0:01  0.01% in.routed."
ucdavis.56.101.14 = "  88 root  1  59  0 1252K  512K sleep   0:30  0.00% cryptorand."
ucdavis.56.101.15 = " 311 root  1  59  0 7260K 1352K sleep   0:05  0.00% Xsun."
ucdavis.56.101.16 = " 166 root  10 34  0 3200K 2444K sleep   0:03  0.00% automountd."
ucdavis.56.101.17 = " 170 root  7  55  0 2812K 1036K sleep   0:02  0.00% syslogd."
ucdavis.56.101.18 = " 326 root  1  59  0 5728K 1396K sleep   0:02  0.00% dtgreet."
ucdavis.56.101.19 = " 241 root  4  38  0 2056K 1092K sleep   0:01  0.00% vold."
ucdavis.56.101.20 = " 286 root  1  58  0 5376K  848K sleep   0:01  0.00% dtlogin."
ucdavis.56.101.21 = " 278 root  7  59  0 4272K  836K sleep   0:01  0.00% httpd."
ucdavis.56.101.22 = " 410 root  1  18  0 1464K  912K sleep   0:00  0.00% in.telnetd."
ucdavis.56.101.23 = "." Hex: 0A
ucdavis.56.102.1 = 0
```

We can use some of the MIB objects found in the `ucdavis.56` MIB group to help identify the `top` command output. The `ucdavis.56.2.1` and `ucdavis.56.3.1` objects contain the command label and the command itself as specified in the agent configuration file. The remaining MIB objects (`ucdavis.56.101.1` to `ucdavis.56.101.23`) are used to represent the command output. Also, the MIB object `ucdavis.56.101.1` shows the return status of the `top` command. In this example, a `0` indicates that the `top` was executed successfully.

Another powerful feature of the UCD agent is the `pass` command. With this command, control of a MIB tree can be given to a program that the agent executes.

As you can see, the `exec` command can be used to extend that agent-monitoring coverage to include additional operating system tools and application functions. This is perhaps the agent's most powerful feature

Sample Agent Configuration File

A sample agent configuration file is provided below (see Listing 5.4). This might be a good starting point for those who want to deploy the agent environment where monitoring some of the standard Unix processes is critical. Also, the configuration includes call functions, which are also listed, to automatically limit certain system processes so that the system doesn't become overloaded as a result.

Listing 5.4 *Sample Agent Configuration*

```
#
# Sample Configuration
# Monitor these processes..
#
proc mountd
proc nfsd
proc lpsched
#
# Monitor load average above 2.0..
#
load 2
#
# Make sure we have a least 50 MB in root
# and 100 MB in /usr
#
disk  /   50000
disk /usr 100000
#
# Execute the following programs to obtain
# output via the UCD mib...
#
exec MIB top /usr/bin/top
exec MIB lpstat /usr/bin/lpstat
```

Command Line Options

The agent provides a number of command line options, which are listed in Table 5.7. Because the agent in most instances will be started automatically when the system boots, some of these options should be changed in the startup file if they are to become permanent. However, some of the options only make sense when used on the command line.

By default, when `snmpd` is started, it uses the well-known SNMP port `161`. This needs to be changed if other agents are running on the same system or if you are using a master agent. The `-p` option has been provided for this purpose. This option, followed by the port number, will be used by `snmpd` to listen for incoming SNMP requests. If the UCD agent will be used with a master agent, refer to the section below for additional configuration details.

Table 5.7 *UCD Agent Command Line Options*

Option	Description
`-a`	Displays the IP addresses of any system that polls the agent
`-V`	Displays the protocol transactions from the agent
`-d`	Displays the UDP packets that were sent from or received by the agent
`-q`	Displays simplified agent output
`-p`	Opens an alternative port used for SNMP transactions
`-f`	Instructs the agent not to fork from the calling shell
`-l`	Specifies that the agent should log activity to a file
`-L`	Specifies that the agent should log activity to standard out
`-c`	Uses the specified configuration file
`-C`	Doesn't search for any additional configuration files, but uses only the one specified by `-c` option

Several options can be used to assist any debugging efforts that must be done with the agent. The `-a` option is used to display the IP address of any system that has been in communication with the agent, along with date and time information. This is useful for establishing that any configured ACLs are working properly. When an option is used, the agent will display messages like the following:

```
1998-11-21 16:04:17 Received SNMP packet(s) from 10.0.2.126
```

The `-d` option displays the UDP packets sent and received from the agent and is used to help detect SNMP protocol-related problems or other operations issues. Also, this option can be used to examine the MIB object requested from SNMP client applications. A sample of the agent debugging output is shown below:

```
GET
    -- system.sysContact.0
    >> system.sysContact.0 = Steve Maxwell
sent 64 bytes to 10.0.2.126:
0000: 30 82 00 3C  02 01 00 04  06 70 75 62  6C 69 63 A2   0..<.....public.
0016: 82 00 2D 02  04 23 C1 E0  9F 02 01 00  02 01 00 30   ..-..#.........0
0032: 82 00 1D 30  82 00 19 06  08 2B 06 01  02 01 01 04   ...0.....+......
0048: 00 04 0D 53  74 65 76 65  20 4D 61 78  77 65 6C 6C   ...Steve Maxwell
```

In this sample, the agent obtains an SNMP `get` request from the system with the IP address of `10.0.2.126`. The agent displays this string "`--`" to indicate what the remote SNMP entity requests (in this case the `sysContact` object) and the "`>>`" followed by the string shows what the agent returns. The hexadecimal output corresponds to the entire UDP packet, which includes the community string information and any returned object(s). If you want just the protocol transaction and not the UDP packet trace, use the `-V` option. This option will display

```
GET
    -- system.sysLocation.0
    >> system.sysLocation.0 = Graphics Lab 11-B
```

as a result of a request for the `sysLocation` MIB object from a SNMP client application.

The `-q` option, according to the documentation in the UCD package, indicates that this option displays simpler formatting that can be used, for example, to automate parsing of the agent output. Unfortunately, this option doesn't seem to do anything in the release 3.5 of the agent tested.

To further assist with agent debugging, the `-f` option can be used to instruct the agent not to fork from the shell. Without this option, the agent will detach by forking a new process from the current shell and return the shell prompt. The `mibiisa` agent, for example, behaves in this manner. When the `-f` is used, the agent can be terminated by typing the `^C` to the shell that was used to start the agent. Alternatively, if you want to stop the agent, you need to use the `kill` command with the appropriate process id of the agent.

If it becomes necessary to save the debugging information to a file, the `-l` option followed by a file name can be used. The output logged to this file includes both standard output (`STDOUT`) and standard error (`STDERR`). If the `-l` option is used without a file name, then the default `/var/log/snmpd.log`[1] file is used. When conducting a SNMP trace (with the `-V` option), saving the output to a file will come in handy when dealing with a large number of transactions. If, however, you want to log information directed to standard output and standard error, then use the `-L` option. The `-l` and `-L` options are mutually exclusive and therefore shouldn't be used together.

If you want the agent to use a specific configuration file, use the `-c` option followed by the complete path and file name. By default, the agent searches in pre-configured locations for one or more agent configuration files. If you don't want the agent to search for additional configuration files and, instead, only use the one specified with the `-c` option, include the `-C` option as well. This forces the agent to only use the configuration file you provide and is one way of ensuring that any other configuration files are ignored.

UCD MIB

The agent implements MIB objects under the `ucdavis (2021)` enterprise number. The complete path to the UCD tree begins with: `iso.org.dod.internet.private.enterprises` or `1.3.6.1.4.1`. The UCD MIB provides the following important MIB objects and groups:

- procTable
- memory
- extTable
- diskTable
- loadTable
- systemStats
- version
- snmperrors

This MIB definition file can be found in the `/usr/local/share/snmp/mibs/UCD-SNMP-MIB.txt` file after the UCD package has been installed.

---

1. This is the default log file name, but can be changed. You are prompted for an alternative name during the configuration process.

UCD ProcTable

The `procTable` is a table that consists of objects that can be used to obtain a list of system processes that are monitored by the agent and have been placed in the agent configuration file. Figure 5.9 shows a hierarchical representation of these objects as related to the `ucdavis` branch. The process information is accessed via the `prEntry` MIB object.

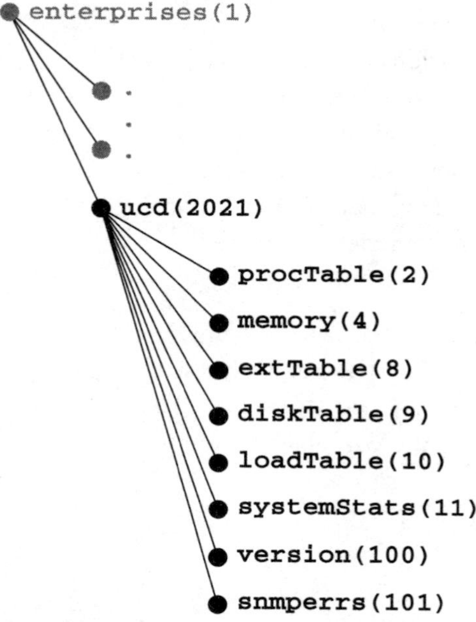

Figure 5.9 *UCD Process Table MIB Tree.*

The `procTable` contains the following set of objects:

Object Name: `prIndex`

OID: `prEntry.1`

Object Type: `PRIndex (Integer)`

Access Mode: `read-only`

Description: Reference index for each monitored system process. Because the `procTable` is in fact a table, the `prIndex` is used access to another instance of the table.

Object Name: `prNames`

OID: `prEntry.2`

Object Type: `Display String [255]`

Access Mode: `read-only`

Description: The name of the process the agent is monitoring. The process name is obtained from the agent configuration file after the `proc` keyword command.

Object Name: `prMin`

OID: `prEntry.3`

Object Type: `Integer`

Access Mode: `read-only`

Description: The minimum number of processes that should be running on the system. If the number of processes is less than the minimum, an error flag is generated in the `prErrorFlag` and `prErrMessage` MIB objects. The minimum value is obtained from the agent configuration after the maximum value has been specified, if any.

Object Name: `prMax`

OID: `prEntry.4`

Object Type: `Integer`

Access Mode: `read-only`

Description: The maximum number of processes that should be running on the system. If the number of processes is greater than the maximum, an error flag is generated in other MIB objects. The maximum value is obtained from the agent configuration after the process name has been specified.

Object Name: `prCount`

OID: `prEntry.5`

Object Type: `integer`

Access Mode: `read-only`

Description: The current number of processes actually running on the system that the agent is presently monitoring.

Object Name: `prErrorFlag`

OID: `prEntry.100`

Object Type: `integer`

Access Mode: `read-only`

Description: This object is set to 1 if the agent detects trouble with the process and set to 0 if no problems are encountered. Possible problems include exceeding the maximum and minimum process count or the process not running at all.

Object Name: `prErrMessage`

OID: `prEntry.101`

Object Type: `DisplayString [255]`

Access Mode: `read-only`

Description: If the agent has detected a problem with a process, this object will contain an error message describing the problem in more detail.

Object Name: `prErrFix`

OID: `prEntry.102`

Object Type: `integer`

Access Mode: `read-only`

Description: If the agent has been configured to support a response to the trouble encountered with a process, setting this object to 1 can be used to instruct the agent to attempt to fix the process problem automatically by executing whatever script or process the agent knows about.

UCD Extensible Agent Table

The extTable is a table that consists of objects that can be used to obtain a list of scripts or programs that the agent will execute and store the results in UCD MIB. Figure 5.10 shows a hierarchical representation of these objects as related to the ucdavis branch. This table contains a MIB object called extEntry, which is used to access each extTable element.

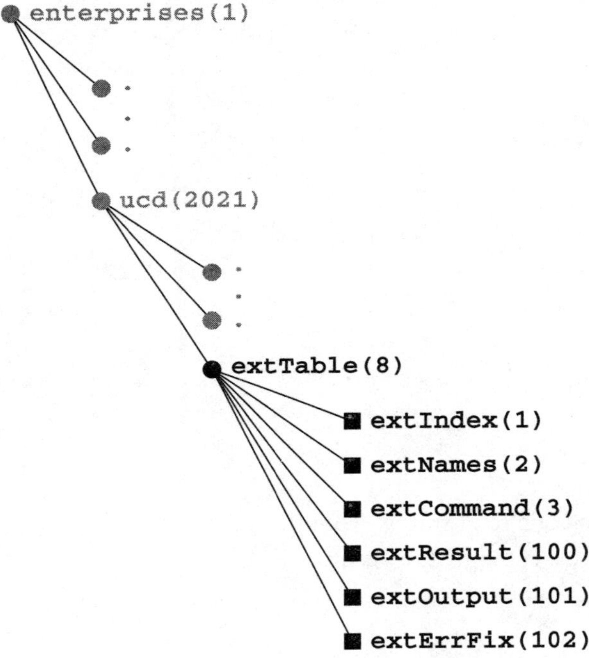

Figure 5.10 *UCD Extensible Table Tree.*

The extTable contains the following set of objects:

Object Name:	extIndex
OID:	extEntry.1
Object Type:	ExtIndex (Integer)
Access Mode:	read-only
Description:	Index into the extTable for each configured extensible script.

Object Name: `extNames`

OID: `extIndex.2`

Object Type: `DisplayString [255]`

Access Mode: `read-only`

Description: A short (single word) description of the extensible command specified in the agent configuration file.

Object Name: `extCommand`

OID: `extIndex.3`

Object Type: `DisplayString [255]`

Access Mode: `read-only`

Description: The extensible command line specified in the agent configuration file.

Object Name: `extResult`

OID: `extIndex.100`

Object Type: `Integer`

Access Mode: `read-only`

Description: The return code (exit status) from the extensible command executed by the agent.

Object Name: `extOutput`

OID: `extIndex.101`

Object Type: `DisplayString [255]`

Access Mode: `read-only`

Description: The first line of output from the extensible command executed by the agent.

Object Name: `extErrFix`

OID: `extIndex.102`

Object Type: `DisplayString [255]`

Access Mode: read-only

Description: Flag to control if the agent should attempt a recovery from problem encountered when running the extensible command.

UCD Disk Table

The diskTable is a table that consists of objects that can be used to obtain a list of all the file systems the agent is monitoring and any related objects. Figure 5.11 shows a hierarchical representation of these objects as related to the ucdavis branch. This table contains a MIB object called dskEntry, which is used to access each diskTable element.

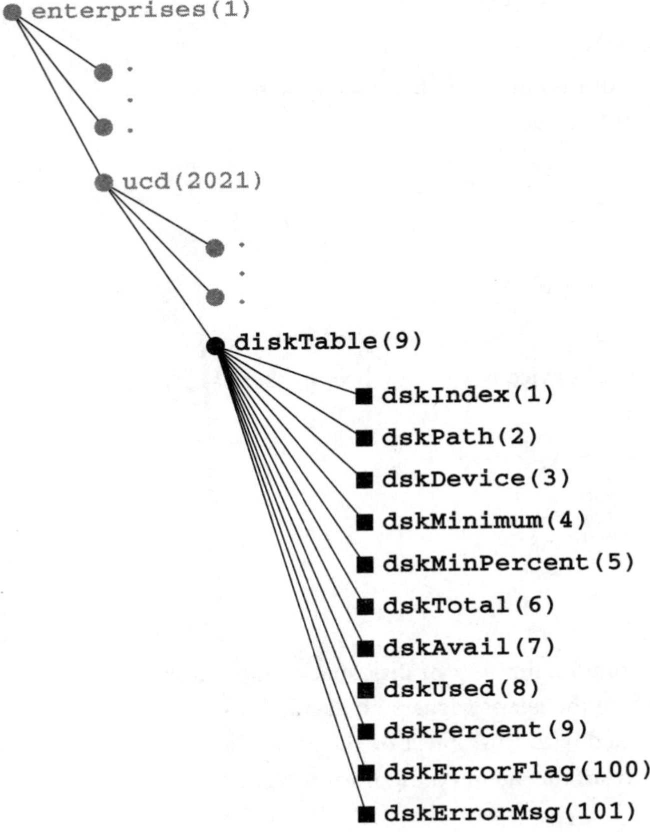

Figure 5.11 *UCD Disk Table Objects.*

The `diskTable` contains the following set of objects:

Object Name: `dskIndex`
OID: `dskEntry.1`
Object Type: `DiskIndex (Integer)`
Access Mode: `read-only`
Description: Index into the `DiskTable` for each file system that is being monitored by the agent.

Object Name: `dskPath`
OID: `dskEntry.2`
Object Type: `DisplayString [255]`
Access Mode: `read-only`
Description: The mount point of the file system being monitored by the agent.

Object Name: `dskDevice`
OID: `dskEntry.3`
Object Type: `DisplayString [255]`
Access Mode: `read-only`
Description: The actual device partition (slice) of the disk mounted.

Object Name: `dskMinimum`
OID: `dskEntry.4`
Object Type: `integer`
Access Mode: `read-only`
Description: The minimum amount of disk space required in Kb before the agent triggers an event. This value is specified with this object or the `dskMinPercent` object from the agent configuration file.

Object Name: dskMinPercent

OID: dskEntry.5

Object Type: integer

Access Mode: read-only

Description: The minimum amount of disk space required in kilobytes before the agent triggers an event. This value is specified with this object or the dskMinimum object from the agent configuration file.

Object Name: dskTotal

OID: dskEntry.6

Object Type: Integer

Access Mode: read-only

Description: Total size of the disk/partition in kilobytes.

Object Name: dskAvail

OID: dskEntry.7

Object Type: Integer

Access Mode: read-only

Description: The total amount of available disk space for the disk/partition in kilobytes.

Object Name: dskUsed

OID: dskEntry.8

Object Type: Integer

Access Mode: read-only

Description: The amount of used space on the disk/partition in kilobytes.

Object Name: dskPercent

OID: dskEntry.9

Object Type: Integer

Access Mode: `read-only`

Description: The amount of used space as a percent on the disk/partition.

Object Name: `dskErrorFlag`

OID: `dskEntry.100`

Object Type: `Integer`

Access Mode: `read-only`

Description: Used to indicate that the disk/partition is under the minimum amount of free disk space as specified by the agent configuration file.

Object Name: `dskErrorMsg`

OID: `dskEntry.101`

Object Type: `DisplayString [255]`

Access Mode: `read-only`

Description: A descriptive warning message and free space summary pertaining to a monitored disk/partition.

UCD System Load Table

The `loadTable` is a table that consists of objects that can be used to monitor the system load. Figure 5.12 shows a hierarchical representation of these objects as related to the `ucdavis` branch. This table contains a MIB object called `laEntry`, which is used to access each `loadTable` element.

The `loadTable` contains the following set of objects:

Object Name: `laIndex`

OID: `laEntry.1`

Object Type: `Integer`

Access Mode: `read-only`

Description: Index into the `loadTable` for each entry.

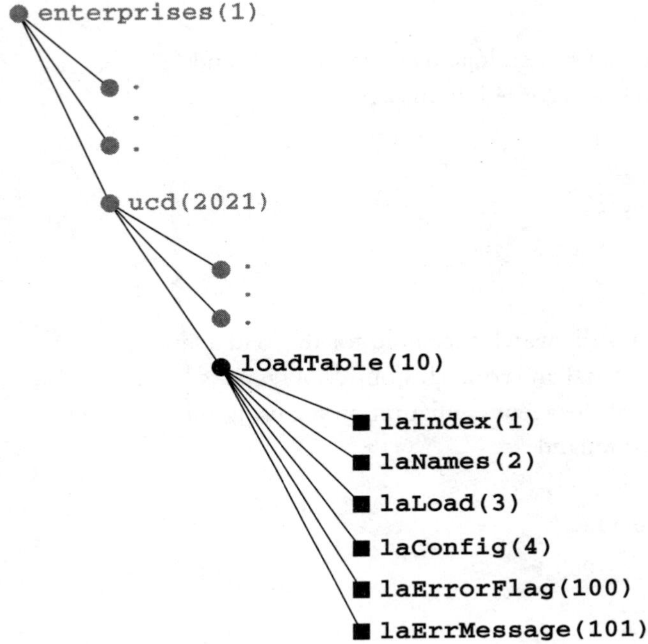

Figure 5.12 *UCD Load Table Objects.*

Object Name: laNames

OID: laEntry.2

Object Type: Display String [255]

Access Mode: read-only

Description: The list of load average names the agent is monitoring. This can be one of the three load average windows that the agent supports and includes 1, 5, and 15 minutes. These are represented as the strings Load-1, Load-5, and Load-15, respectively.

Object Name: laLoad

OID: laEntry.3

Object Type: Display String [255]

Access Mode: `read-only`

Description: The actual system load averages for `1`, `5`, and `15` minutes as recorded by the agent.

Object Name: `laConfig`

OID: `laEntry.4`

Object Type: `Display String [255]`

Access Mode: `read-only`

Description: Contains the watch threshold for the load average to signal an error. This object obtains its value for the agent configuration file using the `load` command.

Object Name: `laErrorFlag`

OID: `laEntry.100`

Object Type: `Integer`

Access Mode: `read-only`

Description: Used to indicate whether the load average threshold (as contained in the `laConfig` object) has been exceeded. If the value is set to `1`, then the value has been crossed; otherwise, it is `0`.

Object Name: `laErrMessage`

OID: `laEntry.101`

Object Type: `Display String [255]`

Access Mode: `read-only`

Description: Descriptive error message indicating the load average and the threshold value that was exceeded.

Agent System Startup

For the SNMP agents to be available at all times, they should be started when the system is initialized or rebooted. The Sun agent ships with a startup script and is set up when the software is installed. The startup script, `init.snmpdx`, which is found in the `/etc/init.d` directory, is used to start the master agent automatically. After the master agent is running, it starts any configured subagents and, by default, starts the `mibiisa` system agent. The startup script is shown in Listing 5.5:

Listing 5.5 *Agent Startup Script*

```
#!/sbin/sh
# Copyright 01/17/97 Sun Microsystems, Inc. All Rights Reserved.
#pragma ident  "@(#)init.snmpdx 1.11 97/01/17 Sun Microsystems"

#
# Return pid of named process in variable "pid"
#
pidproc() {
        pid=`/usr/bin/ps -e |
                /usr/bin/grep $1 |
                /usr/bin/sed -e 's/^  *//' -e 's/ .*//'`
}

#
# Kill named process(es)
#
killproc() {
        pidproc $1
        [ "$pid" != "" ] && kill -9 $pid
}

case "$1" in

'start')
        if [ -f /etc/snmp/conf/snmpdx.rsrc -a -x /usr/lib/snmp/snmpdx ]; then
                /usr/lib/snmp/snmpdx -y -c /etc/snmp/conf
        fi

        ;;
'stop')

        killproc snmpdx
        killproc snmpv2d
        killproc mibiisa
        ;;
```

(Cont'd)

Listing 5.5 *Agent Startup Script (Cont'd)*

```
36
37  *)
38          echo "Usage: /etc/init.d/init.snmpdx { start | stop }"
39          ;;
40  esac
41  exit 0
```

Like most startup scripts on Solaris, this script provides the ability to either start or stop the master agent and subagents. A case statement is used to provide the logic to determine which argument is given on the command line and takes appropriate action. If the string `start` is specified, then everything between lines `25-29` is executed. If the `stop` string is used, then everything between lines `31-35` is executed. When the system starts, it executes this script with the `start` argument. When the system is being brought down, the script is started with the `stop` argument. The `*)` label (on line `37`) is provided when the script is being executed on the command line. If either the `start` or `stop` argument isn't provided, the script uses this to match anything that results in a usage string being displayed.

When the script is going to start the agent processes, it first checks to ensure that the `/etc/snmp/conf/snmpdx.rsrc` file exists and is a regular file, and checks to see if the `/usr/lib/snmp/snmpdx` is executable. If either of these tests is false, the script just silently stops without starting the agents.

When the script is invoked to stop the agent processes, it uses the `killproc` (lines `8-12`) function with the name of each agent name to stop the agents. Before the `killproc` function actually kills each agent process it checks to see if each of these processes is in fact running by invoking the `pidproc` function. This function executes the `ps` command followed by a `grep` for the match of the agent name. If the agent is running, it will return a process id. If not, the null string "" is returned. The last step is to issue the `kill -9` with the process id of each running agent.

The script is designed to be used both during and after the system has been booted. For example, to stop the agent processes, use the following command:

```
# init.snmpdx stop
```

To start the agents, use the following:

```
# init.snmpdx start
```

The UCD agent must also be configured to start when the system is brought up. The version of the UCD package described in this book doesn't contain a startup script and as a result, the Sun agent startup script has been altered to include the UCD agent. The code fragment to start the UCD agent is included below (see Listing 5.6) and can be included in its own startup script:

Listing 5.6 *UCD Agent Startup*

```
#
# Start the UCD Agent
#
if [ -f /usr/local/share/snmp/snmpd.conf -a -x /usr/local/sbin/snmpd
]; then
        /usr/local/sbin/snmpd
fi
```

By default, the UCD agent listens on well-known port `161`. If the agent must use another port, change the command above by including the `-p` option followed by the new port number.

Sun Agent Package Information

The Sun agents started shipping standard with Solaris 2.6. The binary package is available for both SPARC and Intel; therefore, it can only be installed on Solaris systems on either of these platforms. The standard Solaris 2.6 and 2.7 CD-ROMs contain the packages for the Sun Enterprise agents. The agents are also available and can be downloaded via the Sun Website if you don't have access to the Sun Solaris CD-ROM. The agents can be installed on

Solaris 2.4 and 2.5 versions. Because previous releases didn't include the agent, installation of these versions of Solaris will require the `pkgadd` system utility. The packages required and a list of the components within the package for the Sun agents are listed below:

- SUNWascom
- SUNWsasnm
- SUNWsadmi
- SUNWmibii

SUNWascom
Contains configuration and common files for the other packages, which can be found in the `/etc` and `/var` directories. These include `/etc/snmp/conf/snmpd.conf` and `/var/snmp/mib/sun.mib`.

SUNWsasnm
This package contains the `snmpdx` master agent, the master agent MIB file, `snmpdx.mib`, the system startup file, `init.snmpdx`, and additional system libraries.

SUNWsadmi
Contains the DMI portion of the agents. Despite the fact that the DMI functionality won't be used, it should be installed as well.

SUNWmibii
This package contains the `mibiisa` system agent.

Obtaining the Sun Agents from the Internet

As previously stated, the Sun agents can be downloaded from the Sun Website using the following URL:

```
http://www.sun.com/solstice/products/ent.agents/
```

Sun Agent Installation Procedure

To install the Sun agents on an older release of Solaris using the Solaris 2.6 CD-ROM, follow the procedure outlined below and execute the commands as the Super-user.

1. Obtain the Sun software from the site above or from the CD-ROM available with this book.

2. Mount the CD-ROM into the system (or use the volume manager).

   ```
   [mount command here]
   ```

3. Change directory to the CD-ROM:

   ```
   cd /cdrom/sol_2_6_sparc_smcc_svr/s0/Solaris_2.6/Product
   ```

4. Install the `SUNWascom` package:

   ```
   pkgadd -d . SUNWascom
   [lots of output]
   ```

5. Install the `SUNWsasnm` package:

   ```
   pkgadd -d . SUNWsasnm
   [lots of output]
   ```

6. Install the `SUNWadmi` package:

   ```
   pkgadd -d . SUNWadmi
   [lots of output]
   ```

7. Install the `SUNWmibii` package:

   ```
   pkgadd -d . SUNWmibii
   [lots of output]
   ```

8. To activate the agent, reboot the system or use the system startup script:

   ```
   /etc/reboot
   ```

   or

   ```
   /etc/inid.d/init.snmpdx start
   ```

UCD Agent Package Information

The UCD packet is available in the public domain; as such it must be retrieved and subsequently installed. It is provided either in source or binary form. The binary is the easiest to install because the package doesn't need to be compiled. However, if you want to build the UCD from scratch, you will need a compiler and a little bit of patience. The procedures for installing the binary and source releases have been provided below.

Conditions of Use

The following information appears in the `COPYING` file for this distribution:

```
Copyright (c) 1996-1998 by Wes Hardaker
      Copyright (c) 1996 by the University of California, Davis
COPYRIGHT
  Many portions of the code in this package were distributed by
  Carnegie Mellon University.  The copyright for their code can be
  found in the top of most of the source code.
  All other code and changes to the original code written by Wes
  Hardaker at the University of California at Davis is copyrighted
  under the following copyright:
    Permission to use, copy, modify, and distribute this software and
    its documentation for any purpose and without fee is hereby
    granted, provided that the above copyright and the statement
    "Portions of this product were obtained from the ucd-snmp package
    written by Wes Hardaker at the University of California, Davis."
    appear in the supporting documentation of the product.  It may be
    included in a software compact disk set provided that the author
    is contacted and made aware of its distribution.
```

Directory Layout

The layout of the directory structure of the UCD package (version 3.5) includes the following:

- agent
- apps
- etc
- local
- m
- man

- mibs
- ov
- s
- snmplib
- win32

The agent, apps, local, m, and s directories contain source code, shell scripts, and header files, which constitute the bulk of the package. In particular, the apps location contains the source for all the SNMP tools (such as snmpget and snmpset) and the agent location is where the SNMP agent and trap handler source files (snmpd and trapd) reside. The snmplib directory contains the source to the SNMP APIs. The mibs directory contains a list of MIB files that the agent supports and the ov directory contains files that are used for integration into the HP OpenView software package. The etc directory contains the agent configuration files needed to implement SNMP security. The win32 directory contains source code and Dynamically Loadable Library (DLL) modules of the UCD agent and applications for the Windows 95/NT system.

Before attempting to install and compile the UCD package, you will need the following:

- C compiler (gcc, for example)
- gnunzip utility

Obtaining UCD Agent from the Internet

The UCD package may be obtained from several FTP sites on the Internet:

```
ftp://ftp.ece.ucdavis.edu/pub/snmp/ucd-snmp.tar.gz
ftp://sunsite.cnlab-switch.ch/mirror/ucd-snmp/ucd-snmp.tar.gz
ftp://ftp.win.or.jp/pub/network/snmp/ucd-snmp/ucd-snmp.tar.gz
```

Also, it can be obtained from the WWW site:

```
http://www.ece.ucdavis.edu/ucd-snmp
```

The UCD Agent Installation Procedure

The installation procedures for the UCD package include the following:

1. Obtain the UCD package from one of the sites above or from the CD-ROM provided with this book.

2. Uncompress the GNU archive:

   ```
   gunzip ucd-snmp-3.5.tar.gz
   ```

3. Untar the archive into the directory you will be using:

   ```
   tar xvf ucd-snmp-3.5.tar
   ```

4. Normally, the untarring will create a new directory named `ucd-snmp` plus the software version number. Change to this directory:

   ```
   cd ucd-snmp-3.5
   ```

5. Next, run the `configure` command from this directory:

   ```
   ./configure
   [lots of output]
   ```

   After several pages of output, the configure program will ask a small number of questions as shown below:

6. If no errors were encountered, run the `make` command:

   ```
   make
   [lots of output]
   ```

7. After the `make` has completed and no serious errors were displayed, install the package by running:

   ```
   make install
   [lots of output]
   ```

If you encounter a problem during the installation, consult the Frequently Asked Questions (FAQ) file and additional documentation that come with the package. The `FAQ.txt` file is located at the top level of the installation directory.

06

Simple Network Management Protocol Tools

As the previous chapter discusses system tools and utilities, this chapter focuses on network tools that can help manage both systems and other networking devices such as switches, routers, probes, hubs, and other SNMP-compliant devices. The tools in this section will likely become a welcome addition to the suite of software that you have now.

Tools discussed in this chapter include:

- UCD SNMP Commands
- The Snmpconf Command

Taken collectively, these commands provide both monitoring and administration functions and can be used to:

- Determine SNMP System Heartbeat
- Determine System Up/Down Messages
- Obtain Protocol Statistics
- Obtain Interface Performance Measures
- Monitor System Process Activity
- Monitor Routing
- Configure Networking Devices

Monitoring/Administration Functions

System Heartbeat

A system heartbeat is an SNMP get-request that a manager uses to determine the general reachability of the agent and the system. For example, the network manager may poll the system clock MIB variable of the agent to determine that each successive poll is older than the previous one. Each successive poll should indicate that time is moving forward. The MIB variable that can be used for this purpose is the `unixTime` object, part of the `sunSystem` group of the Sun system agent. As an alternative, the `sysUpTime` object from the MIB-2 `system` group can be used and should be available from all SNMP agents.

System Up/Down Messages

Should the system be brought down and rebooted for any reason, a message will be sent to the designated network management system in the form of a trap. Recall that a trap is an unsolicited message emitted from the agent indicating some special condition or event. Receiving these messages, the manager can be informed, for example, of system outages and take appropriate action. The UCD agent configuration file and additional tools can be used to forward trap messages to one or more network management systems.

Protocol Statistics

Because many SNMP agents support the MIB-II standard, protocol performance and system monitoring is possible. This includes IP, ICMP, TCP, SNMP, network interface counter, and some Sun system performance objects.

System Process Activity

With the Sun MIB extensions and the UCD agent, the monitoring of system processes is also possible. Process objects can be used to establish the overall health of the network or the condition of an individual system by monitoring critical processes.

Route Monitoring

The route monitoring agent can be used to determine the routing configuration of a system and report any errors found. For example, if an organization has determined that each machine must have a default route, this can be verified by probing the SNMP agent within these devices.

Interface Performance

MIB-2 also provides objects that contain performance information for each of the interfaces installed within an SNMP device. It is possible to retrieve this information and monitor the performance of active interfaces.

Configuration Control

Many networking devices (e.g., routers and switches) must be configured before they can be effectively used on the network. Also, as network requirements change, so too the configurations within networking devices must change. The tools listed here provide some support for device configuration changes.

UCD Commands

General Description

The UCD package not only provides a robust and powerful SNMP agent, it also provides a series of handy tools that can be used to manage SNMP-enabled networking devices. These tools support SNMPv1, SNMPv2, and, in a limited fashion, SNMPv3. You can select which version is used with a command line option. Further, these tools can be used to build scripts or other programs to accomplish complex network management functions or customized tasks. For example, the `snmpget` command can monitor certain critical interfaces to determine if one or more of them becomes inoperable. In such a case, the appropriate support staff would be notified automatically by the monitoring software.

If the UCD distribution has been completely installed, a full set of Unix manual pages that cover all the UCD tools presented in this chapter will also be installed. The default location for these man pages is `/usr/local/man`.

The tools and utilities that are supplied with the UCD package, along with a general description, are listed in Table 6.1.

Table 6.1 *UCD SNMP Tools*

UCD Tool	Description
`snmpbulkwalk`	Obtains MIB object with SNMP bulk request
`snmpdelta`	Monitors changes of SNMP variables
`snmpget`	Obtains one or more MIB objects
`snmpgetnet`	Continuously walks an SNMP MIB tree and obtains all supported MIB objects
`snmpnetstat`	Obtains agent interface configuration information
`snmpset`	Sets one or more MIB objects to specified value
`snmpstatus`	Obtains important MIB object information
`snmptable`	Obtains a complete SNMP table
`snmptest`	Communicates with an SNMP agent entity
`snmptranslate`	Converts MIB objects into more meaningful information

(Cont'd)

Table 6.1 *UCD SNMP Tools (Cont'd)*

UCD Tool	**Description**
`snmptrap`	Sends SNMP trap messages to one or more managers
`snmptrapd`	Retrieves SNMP traps from the network
`snmpwalk`	Obtains a group of related MIB objects

The basic syntax of the UCD tools is:

```
snmpcmd protocol_version [additional_options] hostname community
object [object]
```

The word `snmpcmd` is a placeholder and represents one of the UCD commands as listed in the above table.

The word `protocol_version` is `1`, `2c`, or `2p`. This string identifier specifies which SNMP version should be used. A `1` represents the standard SNMPv1. A `2c` indicates differences within the supported SNMP protocol data units, but uses the same community-based approach as in SNMPv1. A `2p` indicates SNMPv2 with party-based security.

The `additional_options` are listed in Tables 6.2 and 6.3 and control the operation and display attributes of the UCD tools. The most commonly used command line options are described more fully below.

The word `hostname` can be replaced with the name of any host on the network that contains an SNMP agent that matches the `protocol_version` information specified on the command line. A valid IP address, expressed in dotted notation, may be used instead of a hostname.

The word `object` represents the MIB OID that should be retrieved (in the case of an SNMP GET) or altered (in the case of an SNMP SET). It may be expressed in either dotted numeric or dotted named notation. In the case of an SNMP SET operation, additional object information will be required, as discussed in the "SNMP Set" section below. Note that one or more objects may be specified on the command line.

Common Command Line Options

UCD tools share a common number of command line arguments. Having a core set of options makes it easier to remember and use the tools. The arguments supported by all the tools are divided into two categories: operational and display options. The operational options control the behavior of each of the tools, while the display options control how the MIB objects, associated values, and other information are displayed.

Display Options

The display arguments are listed in Table 6.2; a total of eight are available. However, please note that not all of them are fully described below. For instance, the `-h` option that displays a help string that includes the command line options and meanings is not described because its function is fairly intuitive.

Table 6.2 *Common Display Options*

Option	Description
`-d`	Dumps SNMP packets
`-D`	Displays debugging information
`-h`	Displays a help message
`-f`	Displays full object identifier path
`-q`	Makes it easier to parse for programs
`-s`	Displays only suffix identifiers
`-S`	Displays both suffix identifiers and MIB name
`-V`	Displays version information

Three of the options provided control how MIB path information is formatted and displayed. These options include `-f`, `-s`, and `-S`. The `-f` option is used to display the full object identifier path information. Thus the object,

```
system.sysContact.0
```

will be printed as

```
.iso.org.dod.internet.mgmt.mib-2.system.sysContact.0
```

The `-s` option permits only the suffix to be printed; the last symbolic portion of the MIB object identifier will be shown. For example,

```
.iso.org.dod.internet.mgmt.mib-2.system.sysName.0
```

will be printed as

```
sysName.0
```

Finally, the `-S` option requests that the MIB object be printed with both suffix and MIB names. Thus,

```
.iso.org.dod.internet.mgmt.mib-2.system.sysUpTime.0
```

will be displayed as

```
SNMPv2-MIB:sysUpTime.0
```

Please note, in this example, the `sysUpTime` object is found within the SNMPv2-MIB; this is true when using the UCD tools. However, this object is traditionally found in the MIB-2 tree.

If you need to collect SNMP information from a device and use this information as input into another program, the `-q` option will come in handy. Normally, MIB object information is displayed as shown below:

```
system.sysObjectID.0 = OID: enterprises.9.1.17
system.sysUpTime.0 = Timeticks: (139494644) 16 days, 3:29:06.44
system.sysContact.0 = Matthew Maxwell
system.sysName.0 = remote- gw5
system.sysLocation.0 = Remote Sales Office (San Jose))
system.sysServices.0 = 6
```

The `-q` option, which stands for a quick format, causes the output above to be formatted differently. First, the equal sign (=) is removed; this makes it easier to parse because the data is in column format. Second, notice that both `sysObjectID` and `sysUptime` formats have been changed. The object information in the above example is interpreted while, below, only the raw data is displayed.

```
system.sysObjectID.0 enterprises.9.1.17
system.sysUpTime.0 16:3:24:11.44
system.sysContact.0 Matthew Maxwell
system.sysName.0 remote-gw5
system.sysLocation.0 Remote Sales Office (San Jose)
system.sysServices.0 6
```

To display debugging information, use the -d option. This shows the packet information, including the size, destination, and hex and ascii dump of the packet. The output below is the result of an SNMP GET of the system.sysContact MIB object:

```
sending 51 bytes to 10.0.2.220:161:
0000: 30 82 00 2F  02 01 00 04  06 70 75 62  6C 69 63 A0   0../.....public.
0016: 82 00 20 02  04 41 C9 4A  92 02 01 00  02 01 00 30   .. ..A.J.......0
0032: 82 00 10 30  82 00 0C 06  08 2B 06 01  02 01 01 04   ...0.....+......
0048: 00 05 00                                              ...

received 60 bytes from 10.0.2.220:161:
0000: 30 82 00 38  02 01 00 04  06 70 75 62  6C 69 63 A2   0..8.....public.
0016: 2B 02 04 41  C9 4A 92 02  01 00 02 01  00 30 1D 30   +..A.J.......0.0
0032: 1B 06 08 2B  06 01 02 01  01 04 00 04  0F 4D 61 74   ...+.........Mat
0048: 74 68 65 77  20 4D 61 78  77 65 6C 6C                thew Maxwell
system.sysContact.0 = Matthew Maxwell
```

The first part of the output is the request packet, as indicated by the sending string, and includes the SNMP packet format. Note the visibility of the communication string public. The receiving packet is the response from the agent and it, too, uses the SNMP packet format. In this case, we see both the community string public and the sysContact object string.

Operational Options

The operational arguments are listed in Table 6.3 and, like the display options, eight are available. However, please note that not all of them are fully described below. For instance, the -c option is used to define the clock values with SNMP v2 authentication messages. Because this is not a critical function for using the UCD tools, it is not described in detail.

By default, MIB objects are located in standard, well-known places. Consider, for example, the system.sysContact.0 MIB object, which is normally found within the .iso.org.dod.internet.mgmt.mib-2 tree. The UCD tools support a concept of random

Table 6.3 *Common Operational Arguments*

Option	Description
`-c`	Sets the clock values
`-m`	Specifies a list of MIB modules to load
`-M`	Specifies a list of directories to search for MIB files
`-p`	Uses the specified port to communicate with agent
`-r`	Specifies the number of retries
`-R`	Requests random access to the agent MIB table
`-t`	Specifies the timeout between retry attempts
`-v`	Specifies the protocol version

access MIBs. Using this approach, the `system.sysContact` MIB object may be entered as `sysContact`—without the `system` group name. To specify a single search of a MIB object, because it might appear more than once, specify the name of the MIB followed by the object, such as `SNMPv2-MIB:sysContact.0`. To enable random access, use the `-R` command line option. This feature is most useful when searching for MIB objects that are not located in standard places or when more than one instance of the same object name exists within the agent.

As with any software tool that communicates with an SNMP agent, some method must be provided to convert the numeric dotted notation (such as 1.3.6.) of the MIB object tree into the notation that uses names (such as `.iso.org.dod.internet.mgmt.mib-2`). Normally, without the MIB files, the UCD tools display MIB information using the numeric form. This is because these tools obtain only the numeric form from the agent; they don't know how to map these identifiers into the corresponding string names. To illustrate, when an SNMP GET is done against an agent with the MIB files not available, then the following output snippet may be displayed:

```
.iso.3.6.1.2.1.1.1.0 = "Cisco Internetwork Operating System Software
..IOS (tm) 4500 Software (C4500-J-M), Version 11.1(5), RELEASE SOFT-
WARE (fc1)..Copyright (c) 1986-1996 by cisco Systems, Inc...Compiled
```

```
Mon 05-Aug-96 13:17 by mkamson"
.iso.3.6.1.2.1.1.2.0 = OID: .iso.3.6.1.4.1.9.1.50
.iso.3.6.1.2.1.1.3.0 = Timeticks: (99491814) 11 days, 12:21:58.14
.iso.3.6.1.2.1.1.4.0 = "Steve Maxwell"
.iso.3.6.1.2.1.1.5.0 = "remote-gw"
.iso.3.6.1.2.1.1.6.0 = "Remote Sales Office (Florida)"
.iso.3.6.1.2.1.1.7.0 = 78
```

The output above is from a query from a Cisco router and, as you can see, the MIB object path information contains numeric strings only. This is because the query by default understands only a core set of MIB definitions. When it comes to non-standard or vendor-specific MIBs, only the numeric form is available. To address this issue, the `-m` and `-M` options are provided. The `-m` option is used to specify a list of MIB modules that should be loaded before the UCD tool attempts any SNMP queries on an agent. When more than one MIB module is listed, the modules must be separated by the colon (`:`) character. A MIB module is just a file that contains the MIB definitions for an agent. Using the `-m` option, we can supply the correct MIB modules so that our snippet output above will contain all string names. The `-M` option helps because we can supply a list of directories in which to search for MIB files. Thus the command,

```
snmpwalk -M /var/mibs cisco-gw1 public system
```

will search the directory `/var/mibs`. Assuming that it finds the standard MIB files, it will display the following:

```
system.sysDescr.0 = Cisco Internetwork Operating System Software
IOS (tm) 4500 Software (C4500-J-M), Version 11.1(5), RELEASE SOFTWARE
(fc1)
Copyright (c) 1986-1996 by cisco Systems, Inc.
Compiled Mon 05-Aug-96 13:17 by mkamson
system.sysObjectID.0 = OID: enterprises.9.1.50
system.sysUpTime.0 = Timeticks: (99487614) 11 days, 12:21:16.14
system.sysContact.0 = Steve Maxwell
system.sysName.0 = remote-gw
system.sysLocation.0 = Remote Sales Office (Florida)
system.sysServices.0 = 78
```

There is also a shorthand way to specify all MIB modules (as opposed to supplying a list) using the `all` command. This overrides the `MIBS` environment variable, discussed in the next section.

Environment Variables

Each of the UCD tools uses a small set of environment variables that help establish global values of certain operating parameters or shortcuts for command line options. These include the following:

- PREFIX
- MIBS
- MIBDIR
- SUFFIX

The PREFIX variable is a standard way to define the prefix of MIB object identifiers. The default value is .iso.org.dod.internet.mgmt.mib-2. If this variable is defined, the contents of the variable are added to the beginning of the MIB object being referenced with one of the UCD tools. Defining this value will help in situations in which a non-standard MIB is used. For example, if we are polling the Sun system agent, we will encounter MIB objects that are defined within the Sun MIB. Without the PREFIX definition, when polling for a specific Sun object, we get:

```
snmpget 10.0.2.220 public system.sysDescr.0 system.UpTime.0
sub-identifier not found: UpTime
Invalid object identifier: system.UpTime.0
```

But, when we define the PREFIX variable to:

```
setenv PREFIX iso.org.dod.internet.mgmt.mib-2.enterprise.sun
```

and then attempt the same poll as above, we get:

```
UpTime
system.UpTime.0
```

The MIBS and MIBDIR variables provide a way to load in additional MIB modules. The variable MIBS functions the same way as the -m command line option. The MIBDIR variable functions the same way as the -M option. Both are a convenience because they work with all UCD applications.

The SUFFIX variable is used to toggle the -s command line option, which displays the suffix, or last component, of the MIB object path.

Snmpbulkwalk

The `snmpbulkwalk` tool is used to communicate with a network entity using SNMPv2 SNMP GET BULK requests. Like the `snmpwalk` tool, `snmpbulkwalk` will walk a MIB tree until the end of the MIB is reached or an error occurs. As previously discussed, the BULK request provides a more efficient mechanism to transfer a large amount of data than the regular SNMPv1 GET request. For example, assume we would like to retrieve the MIB-2 `interface` group. The SNMPv1 `snmpwalk` command will obtain the information with 157 packets, while the `snmpbulkwalk` will obtain the same information with just 4 packets! This is a tremendous savings in terms of network bandwidth and increased SNMP performance for the agent and manager.

To walk the entire MIB tree of the device called `cisco-gw1`, use the following command:

```
snmpbulkwalk -v 2c cisco-gw1 public
```

The `snmpbulkwalk` command only works with SNMPv2 agents. This is because the GET BULK facility was not implemented until SNMPv2. Using this command on an SNMPv1 agent will, therefore, generate an error.

For instance, the following command attempts to walk the MIB tree of a device called `remote-gw` starting from the `system` group. In this example, `remote-gw3` only supports the SNMPv1.

```
snmpbulkwalk -v 2c remote-gw3 public system
```

Because this device doesn't understand the SNMP GET BULK request, it eventually times out and the following message is displayed following the `snmpbulkwalk` command:

```
Timeout: No Response from remote-gw3
```

A timeout error occurs because the requests are sent to the device, but the agent residing in the device doesn't understand the SNMP request format. As a result, the packet was not answered and thus timed out.

Note that `snmpbulkwalk` requires that one of the two SNMPv2 names be used (either `2p` or `2c`). If you attempt to invoke `snmpbulkwalk` without specifying which version of the SNMPv2 protocol is to be used, the following error will be displayed:

```
snmpbulkwalk: Cannot send V1 PDU on V2 session
```

Snmpdelta

The `snmpdelta` command collects changes in MIB integer values from an SNMP agent entity. This command monitors the specified integer objects and displays changes to the objects that occur over time. This is very useful in tracking networking errors. You might, for example, want to determine the number of packets discarded from an interface; i.e., the `ifInDiscards` MIB object. To monitor this object from the device `remote-gw`, for example, the following command may be used:

```
snmpdelta -R remote-gw public ifInDiscards.1
```

This command will produce the following:

```
ifInDiscards.1 /1 sec: 800
ifInDiscards.1 /1 sec: 8353
ifInDiscards.1 /1 sec: 449
ifInDiscards.1 /1 sec: 3883
ifInDiscards.1 /1 sec: 541
ifInDiscards.1 /1 sec: 8316
ifInDiscards.1 /1 sec: 4576
ifInDiscards.1 /1 sec: 8763
ifInDiscards.1 /1 sec: 9568
```

This command supports a number of additional command line arguments over the common options previously discussed. Table 6.4 contains the available options.

Table 6.4 *Additional snmpdelta Command Line Options*

Option	Description
`-f`	Reads configuration file
`-k`	Displays seconds in output
`-l`	Writes configuration to file
`-m`	Displays the maximum value ever retrieved

(Cont'd)

Table 6.4 *Additional snmpdelta Command Line Options (Cont'd)*

Option	Description
`-p`	Specifies the polling period
`-P`	Specifies the reporting period in number of polling requests
`-s`	Displays timestamp information
`-S`	Logs data to logfile
`-t`	Determines time interval
`-T`	Produces table output

With the `-m` option, `snmpdelta` will display the maximum value obtained from the MIB objects that are being polled. It displays the values of each poll and, when a new high value is received, includes it in the `Max` column. The command

```
snmpdelta -R remote-gw public -m ifOutOctets.1
```

produces the following output:

```
ifOutOctets.1 /1 sec: 25784      (Max: 25784)
ifOutOctets.1 /1 sec: 21287      (Max: 25784)
ifOutOctets.1 /1 sec: 2743       (Max: 25784)
ifOutOctets.1 /1 sec: 8611       (Max: 25784)
ifOutOctets.1 /1 sec: 4473       (Max: 25784)
ifOutOctets.1 /1 sec: 10939      (Max: 25784)
ifOutOctets.1 /1 sec: 1882       (Max: 25784)
ifOutOctets.1 /1 sec: 9258       (Max: 25784)
ifOutOctets.1 /1 sec: 22751      (Max: 25784)
ifOutOctets.1 /1 sec: 28615      (Max: 28615)
ifOutOctets.1 /1 sec: 18599      (Max: 28615)
ifOutOctets.1 /1 sec: 28459      (Max: 28615)
ifOutOctets.1 /1 sec: 2662       (Max: 28615)
```

Notice that, when the new maximum value was obtained, it was updated in the `Max` column accordingly.

When monitoring a large number of MIB objects or data, you might find it helpful to save the information in a log file. The `-l` option saves the data in a file in the format:

```
{device}-{MIB object}
```

Thus, the command

```
snmpdelta -R monet public -l ifOutOctets.1
```

will log `ifOutOctets` deltas in the file called `monet-ifOutOctets.1`.

Inspection of this file will reveal the same format and data that are normally displayed.

If you need to display the output of `snmpdelta` in a more structured format, use the `-T` option. For instance, if it becomes necessary to monitor several MIB objects and add the data to a spreadsheet or other program, `snmpdelta` can display in a tabular format as shown below. Thus, this command and output:

```
snmpdelta -R remote-gw public -T ifInDiscards.1 ifInDiscards.2
        ifInDiscards.1  ifInDiscards.2
        1592.00 9950.00
        9136.00 2506.00
        3338.00 5.00
        6338.00 2624.00
        8665.00 9971.00
        5609.00 569.00
        9282.00 7086.00
        9153.00 8374.00
        8653.00 8195.00
        9877.00 3827.00
```

is a display of the number of discarded packets from two interfaces and is presented in a columnar format.

Snmpget

The `snmpget` command is used to retrieve information from an SNMP agent entity. It uses the SNMP GET request with one or more fully qualified object names as arguments and returns their associated values. If an error occurs, a descriptive message will be shown to help pinpoint the problem. If one or more MIB object values can't be retrieved, only those objects whose values can be retrieved are displayed. The MIB object name is given in the format specified in the `variables` format.

The command syntax includes:

```
snmpget  [common arguments] MIB-object [MIB-object]
```

To retrieve the MIB objects `sysDescr` and `sysContact` from a Cisco router, the following command could be used:

```
snmpget remote-gw public system.sysDescr.0 system.sysUpTime.0
```

Depending on the router model and configuration the command is used against, output similar to the following is displayed:

```
system.sysDescr.0 = Cisco Internetwork Operating System Software
IOS (tm) 3000 Software (IGS-INR-L), Version 11.0(17), RELEASE
SOFTWARE (fc1) Copyright (c) 1986-1997 by cisco Systems, Inc.
Compiled Thu 04-Sep-97 14:17 by richv
system.sysUpTime.0 = Timeticks: (134381144) 15 days, 13:16:51.44
```

Notice that the Cisco router contains a rather long `sysDescr` string. This can be very useful when attempting to identify the model and present internetwork operating system (IOS) version running on the system. The IOS is Cisco's system software and provides all the routing and processing functions for a large array of Cisco hardware devices. In this example, the system model is a 3000 running version 11.0 and has been up for the last 15 days.

Snmpgetnext

The `snmpgetnext` command is used to retrieve one or more MIB objects using SNMP GET Next requests. For each object specified on the command line, `snmpgetnext` gets the next lexicographical MIB object found in the MIB tree. This tool is very useful for returning a series of related objects when you know the exact structure of the MIB object that is being retrieved. To illustrate, the following command will obtain the next MIB object after the `sysContact.0` object. The command:

```
snmpgetnext 10.0.2.220 public system.sysContact.0
```

will display

```
system.sysName.0 = remote-gw
```

As you can see, the `sysName.0` object is lexicographical next to the `sysContract.0` object.

Snmpnetstat

The `snmpnetstat` command is similar to the Unix `netstat` command and provides some of the same basic information about attached device interfaces and routing tables. What is remarkable about this utility is that the utility makes it very easy to obtain interface information for any SNMP device. This includes, for example, devices such as routers, switches, network monitoring probes, and other devices that support standard SNMP MIBs. This is very powerful; determining interface information on SNMP devices requires polling a number of individual MIB objects or accessing the device directly and running complicated system commands. Like its Unix counterpart, `snmpnetstat` supports a number of command line options that control what is displayed. Table 6.5 lists the available command options.

Table 6.5 *Snmpnetstat Command Line Options*

Option	Description
`-a`	Shows the state of all socket connections
`-i`	Shows the state of all interfaces defined on the system
`-I`	Displays information on the specified network interface
`-o`	Displays an abbreviated status of interfaces
`-n`	Displays network addresses as numbers
`-p`	Shows statistics sorted by the network protocol
`-r`	Displays routing table information
`-s`	Shows per-protocol network statistics

To show the configuration of all network interfaces, use the `-I` option. In the example below, the `snmpnetstat` command is used to query a local Cisco router called `cisco-gw3`.

```
snmpnetstat -i cisco-gw3 public
Name     Mtu  Network          Address            Ipkts Ierrs   Opkts Oerrs Queue
Ethern  1500 10.0.2           10.0.2.1           13377   315   132503   501   115
Serial  1500 135.111.81       135.111.81.2      431375   127   462082   816    50
Serial* 1500 none             none                 1934 154465   57336   998   150
```

As you can see, the output should be familiar; it mirrors the Unix `netstat` output. The only major differences are the names of the interfaces and the removal of the column that represents the total number of collisions on the interface. In the case of the interface names, the Cisco software uses the type of interface and index number as the full interface name (such as `serial1`). However, in the example, the names are both truncated and are derived from the interface type, not the actual Cisco interface name. Thus, when displayed with the `snmpnetstat` command, the entire interface name is not displayed nor are the index numbers shown.

To list the available interfaces in an abbreviated short display form, use the `-s` option. As you can see from the output below, only the columns of incoming and outgoing octets are listed. Compare this to what is displayed with the `-i` option.

```
snmpnetstat -o cisco-gw4 public
Name    Network           Address                  Ioctets        Ooctets
Ethern  10.0.2            10.0.2.1                  487708       12778317
Serial  135.111.81        135.111.81.2             4331197         559999
```

The `cisco-gw4` device only contains two interfaces: one Ethernet and one Serial.

To list an individual interface, use the `-I` option followed by the interface name. This option is also used in conjunction with an `interval`. When `snmpnetstat` is invoked with the `interval` argument, it shows a running count of network statistics relating to the interface specified. The information displayed includes one column for the specified interface, and another column summarizing information for all other interfaces. The first line of output presents summary information since the device was last rebooted. All additional lines represent values that are changing over the specified interval. The command

```
snmpnetstat -I Ethernet cisco-gw4 public 10
    input   (Ether     output              input  (Total)     output
 packets  errs  packets  errs colls  packets  errs  packets  errs colls
   68355 39800   131733   198     0   499131  3924   648945   730     0
     178    62       93    68     0      376   255      236    22     0
      46    58      142    84     0      172   167      268    42     0
      93    63       67    60     0      210   134      359    14     0
     119    49      169    85     0      326   187      385    18     0
```

displays a running count of packet activity on the Ethernet interface contained on `cisco-gw3`. The command will continue displaying this output until a `control-C` (`^C`) is typed. The first two columns represent the number of input packets and input errors for the Ethernet interface, while the next two represent the number of output packets and output errors. The fifth column provides the number of collisions. The remaining five columns are cumulative totals for all interfaces defined within the device.

To display the routing information from the same device, use the `-r` option, as in the following example:

```
snmpnetstat -r cisco-gw3 public
Routing tables
Destination              Gateway           Flags   Interface
default                  161.135.59.1      UG      if0
155.161.75/25            161.135.59.9      U       Serial0
155.161.114.128/26       rembrandt         U       Ethernet0
161.135                  161.135.59.1      UG      if0
161.135.59/26            161.135.59.9      U       Serial0
161.135.59.64/26         161.135.59.8      UG      if0
161.135.59.128/26        rembrandt         U       Ethernet0
170.5                    161.135.59.1      UG      if0
```

The statistics for each network protocol are also supported with this command. Thus, using the `-s` and `-P` options, a listing of just the IP protocols may be obtained, as shown in this example:

```
snmpnetstat -s -P ip monet public
ip:
        39787 total datagrams received
        188 datagrams with header errors
        148 datagrams with an invalid destination address
        105 datagrams forwarded
        248 datagrams with unknown protocol
        180 datagrams discarded
        39942 datagrams delivered
        39626 output datagram requests
        208 output datagrams discarded
        256 datagrams with no route
        236 fragments received
        277 datagrams reassembled
        305 reassembly failures
        330 datagrams fragmented
        239 fragmentation failures
        225 fragments created
```

Snmpset

The `snmpset` is one of the most useful and powerful commands within the UCD package. Many of the tools in this chapter focus on obtaining object values from an SNMP agent. However, this tool is used to alter modifiable MIB agent objects. The ability to alter a MIB object is profound in it implications, because doing so changes the configuration or operating state of a managed agent. Consider, for example, a router with several interfaces that serve as remote connection points between important distant office networks. A single `snmpset` command executed against one or more of the interfaces on this router could sever the network connectivity between the local network and the remote office(s). Because the `snmpset` command is powerful, caution should be exercised when this command is used on an active network.

The basic syntax of the `snmpset` command is:

```
snmpset [common arguments] MIB-objectID type value [MIB-objectID type value]
```

The `MIB-objectID` is the MIB object that will be given a new value. The `type` argument represents the type of object that should be altered and the `value` represents what the new value of the object should be changed to. The `type` is a single character that represents object types that were derived from the types found in the ASN.1. The types supported by `snmpset` are listed in Table 6.6.

Table 6.6 *snmpset Object Types*

Character	Object Type
i	INTEGER
s	STRING
x	HEXADECIMAL STRING
d	DECIMAL STRING
n	NULL OBJECT
o	OBJECTID
t	TIMESTICKS
a	IPADDRESS

There are legitimate reasons to use the `snmpset` command; a few of them are listed below:

- To disable or enable a network interface
- To update a device with new administration information (`sysContact`, for example)
- To reset certain counters
- To restart a device or agent
- To modify some configuration parameter

You may recall an earlier scenario in which a disabled interface caused a network problem. There are also situations when not disabling an interface can cause a network problem. For example, during a broadcast storm or when a hacker is attempting to penetrate the network, shutting down a network or interface might be the only way to prevent the problem from spreading to other parts of the network. However, before resorting to turning off interfaces, watch out for the *set of no return* syndrome. Consider the sample network found in Figure 6.1 on page 260.

In this sample network, we have two routers, `R1` and `R2`. Our only access to `R2` is via router `R1`, `serial1` interface. From device `Node A`, we issue an `snmpset` command to disable the `serial0` interface from `R2`. This stops the broadcast storm, but it also causes a connectivity loss from the remote office. The problem is then: How do we enable the interface on `R2` after the broadcast storm has been fixed? The *set of no return* means that access to the device has been cut off from the only means of access. Remote access to the router has been lost, unless some dial-up capability can be used. In this case, the port must be enabled from the local side, which could require instructing someone to enable the port or reboot the device to reset the port.

The best solution to avoid the *set of no return* mentioned above is to disable the local `serial1` interface on `R1` or the remote `ethernet1` interface of `R2`. This way, the broadcast problem is contained, yet we still maintain access to the devices.

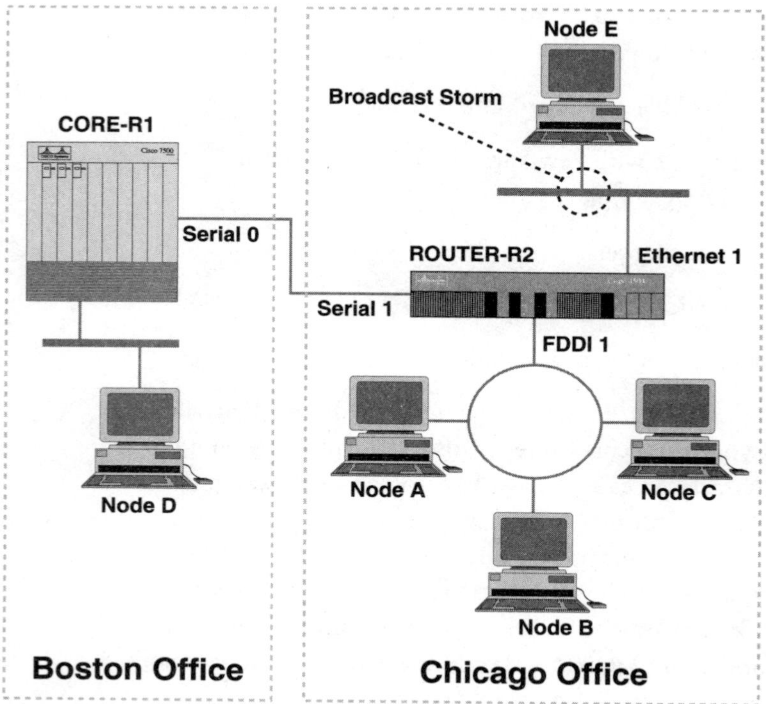

Figure 6.1 *Example of "Set of no return."*

To disable a `serial0` interface on router `R1`, a modification of the `ifOperStatus` object must be made. This includes setting the object to zero (`0`) to disable the interface from an administrative perspective, thus disabling the flow of traffic to and from this interface.

```
snmpset monet private interfaces.ifTable.ifEntry.ifAdminStatus.2 i 0
interfaces.ifTable.ifEntry.ifAdminStatus.3 = 0
```

Other MIB objects that are read/write may also need to be modified. For example, consider the `sysContact` and `sysLocation` objects. Let's assign new values to these objects using a single `snmpset` command:

```
snmpset cisco-gw10 private system.sysContact.0 s "NCC Support" \
system.sysLocation.0 s "3rd Floor Closet"
system.sysContact.0 = NCC Support
system.sysLocation.0 = 3rd Floor Closet
```

Snmpstatus

The `snmpstatus` command obtains important information from an SNMP network entity using the `snmpget` command. The syntax of the command is:

```
snmpstatus host community
```

When the remote agent utilizes the generic community string of `public`, it may be dropped from the SNMP commands, because `public` is used by default. When this command is used against a device, it displays the following information:

- The IP Address of the device
- The `SysDescr` MIB Object
- The `sysUpTime` MIB Object
- The number of packets received and transmitted on all active interfaces (i.e., the sum of `ifInUCastPkts.*` and `ifInNUCastPkts.*`)
- The number of IP packets received and transmitted (i.e., `ipInReceives.0` and `ipOutRequests.0`)
- The number of active interfaces
- The number of interfaces that have been disabled

Thus, running this command on a device called `switch-2200`:

```
snmpstatus switch-2200 private
```

will reveal the following:

```
[10.0.2.240]=>[Model: LinkSwitch 2000, h/w rev: 02-03, s/w rev: 07-
01-00-00] Up: 90:23:02
Interfaces: 17, Recv/Trans packets: 56034/59048 | IP: 39025/47234
8 interfaces are down!
```

Using this tool is a good way to obtain a quick snapshot of a network device without knowing a lot about the device or some of the specific MIB objects to poll. As you can see, the device is a LinkSwitch 2000 (made by 3Com) running version 7.1 of the switching software. The device has been running for 90 hours and 23 minutes. Notice that `snmpstatus` has detected eight interfaces that are down. This isn't a problem in this case, because the device is an Ethernet switch where interfaces are attached to personal computers or workstations. As a result, some users reboot their systems more often and power down their systems when they leave the office each evening. This causes the switch ports to be marked as down, which is why they show up in the `snmpstatus` output.

Snmptable

The `snmptable` command provides the ability to obtain a complete MIB table using the SNMP GETNEXT request. The syntax of the command includes:

```
snmptable [common options ] [additional options] host community tableID
```

The minimum required arguments include the `host`, `community`, and `tableID`. The `tableID` must be a real SNMP table, such as the `interfaces.ifTable`. The `ifTable` table contains a series of MIB objects that contain performance and characteristics of the interfaces within a device. Within MIB-2, the following tables are defined and can be displayed with this command:

```
The Interface Table (interfaces.ifTable)
The IP Address Table (ip.ipAddrTable)
The IP Routing Table (ip.ipRouteTable)
The IP Net Media Table (ip.ipNetToMediaTable)
The TCP Connection Table (tcp.tcpConnTable)
The UDP Listener Table (udp.udpTable)
```

The basic purpose of this command is to give the user the ability to display SNMP tables and import the data into other programs for additional reporting and manipulation. For example, to display the TCP connection table, `tcpConnTable`, use the following command:

```
monet# snmptable 10.0.2.240 public tcp.tcpConnTable
SNMP table: tcp.tcpConnTable
 tcpConnState tcpConnLocalAddress tcpConnLocalPort tcpConnRemAddress tcpConnRemPort
       listen             0.0.0.0               23           0.0.0.0              0
       listen             0.0.0.0              111           0.0.0.0              0
       listen             0.0.0.0              513           0.0.0.0              0
  established          10.0.2.240               23         10.0.2.75          33441
```

Note: This command expects a valid SNMP table. If a non-table object is supplied, an error will be generated. Thus, the example below will show:

```
monet# snmptable 10.0.2.240 public system.sysContact.0
Was that a table? system.sysContact.0.1.1
```

Here we provide the MIB object, `system.sysContact.0` (which is definitely not a MIB table), with the `snmptable` command. As you can see, an error is displayed that includes what should be the first element within the table (i.e. `.1.1`).

This command supports a few additional command line arguments that can be used to control the formatting of the output. The additional options are listed in Table 6.7.

Table 6.7 *snmptable Additional Command Line Options*

Option	**Description**
`-b`	Displays a brief heading
`-f`	Specifies a character separator
`-h`	Prevents display of heading information
`-H`	Displays only table heading information
`-w`	Specifies the width of the table being displayed
`-x`	Prepends the MIB index to each entry listed

One of the most useful options is `-f`. This can be used to specify an alternative column separator character. Thus, to use the colon (:) as the field separator when displaying the same TCP table above, use the following command:

```
monet# snmptable 10.0.2.240 public -f : tcp.tcpConnTable
SNMP table: tcp.tcpConnTable
tcpConnState:tcpConnLocalAddress:tcpConnLocalPort:tcpConnRemAddress:t
cpConnRemPort
listen:0.0.0.0:23:0.0.0.0:0
listen:0.0.0.0:111:0.0.0.0:0
listen:0.0.0.0:513:0.0.0.0:0
established:10.0.2.240:23:10.0.2.75:33441
```

Each of the columns is now separated by the : character, making it very easy to use this information as input into other programs. The -b option can be used to provide a more descriptive column label as shown below. This at.atTable table contains the address translation mappings between IP addresses and physical addresses. In this case, three column labels are displayed, including IfIndex, PhysAddress, and NetAddress. The ifIndex is the index in the interface table and shows what interface these mappings originated from. The PhysAddress is the datalink address (Ethernet in this case) and the NetAddress is the IP address associated with each device on the network.

```
snmptable cisco-gw5 public -b at.atTable
SNMP table: at.atTable
 IfIndex           PhysAddress          NetAddress
       2 "08 00 20 8D 81 82 "           10.0.1.100
       2 "00 60 47 1F 76 8A "           10.0.1.120
      14 "00 60 08 91 4A 64 "           10.0.2.110
      14 "00 60 95 AD F2 1F "           10.0.2.111
      14 "00 80 5F E2 8B 3D "           10.0.2.117
      14 "00 60 08 94 37 FC "           10.0.2.200
      14 "08 00 20 86 2F C2 "           10.0.2.221
      14 "00 60 08 62 C7 3E "           10.0.2.226
      14 "08 00 20 7A CA 49 "           10.0.2.234
      14 "08 00 20 25 70 E7 "           10.0.2.250
      14 "00 20 AF CA E6 99 "           10.0.2.251
      14 "00 60 08 1D FD 4D "           10.0.2.252
      14 "00 80 A3 03 4E 9B "           10.0.2.257
```

Snmptest

The snmptest command provides a simple shell-like facility that makes it easy to communicate with a network entity using SNMP. Unlike most other UCD tools, snmptest is interactive, prompting for information to accomplish its tasks.

The software supports three operating modes: get, getnext, and set. Issuing the $N command will place snmptest in GETNEXT mode, while using the $S puts the command in SET mode. To get back to GET mode, use the $G command. By default, snmptest is placed in SNMP GET mode, in which the user is prompted for a MIB object to retrieve from an SNMP device.

Snmptranslate

The `snmptranslate` tool is used to translate SNMP MIB objects into more readable text. When this command is run with a MIB object, it will translate the object into either the SMI value or symbolic form. When no options are specified, it defaults to displaying the SMI value. Several command line options are supported with this tool. They are listed in Table 6.8. The primary use of the command is to help display the full characteristics of MIB objects, without resorting to reading the appropriate MIB definition files.

Table 6.8 *Snmptranslate Command Line Options*

Option	Description
`-d`	Displays a description of the object
`-p`	Displays the symbol table from the loaded MIB files
`-n`	Displays objects in symbolic format
`-s`	Displays only the last symbolic part of the OID
`-R`	Uses random access when accessing the objects
`-w`	Displays warnings when symbol conflicts occur
`-W`	Displays more verbose warnings than `-w` displays

Using `snmptranslate` without any command arguments displays the numeric dotted object notation. Thus, translation of the `system.sysDescr` MIB object can be accomplished with the command

```
snmptranslate system.sysDescr
```

which results in:

```
.1.3.6.1.2.1.1.1
```

To display a fairly complete description of a MIB object, use the `-d` option. To illustrate, consider the following command:

```
snmptranslate -d system.sysDescr
```

When executed, it will produce the following:

```
.1.3.6.1.2.1.1.1
SYNTAX  OCTET STRING
DISPLAY-HINT    "255a"
MAX-ACCESS      read-only
STATUS  current
DESCRIPTION     "A textual description of the entity.  This value
should include the full name and version identification of the
system's hardware type, software operating-system, and networking
software."
```

Snmptrap

The `snmptrap` command will emit an SNMP trap to a designated SNMP manager. This tool is very useful when embedded in a shell script or other program for sending traps to any number of SNMP network managers. One or more object identifiers can be specified on the command line, plus the type and value must accompany each object. The `snmptrap` supports both SNMPv1 and SNMPv2 formats. The basic syntax of the command is:

```
snmptrap -v 1 [command arguments] enterprise-oid agent generic-trap
specific-trap uptime [object ID type value]
```

The `enterprise-oid` field identifies the network management subsystem that generated the trap. The `agent` is the host that is emitting the trap. The `generic-trap` corresponds to one of the predefined SNMP traps. These traps were listed in Table 2.4 in Chapter 2. The `specific-trap` value indicates more specifically the nature of the trap. The `uptime` field is used as a time-stamp between the last initialization of the device and the issuance of the trap. The object ID, type, and value are used to provide additional information relating to the trap. These additional fields are known as the variable binding and may contain any type of information that is related to the trap.

The `enterprise-oid`, `agent`, and `uptime` need not be specified on the command line. Instead, the empty character sequence `''` may be used to specify the default values for these fields. The default value for the `enterprise-oid` string is `1.3.6.1.4.1.3.1.1` (or `enterprises.cmu.1.1`). The default agent value is the hostname of the machine running the `snmptrap` command. The `uptime` is obtained from the local system's MIB object `system.sysUpTime.0`.

Consider, for example, that we would like to emit a `link-down` trap to a network management system called `rembrandt`. Further, if we want to communicate that a particular port has gone down, we include the port within the variable bindings of the trap. The command below can be used:

```
snmptrap -v 1 monet public '' monet 2 0 '' interfaces.iftable.ifentry.\
ifindex.1 i 1
```

In this example, we use the default values for the `enterprise-oid` and `uptime` fields. Also, we specify the particular interface (`ifindex.1`) and set the value to `1` (which indicates the second interface with the device). The `2` represents the `link-down` trap and `0` provides a null value for the `specific-trap` value.

If we are reviewing the traps on `rembrandt`, we will see output like the following:

```
1998-11-27 17:48:45 monet [10.0.3.126] enterprises.3.1.1:
        Link Down Trap (0) Uptime: 1:29:06
        interfaces.ifTable.ifEntry.ifIndex.1 = 1
```

In practice, most `link-down` messages are not that meaningful or interesting. However, when they come from critical devices, such as core routers or switches, a downed interface could spell disaster for the network.

Care should be taken when configuring traps from network devices because enabling them can cause a trap flood. A *trap flood* is when a large number of traps are sent because a port is bouncing up and down many times per second. Often, this represents a malfunction with the device transmitting the traps. However, with a little bit of care, this problem can be avoided.

Snmptrapd

The `snmptrap` command will receive and log SNMP traps. Traps that are sent on port `162` are either logged to the Unix `syslog` facility or displayed on the terminal. These messages are sent using `LOG_WARNING` and, if available, are sent to the `LOG_LOCAL0` logging level. This command must be run as superuser because it listens on a reserved system port. Executing the command without any options will cause it to be placed in the background and detached from the calling shell.

The snmptrap command supports a few command line arguments that include -P, -D, -d, and -q. The -P option will instruct snmptrapd to display any traps received on the standard output and the -d option will display a dump of the trap packet. Thus, to show received traps and display the trap packets, use the following command:

```
snmptrapd -P -d
```

If this command is run, using the previous example on the host rembrandt, the proceeding output will be displayed:

```
1998-11-27 22:56:47 UCD-snmp version 3.5
received 69 bytes from 10.0.3.126:-32566:
0000: 30 82 00 41  02 01 00 04  06 70 75 62  6C 69 63 A4    0..A.....public.
0016: 82 00 32 06  08 2B 06 01  04 01 03 01  01 40 04 0A    ..2..+.......@..
0032: 00 03 7E 02  01 02 02 01  00 43 03 24  5C 96 30 82    ..~......C.$\.0.
0048: 00 13 30 82  00 0F 06 0A  2B 06 01 02  01 02 02 01    ..0.....+.......
0064: 01 01 02 01  01                                       .....
1998-11-27 22:56:51 monet [10.0.3.126] enterprises.3.1.1:
        Link Down Trap (0) Uptime: 6:37:09
        interfaces.ifTable.ifEntry.ifIndex.1 = 1
```

The first line shows the current version and when the snmptrapd process was run. Next, the output displays the number of bytes in the trap packet, the host the trap was sent from (monet), and the UDP port (32566, in this case). The contents of the trap include both hexadecimal and ASCII. Finally, the trap information, including the variable-binding information, is shown.

The -D option will display additional debugging information that includes the parsing of MIB files. The user manual reports that -q provides a more verbose output, but it doesn't seem to be implemented in this version of the command.

Snmpwalk

The snmpwalk command will walk an agent MIB tree using the SNMP GETNEXT request. An object variable may be given on the command line to specify with which portion of the MIB space the search will begin. Without an object argument, snmpwalk searches and starts with the MIB-2 objects. Thus, the command

```
snmpwalk monet public
```

will walk the entire system agent on the device `monet`. Since MIB-2 contains a large number of objects, the command will produce a rather long listing. Instead of listing every object supported by the agent, we can limit the search and display only a single group of objects. Thus, we can list all the objects found within the MIB-2 `system` group as shown by the following:

```
snmpwalk cisco-gw5 public system
system.sysDescr.0 = Cisco Internetwork Operating System Software
IOS (tm) GS Software (RSP-JV-M), Version 11.1(13a)CA1, EARLY
DEPLOYMENT RELEASE SOFTWARE (fc1)
Synced to mainline version: 11.1(13a)
Copyright (c) 1986-1997 by cisco Systems, Inc.
Compiled Wed 13-Aug-97 04:12 by richardd
system.sysObjectID.0 = OID: enterprises.9.1.46
system.sysUpTime.0 = Timeticks: (236153209) 27 days, 7:58:52.09
system.sysContact.0 = Steve Maxwell
system.sysName.0 = cisco-gw4
system.sysLocation.0 = Testing Lab
system.sysServices.0 = 78
```

If you need to walk the entire MIB within a given agent and save the output to a file, use the following command:

```
snmpwalk cisco-gw5 public .1 > walk.out
```

The command above uses the `.1` as the start of the `snmpwalk`. Doing this will ensure that every object will be displayed because `.1` is the root of the entire MIB tree and all objects are accessible from this starting point. Walking the entire MIB tree with an agent will help track down certain MIB objects or get an idea of exactly how many objects a particular agent may support. To see the approximate number of objects the `cisco-gw5` supports, count the number of lines in the file. Because the `snmpwalk` displays each MIB object on its own line (unless the line is longer than 80 characters), we can then use the Unix `wc` command to total the number of lines within the `walk.out` file.

Thus the command

```
wc -l walk.out
```

produces the following output:

```
    2242 walk.out
```

As you can see, this command output shows that the agent contained within the `cisco-gw5` device supports roughly 2242 MIB objects. When no object is specified with the `snmpwalk` command, it will search the MIB-2 object tree by default. When a tree search causes the `snmpwalk` command to go beyond the end of the MIB within the agent, the message `End of MIB` will be displayed. This can happen, for example, when a MIB object group is given and the agent doesn't actually support that group.

Snmpconf

General Description

The `snmpconf` command provides the ability to configure devices using the `snmpset` command according to MIB objects defined within a configuration file. The configuration file may contain a list of MIB objects and values that will be set against an SNMP device. This tool provides an automated mechanism to apply standard configuration information to a number of devices or even a single device that must be configured the same way more than once. Consider, for example, the installation of several router devices. It would be easier to create a configuration file that contains many of the common configured objects that the router devices share. Such a configuration could be executed against the device when each of the devices is first installed. Contrast this to manually configuring each router by hand. Using this approach, the amount of time needed to install a device is reduced and the likelihood of possible configuration errors is decreased as well.

The configuration file may contain MIB object entries, comments, and blank lines. Comments may be added by using the hash mark (#). A valid configuration entry consists of a type, OID, value, and comment string. Listing 6.1 contains a sample configuration file:

Listing 6.1 *Sample SNMPCONF File*

```
#
# Setup standard system group information
#
S .1.3.6.1.2.1.1.4.0 Steve-Maxwell      system contact
S .1.3.6.1.2.1.1.5.0 host.dt.com        system name
S .1.3.6.1.2.1.1.6.0 Graphics_Lab       system location
```

Each of the three configuration entries contains the S character in the first field, which identifies the type of MIB object listed in the second field. The S means that the object is of type STRING. This field is interpreted as a string and, therefore, it must not contain any extra spaces. Thus, Virginia-Maxwell is acceptable, but Virginia Maxwell is not. Also, the use of double quotes is not permitted. If the string "Virginia Maxwell" is used, it will result in a configuration error. The snmpconf tool defines two additional types: I for INTEGER and A for IPADDRESS.

The second field is the MIB object that will be changed to the value contained within the third field. Note that only a fully qualified OID expressed in dotted notation is supported by snmpconf. Any other format, such as a dotted name format (e.g., iso.org.dod.internet.mgmt.mib-2.system.sysLocation.0) or abbreviated MIB strings will cause configuration errors.

As stated before, the third field is the value that the MIB object will be set to. As such, it must match the type character specified in the first field. Thus, in this example, each of the configuration lines expects a string in this field. The last or fourth field is for comments. It provides a comment that should be used to identify the MIB object and value. In this case, the MIB objects are the contact (sysContact), name (sysName), and location (sysLocation) objects from the MIB-2 system group.

Once the configuration file contains the needed/required MIB objects and values, it can be used against an SNMP device. The basic syntax of the snmpconf command includes:

```
snmpconf hostname community configuration_file
```

Thus, assume the above configuration is stored in a file called config1 and we would like to apply this file to the device called nicodemus, which also has a community string of private. Given this information, the following command could be used:

```
snmpconf nicodemus private config1
```

When the above command executes, the output shown below is displayed:

```
#
# Setup standard system group information
```

```
#
Set display string 'system contact' to Steve-Maxwell
Set display string 'system name' to host.dt.com
Set display string 'system location' to Graphics_Lab
Done.
```

Notice that defined comments are displayed along with a confirmation that each `set` command was successful. If you would like to verify this, simply execute an `snmpwalk` within the MIB-2 `system` group. Thus, the command

```
snmpwalk nicodemus public system
```

will produce the output listed below:

```
system.sysDescr.0 = unknown
system.sysObjectID.0 = OID: enterprises.ucdavis.ucdSnmpAgent.solaris
system.sysUpTime.0 = Timeticks: (260363) 0:43:23.63
system.sysContact.0 = Steve-Maxwell
system.sysName.0 = host.dt.com
system.sysLocation.0 = Graphics_Lab
system.sysServices.0 = 72
```

The host `nicodemus` is running the UCD SNMP agent and the output above shows only part of the system group. In this example, we can confirm that the `sysContact`, `sysName`, and `sysLocation` objects have been updated according to the `snmpconf` configuration file.

The SNMPCONF software provides a couple of ways to specify the required configuration file. First, the name of the file may be given on the command line as in the preceding example; `snmpconf` will examine the current directory to find the file. Next, the file may be provided with a fully qualified pathname. Finally, if the environment variable `SNMPCONF_LIB` has been set, the software will search the directory specified in this variable.

The `snmpconf` tool provides some basic error checking and, when problems occur, displays useful information. However, it is difficult to determine the cause of certain types of problems. For example, if the incorrect community string is given or the device given isn't currently on the network, the same error message is displayed. Thus, the commands

```
snmpconf didymus private config1
snmpconf monet public config1
```

produce the same errors as shown below, but for different reasons:

```
#
# Setup standard system group information
#
UNABLE to set display string 'system contact' to Steve-Maxwell
UNABLE to set display string 'system name' to host.dt.com
UNABLE to set display string 'system location' to Graphics_Lab
Done.
3 errors encountered.
```

The first command attempts to set MIB objects on the system `didymus`, which isn't presently reachable on the network. That is, the device was powered down when this command was run. The second command uses the wrong community string. In this case, the correct community string is `private`, not `public`. As you can see, the tool doesn't respond differently to a down system and an incorrect community, making it difficult for you to determine the cause of the particular errors. However, with care, you can get around this problem by issuing the `ping` command before executing the `snmpconf`. In this way, you can avoid these kinds of ambiguities and address the separate problems appropriately.

The SNMPCONF software provides two command line options. The first, `-version`, displays version information for both the `snmpconf` tool itself and the CMU support library. The second, `-quiet`, instructs `snmpconf` to squelch messages when executing.

Obtaining Snmpconf from the Internet

The software may be obtained from the Internet as indicated below. Also, because the CMU library is used with SNMPCONF, it must be downloaded and installed as well.

```
ftp://ftp.net.cmu.edu/pub/snmp/snmpconf/snmpconf-V1.1.tar.gz
ftp://ftp.net.cmu.edu/pub/snmp/cmu-snmp-V1.13.tar.gz
```

Also, additional information may be obtained at:

```
http://www.net.cmu.edu/projects/snmp
```

Conditions of Use

The following information appears in the source code files for this distribution:

```
/************************************************************************
 *
 *          Copyright 1997 by Carnegie Mellon University
 *
 *                        All Rights Reserved
 *
 * Permission to use, copy, modify, and distribute this software and its
 * documentation for any purpose and without fee is hereby granted,
 * provided that the above copyright notice appear in all copies and that
 * both that copyright notice and this permission notice appear in
 * supporting documentation, and that the name of CMU not be
 * used in advertising or publicity pertaining to distribution of the
 * software without specific, written prior permission.
 *
 * CMU DISCLAIMS ALL WARRANTIES WITH REGARD TO THIS SOFTWARE, INCLUDING
 * ALL IMPLIED WARRANTIES OF MERCHANTABILITY AND FITNESS, IN NO EVENT SHALL
 * CMU BE LIABLE FOR ANY SPECIAL, INDIRECT OR CONSEQUENTIAL DAMAGES OR
 * ANY DAMAGES WHATSOEVER RESULTING FROM LOSS OF USE, DATA OR PROFITS,
 * WHETHER IN AN ACTION OF CONTRACT, NEGLIGENCE OR OTHER TORTIOUS ACTION,
 * ARISING OUT OF OR IN CONNECTION WITH THE USE OR PERFORMANCE OF THIS
 * SOFTWARE.
 *
 * snmpconf - configure devices using SNMP set requests according to a
 *            configuration file
 *
 * Authors: Erikas Napjus (erikas+@cmu.edu)
 *          Ryan Troll    (ryan+@andrew.cmu.edu)
 *
 ************************************************************************/
```

The Snmpconf and CMU Library Installation Procedure

The installation procedures are as follows:

1. Obtain the SNMPCONF and CMU Library packages from one of the sites above or from the CD-ROM available with this book.

2. Determine a location for the software. Possible directories include:

   `/usr/local/snmp` and `/usr/local/snmpconf`

   Create the appropriate directories:

   `mkdir /usr/local/snmp` and `mkdir /usr/local/snmpconf`

3. Uncompress the CMU archive:

```
gunzip cmu-snmp-V1.12.tar.gz
```

4. Uncompress the snmpconf archive:

```
gunzip snmpconf-V1_1_tar.gz
```

5. Untar the CMU archive into the directory you will be using:

```
cd /usr/local/snmp
tar xvf cmu-snmp-V1.12.tar
```

   a. On Solaris, it is necessary to modify the source.

   b. Add the include file `<sys/sockio.h>` in the `snmp_extra.c` file after the other entries.

   Remove extra spaces next to the line `version.o` in `Makefile.`

6. Next, run the `configure` command from this directory:

```
./configure
[lots of output]
```

   After several pages of output, the `configure` program will ask a small number of questions as shown below:

7. If no errors were encountered, run the `make` command:

```
make
[lots of output]
```

8. If no errors were encountered, run the `make install` command:

```
Make install
[lots of output]
```

9. Untar the SNMPCONF archive into the directory you will be using:

```
cd /usr/local/snmpconf
tar xvf snmpconf-V1_1_tar
```

10. Next, run the `configure` command from this directory:

```
./configure
[lots of output]
```

11. If no errors were encountered, run the `make` command:

```
make
[lots of output]
```

12. After the `make` has completed with no serious errors, install the package by running:

```
make install
[lots of output]
```

13. Invoke a `csh` and add the `/usr/local/lib` library path to the `LD_LIBRARY_PATH` variable.

```
csh
set LD_LIBRARY_PATH /usr/local/lib
```

If you encounter a problem during the installation, consult the `README` and `INSTALL` files that come with the package. These are located at the top level of the directory where the software was installed.

07

Web Enabled Network Management Tools

As the previous chapter discusses network management tools and utilities (largely for the Unix command line), this chapter focuses on network management tools that provide a Web interface. No one can discount the significant impact the Web has had on applications development, specifically in the area of network management. Because of the immense popularity of the Web, it is reasonable to include some tools that can be used with common browsers.

These tools include both SNMP and non-SNMP based software. Non-SNMP tools have been selected for those sites that have yet to implement SNMP functionality or just need a system tool that can be implemented without a lot of fuss. For those who are already using SNMP, the tools in this section will be a welcome addition to any existing suite of software.

This section includes the following tools:

- MRTG
- NTOP

MRTG

General Description

The Multi Router Traffic Grapher (MRTG) is a tool that can be used to monitor and graph network traffic obtained from networking devices that use SNMP. As the name implies, it displays traffic utilization and other statistical information gathered from routers and other networking devices. It generates HTML pages and GIF images, providing a visual representation of network performance via a Web browser. Network performance is one of the most important aspects of network management. This tool will make it easy to pinpoint both device and network performance problems.

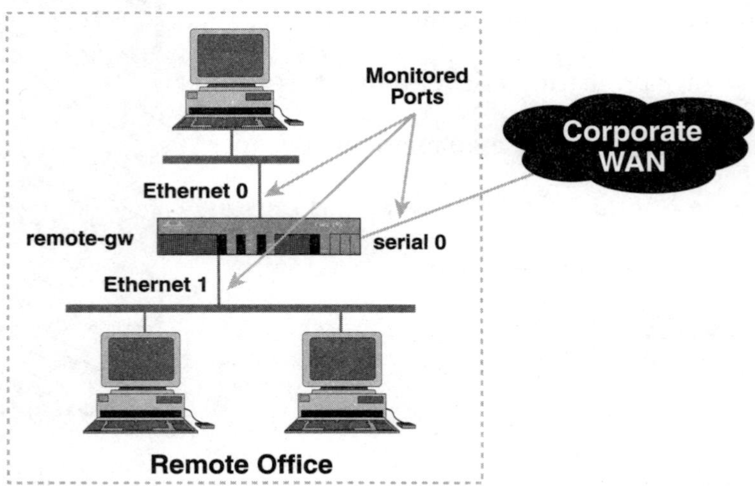

Figure 7.1 *Remote Office Network.*

For example, given the network topology shown in Figure 7.1, MRTG can be used to monitor the network from the remote router call `remote-gw`. Because this network is critical, it is important to monitor the network traffic going to and from the router. Specifically, it is important to monitor the serial interface and both Ethernet interfaces to ensure they do not become overloaded.

Because MRTG can monitor any router or networking device that supports SNMP, it can be put to use monitoring both edge and backbone routers as well as other devices. The primary method MRTG uses to collect information is the `snmpget` command. However, MRTG can be customized to display information derived through other means as well. For example, MRTG can be used to display Unix system load and disk space utilization. Further, because MRTG can poll any SNMP MIB object, many additional performance metrics and MIB object polls can be made. As a result of these capabilities, there are many practical uses for MRTG, including, but not limited to, the following:

- Displaying system CPU load on networking devices
- Displaying system memory utilization on network devices
- Displaying modem usage on remote access servers

Conceptually, MRTG polls specific performance MIB objects from devices and displays the data in a graphical format using HTML. The operation of MRTG is shown in Figure 7.2.

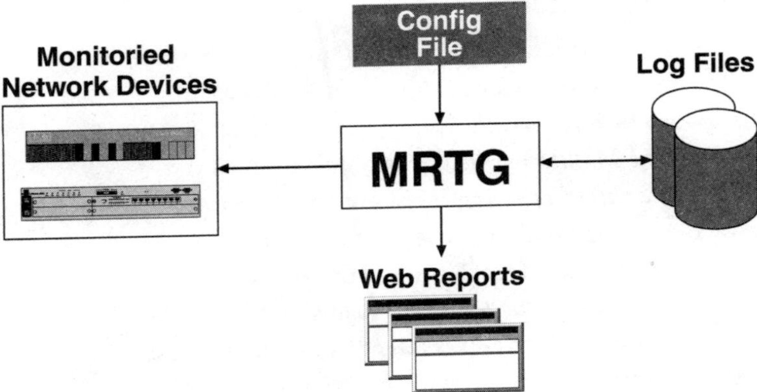

Figure 7.2 *Basic Operation of MRTG.*

Web Page Overview

MRTG displays the results of network performance polls in a series of graphs, along with other additional device information for each monitored interface. A total of four graphs is provided, showing bytes per second in Daily, Weekly, Monthly, and Yearly averages. Figure 7.3 shows only a partial MRTG report, containing some device information plus the Daily usage graph.

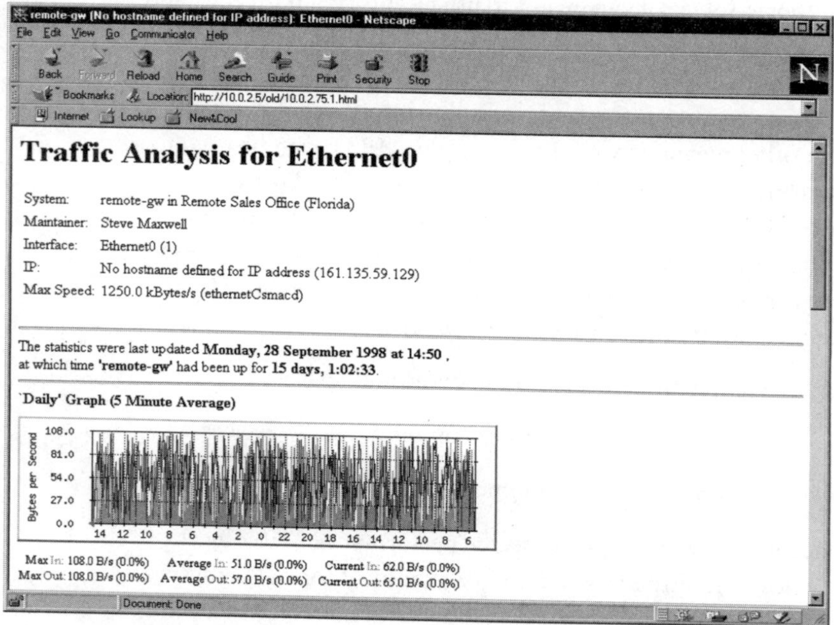

Figure 7.3 *MRTG Web Report.*

This report includes information that was obtained via SNMP from the MIB-II system and interface groups from the device `remote-gw`. The *System* field is derived from the `sysName` and `sysLocation` objects while the *Maintainer* field was obtained from the `sysContact` object. The *Interface* string represents the physical hardware interface contained within the device and the number (1) indicates that this is the first interface. Notice in the above example that the interface is labeled *Ethernet0,* which means that this is the first Ethernet interface on the device. It is labeled this way because Cisco routers always number their interfaces starting at zero. The *IP* string indicates that no associated hostname was found for the

IP address of this device. This is not really a problem because, most of the time, connectivity to many networking devices is via the IP address, not the hostname.

The *Max Speed* field is calculated from the `ifSpeed` object that was divided by eight. This represents the maximum number of bytes per second the interface can theoretically support. The value of eight was selected because there are eight bits in a single byte. The *Max Speed* field also confirms that this interface is Ethernet by displaying the type as `ethernetCsmacd`, which is derived from the `ifType` object. The report also displays the date and time the report was updated and how long the device has been running since it was last rebooted or when the network management component of the device was last reset.

The Daily graph shows bytes per second over an approximate 36-hour period using a 5-minute average. This average is the difference between each successive poll of bytes transmitted or received, not cumulative totals or raw counts. In other words, the displayed value is the difference between the current and previous values and is divided by the time elapsed between these readings. The horizontal (x-axis) shows time in 2-hour increments, while the vertical (y-axis) shows bytes that range from `0` to a given maximum value. The graph displays bytes transmitted in and out of the interface, obtained from `ifOutOctets` and `ifInOctets` MIB objects, respectively.

The bottom of the report shows the legend; in this case, incoming traffic is displayed in green while outgoing traffic is displayed in blue. However, because this book is in black and white, the green in the graph appears gray and the blue appears black. Later on, we will show how to change the colors used in the graphs. Also, the bottom of the graph contains a short summary that lists the maximum, average, and current incoming and outgoing bytes per second. Using the customization options available with MRTG, these colors, as well as many other report and graph attributes, may be changed. Consult the MRTG customization section below for additional information.

In a complete MRTG report, additional graphs for Weekly, Monthly, and Yearly totals are also included. The Weekly graph contains weekly averages for the past seven days, with the current day displayed on the left. The Monthly report shows the last five weeks, with the current week on the left and the previous weeks to the right. The data in this graph has been averaged over a two-hour period. The Yearly graph spans the last 12 months, with the current month shown on the left, and shows the data as a daily average. These three graphs are shown in Figure 7.4.

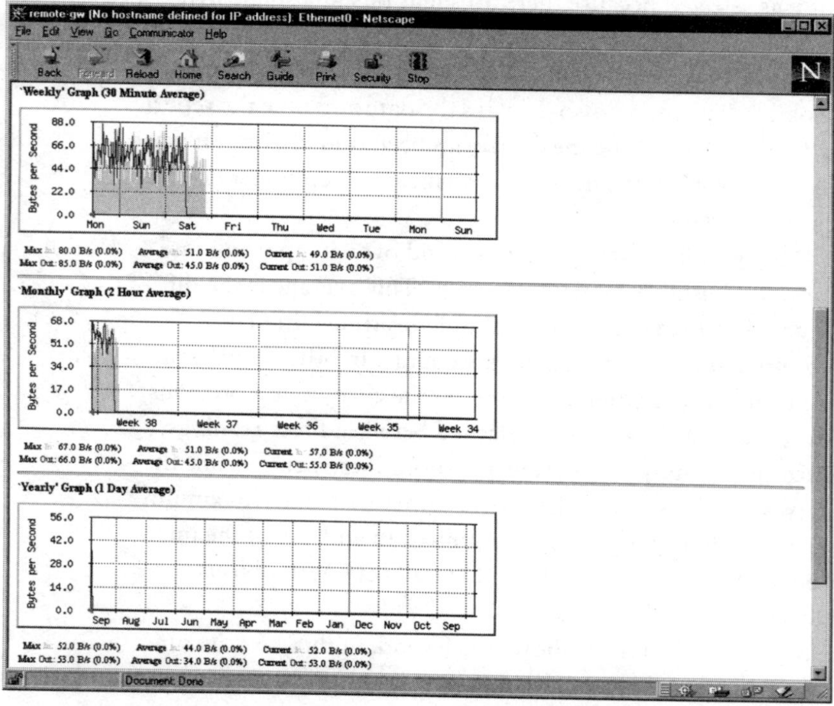

Figure 7.4 *MRTG Weekly, Monthly, and Yearly Reports.*

As you can see, all the graphs grow from the left, which is the default. The graphs can be made to grow from the right by enabling one of the MRTG command options. Also by default, the report pages are updated automatically every five minutes when new information is obtained for each of the monitored interfaces. This update interval (or refresh rate) can be customized as well. MRTG customization and configuration are discussed in the next section.

Basic Configuration of MRTG

MRTG uses a configuration file to specify which devices are to be monitored. The MRTG package doesn't come with a predefined configuration because the devices listed wouldn't likely match those at your site. Instead, the package includes a utility program called `cfgmaker`, which is used to build a basic configuration so you don't have to create one from scratch. The purpose of this utility is to poll a network device for specific SNMP objects (e.g., `interfaces`) and build a configuration file suitable for MRTG. The syntax of `cfgmaker` is:

```
cfgmaker community@device
```

Two arguments are required—the device's community string and hostname (or IP address). Because `cfgmaker` writes to STDOUT, the output should be redirected to a file when you want to save the results. To illustrate the use of this utility, let's assume that we want to monitor a single router in a remote office. In this case, we have a Cisco 2500 series router, called `remote-gw` with a community string of `louvre`. Thus the command:

```
cfgmaker louvre@remote-gw >> cisco.conf
```

builds the MRTG configuration file and calls it `cisco.conf`. Assuming the arguments provided to the `cfgmaker` are correct and the device responds to the SNMP requests, Listing 7.1 showns the configuration that was generated (minus any comments) by the `cfgmaker` script:

Listing 7.1 *Sample Configuration File*

```
Target[10.0.2.75.1]: 1:public@10.0.2.75
MaxBytes[10.0.2.75.1]: 1249994
Title[10.0.2.75.1]: remote-gw (No hostname defined for IP address):
Ethernet0
PageTop[10.0.2.75.1]: <H1>Traffic Analysis for Ethernet0
 </H1>
 <TABLE>
   <TR><TD>System:</TD><TD>remote-gw in Graphics Lab 11-B</TD></TR>
   <TR><TD>Maintainer:</TD><TD>Steve Maxwell</TD></TR>
   <TR><TD>Interface:</TD><TD>Ethernet0 (1)</TD></TR>
   <TR><TD>IP:</TD><TD>No hostname defined for IP address
```

(Cont'd)

Listing 7.1 *Sample Configuration File (Cont'd)*

```
(161.135.59.129)</TD></TR>
   <TR><TD>Max Speed:</TD>
       <TD>1250.0 kBytes/s (ethernetCsmacd)</TD></TR>
  </TABLE>
#-------------------------------------------------------------
Target[10.0.2.75.2]: 2:public@10.0.2.75
MaxBytes[10.0.2.75.2]: 6982
Title[10.0.2.75.2]: remote-gw (No hostname defined for IP address):
Serial0
PageTop[10.0.2.75.2]: <H1>Traffic Analysis for Serial0
 </H1>
 <TABLE>
   <TR><TD>System:</TD><TD>remote-gw in Graphics Lab 11-B</TD></TR>
   <TR><TD>Maintainer:</TD><TD>Steve Maxwell</TD></TR>
   <TR><TD>Interface:</TD><TD>Serial0 (2)</TD></TR>
   <TR><TD>IP:</TD><TD>No hostname defined for IP address
(161.135.59.9)</TD></TR>
   <TR><TD>Max Speed:</TD>
       <TD>6982.0 Bytes/s (rfc877x25)</TD></TR>
  </TABLE>
#-------------------------------------------------------------
```

Comments are supported in the MRTG configuration file by using the hash (#) character at the beginning of each line. Blank lines are ignored. The configuration file includes one or more polling instances that contain tokens and associated values. Collectively, these tokens represent a single monitored element. Each element represents a polled entity that includes the SNMP objects to query from the device being monitored and additional display formatting for the resulting information. They are usually separated by a single hash (#) followed by a line of - characters. This particular router contains only a few network interfaces and the `targets` correspond to each router interface. This is a key observation because any data that is going to be monitored and displayed by MRTG requires a `target` entry.

This particular router contains three interfaces—one Ethernet and two Serials—but `cfgmaker` only reports two working interfaces. Because the third interface is administratively down, it wasn't configured within the router or it was disabled on purpose when the `cfgmaker` script was run. In any event, `cfgmaker` includes the first two interfaces, but it inserts a comment character in front of the third interface in the `cisco.conf` file so that it will not be polled with the MRTG software, as shown in Listing 7.2:

Listing 7.2 *Commented Interface Entry*

```
#########
######### This Interface is one of the following
######### - administratively not UP
######### - it is in test mode
######### - it is a softwareLoopback interface
######### - has a unrealistic speed setting
######### It is commented out for this reason.
#########
#
# Target[10.0.2.75.3]: 3:public@10.0.2.75
# MaxBytes[10.0.2.75.3]: 193000
# Title[10.0.2.75.3]: TYO-RErp01.network.fedex.com (): Serial1
# PageTop[10.0.2.75.3]: <H1>Traffic Analysis for Serial1
#  <BR></H1>
#  <TABLE>
#    <TR><TD>System:</TD><TD>TYO-RErp01.network.fedex.com in
</TD></TR>
#    <TR><TD>Maintainer:</TD><TD></TD></TR>
#    <TR><TD>Interface:</TD><TD>Serial1 (3)</TD></TR>
#    <TR><TD>IP:</TD><TD> ()</TD></TR>
#    <TR><TD>Max Speed:</TD>
#        <TD>193.0 kBytes/s (propPointToPointSerial)</TD></TR>
#   </TABLE>
#
#--------------------------------------------------------------
```

This is a good thing, because it is not reasonable to have MRTG poll interfaces when there is no traffic and thus produce empty graphs. Also, should the interface be enabled and put into service at some future date, it is a simple matter of "un-comment" the interface entry, thus permitting MRTG to monitor the port.

The MRTG configuration file is displayed in the HTML formatting language and, in particular, uses a table to format the device information, as denoted by the `<TABLE>` and `</TABLE>` tags.

The MRTG configuration includes one or more keywords that control which devices are monitored and how data is graphed. Each keyword contains the following syntax:

```
Command [label] args
```

where command is one of the commands defined below, followed by a label enclosed with brackets and one or more arguments or command options.

Each element or interface within the configuration file usually contains the following keywords:

- `Target`
- `MaxBytes`
- `Title`
- `PageTop`

The `Target` keyword indicates to MRTG what it should monitor. The basic format includes:

```
Target[label]: port:community@device
```

The `label` is used as an identifier, so that MRTG can display a group of keywords on one HTML page. The `label` is a combination of the device IP address and interface number. The `port` is the interface number as defined in the `device` that MRTG should poll with the SNMP community string of `community`. The port or interface number must be a valid interface on the device being polled. You can determine the valid interfaces on a given device with the MRTG `cfgmaker` program. By using this program, you will determine that all defined interfaces within a given device are discovered automatically. Alternatively, using a MIB browser, you can peruse the MIB tree of the device and examine the interface table to discover the interfaces manually. However, if you already know which interfaces you want to monitor, specifying them manually might be the simplest approach. Using the configuration example above, consider the following `Target` command:

```
Target[10.0.2.75.1]: 1:public@10.0.2.75
```

This command will define the label `10.0.2.75.1` and instruct MRTG to monitor traffic from the first interface of the device with the IP address of `10.0.2.75` using the community string of `public`. By default, MRTG polls the MIB objects `ifInOctets` and `IfOutOctets` from the specified device and graphs this data over time.

The `Maxbytes` keyword is used to define the upper limit for any monitored traffic statistics and is used to determine the y-axis range for unscaled graphs. For any interface, the `Maxbytes` keyword is normally specified in bytes per second, which can be calculated by dividing the maximum bandwidth of the interface by eight. For example, because Ethernet has a maximum bandwidth of 10 Mbits (megabits) per second, dividing this by eight (`8`), we get `1250000` or `1250K` (`10,000,000 / 8 = 1,250,000`). Setting this value correctly is very important, because this will ensure that the graphs will display realistic information. For example, commands taken from the sample configuration above,

```
MaxBytes[10.0.2.75.1]: 1250000
```

will define the maximum bytes of 1,250,000 for the device associated with the label `10.0.2.75.1`. Recall that the `cfgmaker` program assigns the `MaxBytes` value and the reason this value was chosen is because the interface is of type Ethernet. Because knowing that bytes per second is important, this value, for some of the most common networking interface types, is included in Table 7.1. This information has been included here because MRTG doesn't include the maximum bytes per second for the graphs; this is to ensure that they are readable when small traffic loads are graphed.

Table 7.1 *Bytes Per Second for Different Interfaces*

Network Type	Bytes Per Second
ATM (OC-3)	1944000000
Giga Ethernet	125000000
Fast Ethernet	12500000
FDDI	12500000
T3	5593250
Ethernet	1250000
Token Ring (16MB)	2000000
Token Ring (4MB)	500000
T1	193000
56K	7000

The `MaxBytes` value is also used by MRTG to detect invalid responses when polling devices for interface traffic statistics.

The `Title` keyword is used to label the report page and usually includes some information regarding the particular interface that is being monitored. The example

```
Title[10.0.2.75.1]: remote-gw (No hostname defined for IP address): Ethernet0
```

defines the title that is associated with the system 10.0.2.75. It contains the hostname, plus the interface (i.e., `Ethernet0`).

The final keyword, `PageTop`, is used to include additional information that will be placed at the top of the report. This allows more description information regarding the interface or other information to be placed on the report.

```
PageTop[10.0.2.75.1]: <H1>Traffic Analysis for Ethernet0
 </H1>
```

In this example, the string `Traffic Analysis for Ethernet0` is included when the `cfgmaker` script is executed and further describes what the report represents. The `<H1>` and `</H1>` markers are HTML heading tags. The browser may choose to display the string between these markers in one of many different formats that might include centering, bold text, a large font, italics, color, or underlining. Multiple lines may be added to this keyword and, since HTML normally removes new-line characters, the `\n` sequence must be used if new lines are required.

Using MRTG

After a basic configuration file for the devices has been prepared, it is time to start using MRTG to monitor performance and produce reports on these devices. The program that polls the devices for performance statistics and builds the HTML pages is called `mrtg`. However, before we can run this command, we must make sure to include the `WorkDir` keyword entry command in the configuration file. This keyword tells MRTG where to create the log files and HTML pages. The syntax of this command includes:

```
WorkDir: path
```

where `path` is the absolute pathname of the target directory. After this command has been added to the configuration file, it is time to run the `mrtg` program with the new configuration to ensure that no syntax errors or other problems have been introduced. This is an important step. It helps to ensure that we catch any problems before we start executing `mrtg` on a more or less permanent basis. Assuming the configuration file being used is called `cisco.conf`, the command

```
mrtg cisco.conf
```

runs `mrtg` with this file and immediately attempts to collect SNMP data from the device listed. After the `mrtg` command has completed, it creates a series of files in the directory specified by the `WorkDir` command. Assume for example, the `cisco.conf` file contains the following sample entries:

```
WorkDir: /usr/mrtg/www
Target[10.0.2.75.1]: 1:public@10.0.2.75
```

The following files will be created in the `/usr/mrtg/www` directory:

```
10.0.2.75.1-day.gif
10.0.2.75.1-month.gif
10.0.2.75.1-week.gif
10.0.2.75.1-year.gif
10.0.2.75.1.html
10.0.2.75.1.log
10.0.2.75.1.old
```

All of these files have the prefix of the IP address and interface number and represent the device and port being monitored by MRTG. The `10.0.2.71.1-html` file contains the high level report, in HTML, previously shown in Figure 7.1. When viewing the MRTG reports, use this file and a standard Web browser to display the interface performance graphs. The files with the `gif` extension are the four graphs that show the daily, monthly, weekly, and yearly usage in bytes per second of the device that the `10.0.2.75.1-html` report file uses. The `10.0.2.75.1.log` and `10.0.2.75.1.old` files contain the SNMP polled data, used in building the graphs.

For every interface monitored by MRTG, these seven files will be created automatically. Another good thing about MRTG is that the reports and data files don't consume a large amount of disk space. In fact, MRTG uses a unique method of data storage to minimize the amount of space used in the historical graphs.

To ensure that MRTG captures consistent and complete information from the monitored devices, the mrtg program must be run at regular intervals. One of the best ways to do this is to use the cron facility. Since the daily graph, which is available on the MRTG report, is averaged over a five-minute period, it is reasonable that mrtg should be run every five minutes. A sample crontab entry that would do just this is shown here:

```
0,5,10,15,20,25,30,35,40,45,50,55 * * * * /usr/mrtg/www/mrtg \
/usr/mrtg/www/mrtg.conf
```

This entry will execute the mrtg program every five minutes every day of the week. The * is a wildcard and means all for the four time specifications following the minutes field. See crontab manual page for additional information.

Customizing MRTG Reports

The MRTG package can be customized to produce differently formatted reports and graphs and to control certain operational aspects of MRTG. This is accomplished by using optional target configuration tags (or keywords) within the MRTG configuration file. The keywords can be divided into two groups: optional global commands and optional target commands. The global commands affect the operation or behavior of MRTG as a whole, while the optional target commands apply specifically to individual targets or device reports and graphs.

Global Commands

There are four global commands supported by MRTG. They are listed in Table 7.2. These are optional keywords and are placed in the configuration file that is used with the mrtg program.

The Refresh keyword specifies how often, in seconds, the browser should reload the MRTG report page. The default value is 300 seconds, which is five minutes. This is a very useful option when it becomes important to precisely control the granularity for the update of the MRTG reports. For example, if it is necessary to have nearly real-time performance information on certain critical devices, lowering the Refresh to as little as 60 seconds may be

Table 7.2 *Optional Global Commands*

Option	Description
`Refresh`	Specifies how frequently (in seconds) to update the MRTG report
`Interval`	Specifies how often `mrtg` is called
`WriteExpires`	If set to `YES`, will generate meta files that control expiration tags for the MRTG reports
`IconDir`	Tells MRTG to look in an alternative location for GIF images

appropriate. On the other hand, the `Refresh` should be larger for those devices that might be less critical and don't require up-to-the-minute reporting. To reduce the browser refresh rate to one minute, place the following command in the MRTG configuration file:

```
Refresh: 60
```

In order for the refresh value to be effective, it should match closely the interval that the `mrtg` is executed when polling devices. The `crontab` entry previously specified in this section runs `mrtg` every five minutes. If the refresh value is decreased from its default value, the `crontab` entry should also be updated with the same value as well. Consider the situation in which the refresh value is one minute while the execution of the `mrtg` is every five minutes. In this scenario, there would be no point in refreshing the MRTG reports because the data would only be updated every five minutes by `mrtg`. Clearly, to increase the granularity of the MRTG reports means running the `mrtg` program more often to collect additional data points from the devices being monitored.

The `Interval` command specifies how often MRTG is executed. The purpose of this command is to generate a meta header in the MRTG report which is used to control the time-to-live of the report for caching purposes. Also, it is used to document the HTML pages with the correct calling interval. If the Web browser being used requires the generation of meta files that control the expiration of the MRTG reports, use the `WriteExpires` command. These meta files contain tags that specify the expiration of both the HTML and GIF files. Enabling `WriteExpires` will cause MRTG to create additional files in the working directory.

The `IconDir` can be used to specify an alternative directory (instead of the working directory) to contain icons used by MRTG. It is useful to separate the device report files from the GIF images used with the reports. Thus, to use the `graphics` directory to hold all the images, use the following command:

```
IconDir: /graphics/
```

Note that the directory name must include the trailing / character.

Optional Target Commands

Many options control the formatting of the graphs, but only a few affect how the report is displayed. All the keywords described here have the same syntax as the other MRTG commands, such as `Target` and `Maxbytes`. These customization keywords are listed in Table 7.3 and are described below.

Table 7.3 *MRTG Customization Options*

Option	Description
`AddHead`	Like the `PageTop` keyword, this includes the specified entry in the MRTG report. This is a great way to add site-specific information to the MRTG reports
`AbsMax`	Specifies the maximum value ever to be reached when data is to be graphed
`Background`	Controls the background color of the MRTG reports
`Colours`	Overrides the default color scheme
`Directory`	Places all files related to a given label in the directory specified

(Cont'd)

Table 7.3 *MRTG Customization Options (Cont'd)*

Option	Description
`Legend`	Controls the strings for the color legend
`Options`	Enables the use of additional Boolean switches, which further control display attributes of graphs
`ShortLegend`	Overrides the units string, which by default is `b/s`
`Step`	Changes the default step or timeout from five minutes `(5 * 60)`
`Suppress`	Disables the display of daily, weekly, monthly, or yearly graphs on a MRTG report
`Timezone`	Controls the time zone that is used. Standard names are supported, such as `japan`
`Unscaled`	Turns off the vertical scaling of data on graphs on a MRTG report
`Weekformat`	Controls which Unix API function is used to format the weekly information displayed in the monthly graphs
`WithPeak`	Enables display of peak values in graphs on a MRTG report
`XSize/YSize`	Changes the vertical and horizontal sizes of the MRTG report graphs
`XZoom/YZoom`	Increases the number of pixels used with a graph
`XScale/YScale`	Scales both the x and y axes of the graph
`Ylegend`	Overrides the text displayed for the y-axis for the graph

The `AddHead` keyword is used to add HTML code between the `</TITLE>` and `</HEAD>` HTML tags in the resulting HTML. This is a good way to add any site-specific information to the MRTG reports. For example, to add the ability to email an individual from the MRTG report, add the following:

```
AddHead[10.0.2.75.1]: <A HREF="mailto:support@monet">Open Trouble Ticket</A>
```

Notice that this keyword requires a label and is used to match up the `AddHead` to the existing `Target` command entry.

By default, MRTG scales the vertical axis to ensure that data that is much smaller than the `MaxBytes` is displayed in such a way that it is visible on the graph. If you want to disable the scaling function, use the `Unscaled` keyword. This command accepts a single string argument that consists of the first letter of the graph name that should not be scaled. The string includes `d` for daily, `w` for weekly, `m` for monthly, and `y` for yearly. Thus the command

```
Unscaled[10.0.2.71.1]: dw
```

will disable scaling for both the daily and weekly graphs.

The `WithPeak` command instructs MRTG to display peak five-minute rates for both incoming and outgoing traffic on device interfaces. Normally, the graphs only contain the average values of the monitored variables. This command takes a single string, which contains the first letter of the graphs that should display the peak values. The string includes `w` for weekly, `m` for monthly, and `y` for yearly. In the following example, both the weekly and yearly graphs will contain peak information.

```
WithPeak[10.0.2.71.1]: dw
```

The reason the daily graph is not included in this list is that this graph already shows peak information.

Normally, MRTG displays all four graphs on the interface report. With the `Suppress` keyword, one or more of these graphs can be removed from the report. This keyword takes the same argument as both the `Unscaled` and `WithPeak` commands. To block display of the weekly, monthly, and yearly graphs, use the following command:

```
Suppress[10.0.2.71.1]: wmy
```

To provide a way to better organize MRTG reports and data files, the `Directory` command has been supplied. By default, MRTG saves all the files to the directory specified with the `WorkDir` keyword. The `Directory` command accepts a string argument that represents a directory name to save all files associated with the label to this location. Consider:

```
WorkDir: /usr/mrtg/www/devices
Directory[10.0.2.71.1] gw-1
```

will instruct MRTG to save all files associated with the label `10.0.2.71.1` in the directory called `gw-1`. As you can see, this can be useful in managing a large installation of monitored devices and interfaces because each interface may be saved to its own location. The directory specified with the `Directory` command must exist before MRTG is run because MRTG will not create it. If MRTG is run before this directory exists, it will produce an error message and abort.

The `options` keyword provides further capabilities to customize the way the MRTG graphs are displayed. This command accepts several Boolean switches, listed in Table 7.4, that toggle attributes to control various graphing options.

Table 7.4 *Options Boolean Switches*

Option	Description
`growright`	Causes graphs to grow from the right
`bits`	Changes the bits per byte
`noinfo`	Suppresses uptime and device information
`nopercent`	Suppresses usage percentage information
`gauge`	Treats polled values as absolute and not incrementing counters
`absolute`	Used when data sources reset their values when read

The `growright` option will cause data to be added from the right side of the graph instead of from the left, which is the default behavior. This also reverses the x-axis value for all the graphs.

With MRTG, all the monitored values, by default, are displayed in bytes. With the `bits` option, these values may be displayed in bits instead. This has a profound impact on graphs as the `bits` value seems to produce a more impressive graph than the graph of only bytes. The `noinfo` and `nopercent` keywords are used to suppress information from the MRTG report. In the case of `noinfo`, neither uptime nor additional device information will be displayed. The `nopercent` keyword is used to withhold calculated percent information from the graphs.

The `gauge` switch is used to treat gathered values as absolute quantities rather than increments to the values displayed in previous polls. This is useful for monitoring information related to disk space, processor utilization, and the number of users on a system. The `gauge` option is used in the disk space-monitoring example provided below. The absolute switch is used for data sources that reset their value when they are read. This indicates that MRTG doesn't need to calculate the difference between the present value and the previous polled value. The `absolute` value is divided by the elapsed time between the last two polls, which makes it quite different from the `gauge` values previously discussed.

Special Target Names

MRTG provides three special target names, which can reduce the amount of typing within the MRTG configuration file. These special characters include the hat (`^`), dollar sign (`$`), and underscore (_). The text of every keyword that uses the `^` is prepended to every subsequent target that is used. For example, the MRTG sequence

```
PageTop[^]: <H1>The Graphics Lab Network</H1>
```

will be added to every additional `PageTop` keyword command that is found within the configuration file. Thus, given the following:

```
PageTop[10.0.2.75.1]: <H1>Traffic Analysis for Ethernet0</H1>
```

the output on the report will be:

```
The Graphics Lab Network
Traffic Analysis for Ethernet0
```

Whenever MRTG encounters a `target` entry, it adds the string `The Graphics Lab Network` to the beginning of each `target` command.

When the `$` character is used instead of the `^`, the string that follows is appended to any additional keyword. Thus, given the following:

```
PageTop[$]: <H1> <A HREF="mailto:lisa_ellen@think-tech.com">Lisa Ellen/A></H1>
```

The above email link will appear at the end of any `PageTop` entries. Using the example above, the output on the report will be:

```
Traffic Analysis for Ethernet0
Lisa Ellen
```

If you want to replace an existing prepend/append value, simply refine it. For example,

```
PageTop[^]: <H1>The Graphics Lab Network</H1>
PageTop[10.0.2.75.1]: <H1>Traffic Analysis for Ethernet0</H1>
PageTop[^]: <H1>The Engineering Lab</H1>
PageTop[10.0.2.100.1]: <H1>Traffic Analysis for ATM1</H1>
```

In the above output, the second instance of `PageTop[^]` overwrites the first and will be used throughout the entire configuration file unless additional `PageTop[^]` keywords are encountered.

Also, previously defined values with `^` and `$` can be reset to null, or "unset," simply by using the characters without any string definitions. Thus,

```
PageTop[^]:
PageTop[$]:
```

resets the keywords to the default state of no value.

The _ character is used with MRTG keywords; it specifies a default value for that keyword. In the absence of an explicit keyword value, or the prepended/appended value, the default will be used. For example,

```
Target[10.0.2.75.1]: 1:public@10.0.2.75
```

The `Target` definition with the label `10.0.2.75.1` can be replicated without the need to use the label string. So,

```
MaxBytes[_]: 1249991
Title[_]: remote-gw (): Ethernet0
Options[_]: growright
PageTop[_]: <H1>Traffic Analysis for Ethernet0</H1>
```

are all valid MRTG entries—because the underscore points back to the `10.0.2.75.1` label.

To reset the underscore, specify an empty value:

```
Options[_]:
```

Master Index

MRTG can be said to be "interface centric." This means that its main focus is on the interface of the devices being monitored. If MRTG is used to monitor a Cisco router with five interfaces, five separate MRTG reports will be created. Unfortunately, this structure, though sufficient for a small number of interfaces, becomes difficult to use and manage when faced with a large number of interfaces or the combination of many devices and interfaces. To assist with this task, a script has been provided in the MRTG distribution, called `indexmaker`, which produces an index of all the monitored devices and interfaces. The syntax of `indexmaker` is:

```
indexmaker config label interfaces
```

This command accepts three arguments—the MRTG configuration file, the graph label, and the regular expression that includes all the monitored interfaces that should be included within the index. Because `indexmaker` writes to STDOUT, the output should be redirected to a file. Thus, the sample command,

```
indexmaker cisco.conf "Summary of Interfaces" . > backbone.html
```

builds a master interface index for all the interfaces contained within the `10.0.2.75` device using the file `backbone.html`. The new file, when displayed, should look similar to the window shown in Figure 7.5. It shows the daily graph for each interface and contains a link to each of the defined pages, which contain the remaining graphs for that interface.

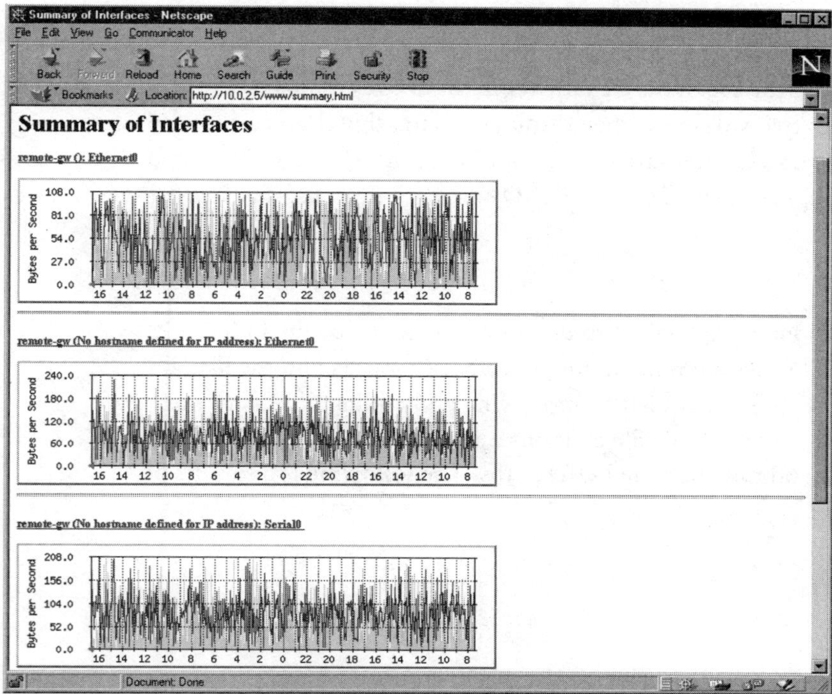

Figure 7.5 *Master Index of Monitored Devices.*

Monitoring Additional Information

MRTG can be used to monitor other information—including additional SNMP objects and non-SNMP information—using the `Target` command. The `Target` command accepts additional input formats, which can be used to monitor and graph information. These formats include direct OID strings, SNMP abbreviated objects, and custom commands. The direct OID format uses Object Identifier (OID) strings, expressed in fully qualified dotted decimal notation, that specify which object should be monitored by MRTG. Fully qualified indicates that the entire path from the root to the object has been supplied. For example, to monitor `ifInErrors` and `ifOutErrors` from the device `10.0.2.200`, use the following command:

```
Target[10.0.2.200.1]:1.3.6.1.2.1.2.2.1.14.1&1.3.6.1.2.1.2.2.1.20.1\
:public@10.0.2.200
```

This command retrieves both input and output error counts on the interface known as `1`.

Notice the use of the `&` character in the above command. MRTG requires two variables when displaying data; this character is used as a separator. Alternatively, one could use the SNMP-abbreviated object names instead of direct OID convention. Thus, this command

```
Target[10.0.2.200.1]:ifInErrors.1&ifOutErrors.1:public@10.0.2.200
```

is functionally equivalent to the previous `Target` command. MRTG knows a limited number of SNMP objects and the list of objects can be expanded by modifying and adding objects to the `mibhelp.txt` file. This file contains mappings between SNMP objects and fully qualified OID paths. The following is a sample of this file:

```
Descriptor:            ifInErrors
Identifier:            1.3.6.1.2.1.2.2.1.14
ASN.1 Syntax:          Counter32

The number of inbound packets that contained
errors preventing them from being deliverable to a
higher-layer protocol.
```

The entry above shows the `ifInErrors` object used in the above command and contains a descriptor, identifier, and ASN.1 syntax of the object. The descriptor names the object that MRTG will use and is associated with the identifier string; it can be any string name as long as it is unique within the `mibhelp.txt` file. The identifier is the fully qualified path name of the object, minus the instance. The ASN.1 syntax refers to the object type and should match the object definition found within the MIB that defines the object. Finally, the entry contains descriptive text, which explains the object definition. Although this text isn't required, it is very useful and its inclusion is recommended when additional objects are added to this file.

SNMP objects that are predefined within the `mbhelp.txt` are listed in Table 7.5.

Table 7.5 *Predefined SNMP MRTG Objects*

SNMP Object	Object Information
ifOperStatus	The current operational state of the interface
ifAdminStatus	The current administrative state of the interface
ifInOctets	The total number of octets received on the interface, including framing characters
ifInUcastPkts	The number of subnetwork-unicast packets delivered to a higher-layer protocol
ifInNUcastPkts	The number of non-unicast (i.e., subnetwork-broadcast or subnetwork-multicast) packets delivered to a higher-layer protocol
ifInDiscards	The number of inbound packets that were chosen to be discarded
ifInErrors	The number of inbound packets that contained errors preventing them from being deliverable to a higher-layer protocol
ifInUnknownProtos	The number of packets received via the interface that were discarded because of an unknown or unsupported protocol
ifOutOctets	The total number of octets transmitted out of the interface, including framing characters
ifOutUcastPkts	The total number of packets that higher-level protocols requested be transmitted to a subnetwork-unicast address, including those that were discarded or not sent

(Cont'd)

Table 7.5 *Predefined SNMP MRTG Objects (Cont'd)*

SNMP Object	Object Information
`ifOutNUcastPkts`	The total number of packets that higher-level protocols requested be transmitted to a non-unicast (i.e., a subnetwork-broadcast or subnetwork-multicast) address
`ifOutDiscards`	The number of outbound packets that were chosen to be discarded even though no errors had been detected to prevent their being transmitted
`ifOutErrors`	The number of outbound packets that could not be transmitted because of errors
`ifOutQLen`	The length of the output packet queue (in packets)

MRTG supports mathematical operations on the SNMP objects or OID strings. This could be used, for example, to group the total number of input errors and output errors for a collection of interfaces instead of just a single interface. Thus,

```
Target[monet]: ifInErrors.0:public@10.0.2.75+ifInErrors.1:public@10.0.2.75\
&ifOutErrors.0:public@10.0.2.75+ifOutErrors.1:public@10.0.2.75
```

computes the sum of interface errors for both the first and second interfaces found on the device `10.0.2.75`.

MRTG also supports the collection of data from custom programs or scripts. For example, MRTG can be used to display disk space usage information. Using the `df2mrtg` script, available in the contributed software directory, it monitors individual disk partitions and provides disk usage and size information. The following command shows this task:

```
Target[monet]: `/usr/mrtg/bin/df2mrtg -u /dev/dsk/c0t3d0s7`
```

When this line and some additional options are placed in a MRTG configuration file, the graph shown in Figure 7.6 is produced.

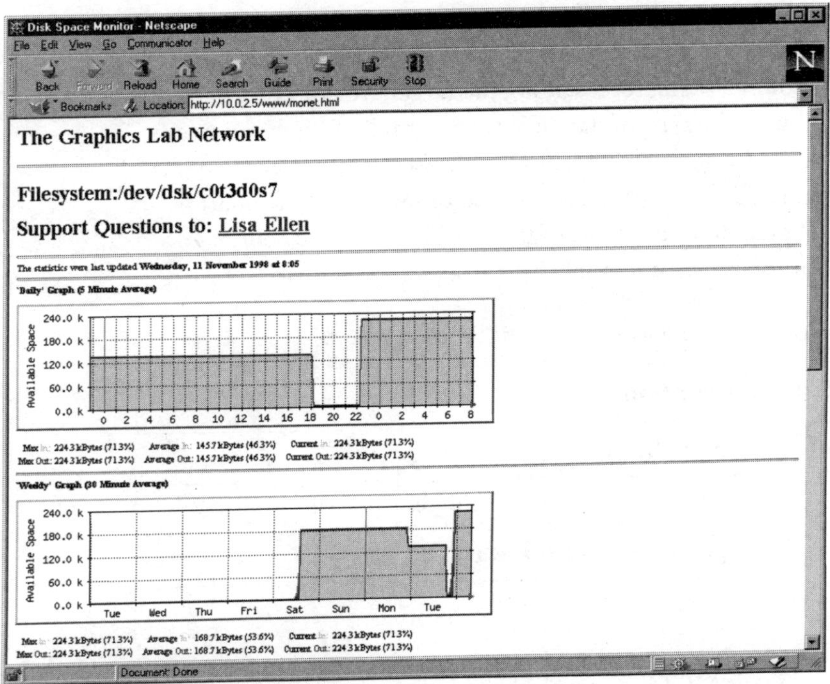

Figure 7.6 *MRTG Report on Disk Space.*

As you can see, having the ability to collect information from other sources is a very powerful feature of MRTG. If you are interested in developing custom programs to monitor non-SNMP information, the data returned from the program must be in a format that MRTG understands. Therefore, the program normally returns four lines of output that include the present state of the first variable, the present state of the second variable, a string indicating the system uptime of the target, and a string indicating the name of the target.

The first two variables are comparable to, for example, incoming bytes per second and outgoing bytes per second. The system update time is indicative of when the system was last rebooted (or when the network management component—the agent—was last restarted). To ensure that the script output is matched with a target, the target name is returned.

In the case of the `df2mrtg` script, the first variable represents the currently used disk space in kilobytes (when the `-u` options are used) and the second variable is a repeat of the first. Because we are only interested in monitoring disk space, the system uptime information and the string representing the target are not needed. Also, depending on the type of data returned with the script, you might need to use the `Options` keyword with either `gauge` or `absolute` as appropriate. This script is also used to report other information regarding the disk partitions of the local system. The command line options are listed in Table 7.6.

Table 7.6 *df2mrtg Script Command Line Options*

Option	Description
`-f`	Reports free disk space in the partition
`-s`	Reports the total size of the disk partition
`-p`	Reports free disk space as a percent
`-u`	Reports used disk space

If you want MRTG to graph the free disk space on a partition, use the `-f` option. The `-s` option will report the total size of the partition.

Because MRTG is used to monitor network interfaces, some of the default values and configuration information should be changed when it is used to monitor disk space or other system information. Listed below is the MRTG configuration that closely matches what would be appropriate when the `df2mrtg` script is used.

```
Title[monet]: Disk Space Monitor
PageTop[monet]: <H1>Disk Space Usage for System:Monet
Options[monet]: gauge,growright
MaxBytes[monet]: 314461
AbsMax[monet]: 400000
WithPeak[monet]: ymwd
YLegend[monet]: Available Space
ShortLegend[monet]: Bytes
Legend1[monet]: Current Disk Utilization
```

Because of the flexibility of MRTG and the `df2mrtg` script, instead of reporting available disk space, we could report percent of disk space available. This is, perhaps, a better measurement because, by displaying the percent utilization, we can obtain a quick status of the condition of the available disk space without doing any math. Figure 7.7 shows the same partition, but uses the `-p` option of the script to report on disk percent.

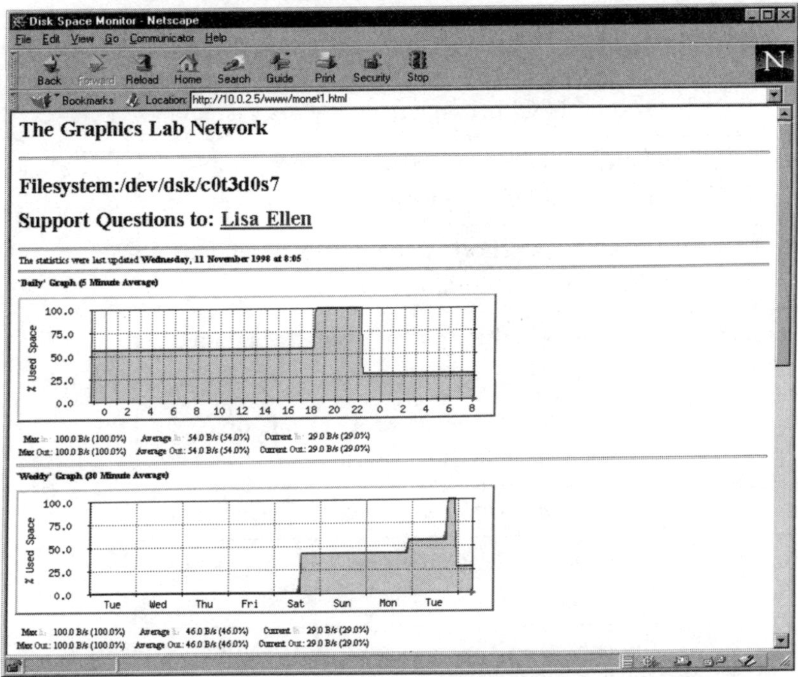

Figure 7.7 *MRTG Report on Disk Usage by Percent.*

As you can see, this graph shows the same information as Figure 7.6, but displaying this information as a percentage is more meaningful and is easier to read.

Contributed Components for MRTG

Several modules have been included in the MRTG package to provide support for additional customization of MRTG and monitoring of additional services and devices. Table 7.7 on page 306 provides a list of these modules found in the `contrib` directory under that main MRTG working directory.

Table 7.7 *Contributed Modules for MRTG*

Module Name	Description
`ascendget`	Provides modem information from Ascend's remote access device
`atmmaker`	Builds MRTG configuration files for ATM devices
`cpumon`	Monitors CPU usage from a Unix system
`distrib`	Builds network traffic distribution graphs given MRTG log files
`get-active`	Produces a report of the most active interfaces that are monitored by MRTG
`get-multiserial`	Monitors dial-in modems on a local Unix system
`GetSNMPLinesUP`	Queries SNMP devices for specific objects and returns values to MRTG
`ircstats`	Collects information on active IRC clients.
`mrtg-archiver`	Archives the MRTG report GIFs given a list of device targets
`mrtg-blast`	Incorporates `tcp-blast` output in MRTG
`mrtg-dynip`	Enables MRTG to monitor dynamic network interfaces
`mrtg-ipget`	Enables MRTG to monitor interfaces expressed with IP addresses instead of instances
`mrtg-mail`	Monitors mail statistics
`mrtgidx`	Generates MRTG index of monitored devices

(Cont'd)

Table 7.7 *Contributed Modules for MRTG (Cont'd)*

Module Name	Description
`mrtgindex.cgi`	Generates MRTG index of monitored devices (an improved script)
`ping-probe`	Displays round trip performance information using `ping`
`portmasters`	Displays modem information from Livingston Portmaster devices
`rdlog2`	Produces traffic displays of devices monitored by MRTG
`rumb-stat`	Obtains low-level statistics from Web servers such as Apache

Installation and operation of these tools is found in the associated directory bearing the same (or similar) name as the script name.

Troubleshooting MRTG Problems

Because the MRTG configuration file consists of plain text, it is relatively simple to introduce syntax or other errors into this file during customization. Also, other conditions might exist that produce errors when executing other MRTG programs. Listed below is a list of some of the most common run-time and configuration problems.

Error Message/Problem:

```
Rateup WARNING: .//rateup could not read the primary log file for 10.0.2.50.1
Rateup WARNING: .//rateup The backup log file for 10.0.2.50.1 was invalid as well
Rateup WARNING: .//rateup Can't remove 10.0.2.50.1.old updating log file.
```

Solution

Don't worry about these errors. They occur once in while, but don't pose any serious problem and can be ignored.

Error Message/Problem:

```
No answer from community@device. You may be using the wrong community
```

Solution

MRTG is having trouble polling a device with the SNMP community string specified in the configuration file.

Error Message/Problem:

```
./mrtg rmon
ERROR: I guess another mrtg is running. A lockfile (rmon_l) aged
264 seconds is hanging around. If you are sure that no other mrtg
is running you can remove the lockfile.
```

Solution

MRTG detected a lock file, which indicates that another copy of MRTG is presently running or ran in the past and failed to remove the lock file. Use the `ps` command to ensure that no additional MRTG process is running. If no additional process is running, remove the lock file.

Error Message/Problem:

```
ERROR: I can't find a "target[10.0.2.50.1]" definition
```

Solution

MRTG reports that the `target` keyword command is missing from the configuration file.

Error Message/Problem:

```
ERROR: "WorkDir" not specified
ABORT: Please fix the error(s) in your config file
```

Solution

The WorkDir command has not been included in the configuration file that was specified with the `mrtg` command. Because this keyword is not optional, MRTG aborts without this definition.

Error Message/Problem:

```
Bareword found where operator expected at (eval 13) line 1, near "1public"
(Missing operator before public?)
Bareword "public" not allowed while "strict subs" in use at (eval 13) line 1.
Array found where operator expected at (eval 13) line 1, at end of line * Prob-
lem with '1public@10.0.2.50': syntax error at (eval 13) line 1, near "1public"
```

Solution

A syntax error was detected in the MRTG configuration file. Check the line indicated within the error message for a missing colon or other syntax errors.

```
Target[10.0.2.50.1]:1public@10.0.2.50
```

Error Message/Problem:

```
SNMP Error:
no response received
SNMPv1_Session (remote host: "10.0.2.200" [10.0.2.200].161
                  community: "public"
                 request ID: 472779887
                PDU bufsize: 8000 bytes
                    timeout: 2s
                    retries: 5
                    backoff: 1)
SNMPGET: Failed to reach target: "1:public@10.0.2.200". I tried multiple times!
```

Solution

This error indicates that the device didn't respond to SNMP requests. Check to ensure the device is alive on the network and the SNMP agent is responding.

MRTG Package Information

The MRTG software may be obtained from the following location:

```
http://ee-staff.ethz.ch/~oetiker/webtools/mrtg/pub/
```

Also, MRTG requires the GD graphics library, which may be obtained from the following location:

```
http://www.boutell.com/gd/
```

Additional information on MRTG may be obtained from:

```
http://ee-staff.ethz.ch/~oetiker/webtools/mrtg/mrtg.html
```

Conditions of Use

The following information appears on the Website regarding this software:

```
MRTG is available under the GNU General Public License.
The only thing I would like to ask happy users to do, is to
```

```
send a Picture Postcard to:
Tobias Oetiker, D-ELEK, ETH Zentrum, CH-8092 Zurich,
Switzerland
```

Installing the MRTG Package

The installation procedures for the MRTG software are included below. Please note that these instructions are for version 2.5.3 of the MRTG package. If you are installing a newer version, these procedures may not be accurate or complete. In this case, consult the installation instructions that accompany the MRTG distribution.

The `df2mrt` script, which is not part of the MRTG distribution, is available on the CD-ROM that accompanies this book.

1. Obtain the MRTG package from the site above or from the CD-ROM available with this book.

2. Obtain the GD graphics package from one of the site above.

3. Uncompress the GD archive:

   ```
   gnzuip gd1.3_tar.gz
   ```

4. Untar the GD archive into the directory you will be using:

   ```
   tar xf gd1.3_tar
   ```

5. Compile the GD programs:

   ```
   make
   [lots of output]
   ```

6. Uncompress the MRTG archive:

   ```
   gnzuip mrtg-2_5_3_tar.gz
   ```

7. Untar the MRTG archive into the directory you will be using:

   ```
   tar xvf mrtg-2_5_3_tar
   ```

8. Change directory into the MRTG distribution:

   ```
   cd mrtg-2.5.3
   ```

9. Edit the `Makefile` to update the GD path information to include the location of the GD software just installed. These changes include:

```
GD_LIB = <path>

GD_INCLUDE = <path>
```

10. Compile the `rateup` program:

```
make rateup

[lots of output]
```

11. Update the MRTG scripts to include the path of the PERL software:

```
make substitute

[output]
```

NTOP

General Description

The `ntop` program provides a way to determine the systems that are active on a network and the types of traffic sent and received by these systems. Network traffic is sorted by protocol and some of the most common network protocols are recognized, including TCP/IP and associated protocols. This tool also supports non-IP protocol types such as Decnet, IPX, AppleTalk, and others. A complete list of network protocols supported by `ntop` is found at the end of this section. This tool differs significantly from the `snoop` utility, because it concentrates on providing statistical data about network packets, not their contents. Also, `ntop` doesn't require the use of a Web server; it supports the HTTP protocol internally.

Why use `ntop`? First, it provides a quick and easy way to get an accurate snapshot of network activity without using a network probe or Sniffer device. In many cases a dedicated probe is necessary to trace-down network problems, but sometimes time is of the essence and `ntop` can be used in situations in which it is not possible to obtain a probe in a timely manner. Second, it might not be possible to attach a probe given certain network configurations, say between a pair of Unix systems interconnected via a WAN. In this situation, `ntop` can be used when deploying a probe might be very difficult, if not impossible. Third, where cost is a major consideration, purchasing probes will be far more expensive than installing a public domain software tool.

On the negative side, there is no such thing as a free lunch! Running `ntop` across a number of systems does pose some problems. First, `ntop` places the interface in promiscuous mode, which means that every network packet is being captured and, as a result, a significant processing load is placed on the system. To address this issue, care should be taken when running `ntop`. Setting up some automated mechanism may remedy any potential problems by ensuring that `ntop` is only run when necessary and, perhaps, not during critical times or peak system usage.

Secondly, using `ntop` may further complicate security policies and procedures because unauthorized access to this tool could result in additional exposure of existing system vulnerabilities and security holes. Luckily, `ntop` has a rudimentary facility to protect the captured network information. It isn't the most rigorous security available, but it provides a reasonable amount of control. This will be discussed further below.

One of the most powerful features of `ntop` is that it provides two viewing modes: Web mode and basic ASCII terminal mode. This is a very unique feature and is one of the first public domain tools that successfully implement multiple robust interface capabilities. In the Web mode, a series of HTML pages are available that provide a number of network traffic statistics reports and additional network related information. In this mode, a standard Web browser is needed to view these reports and to support multiple simultaneous browser connections. This is a very handy feature when using `ntop` in a distributed network environment where access may originate from more than one location by different users at the same time. When a browser is connected to `ntop`, the main page shown in Figure 7.8 is displayed.

For those not wishing to use the Web interface, the second display mode provides terminal output similar to the Unix `top` command. In this mode, network information is presented in a constantly updated window, as shown in Figure 7.9. It contains a running status of network utilization sorted by network protocols. Several display options are available that can be used to toggle the information displayed and otherwise control `ntop`. The list of available keyword commands is described below.

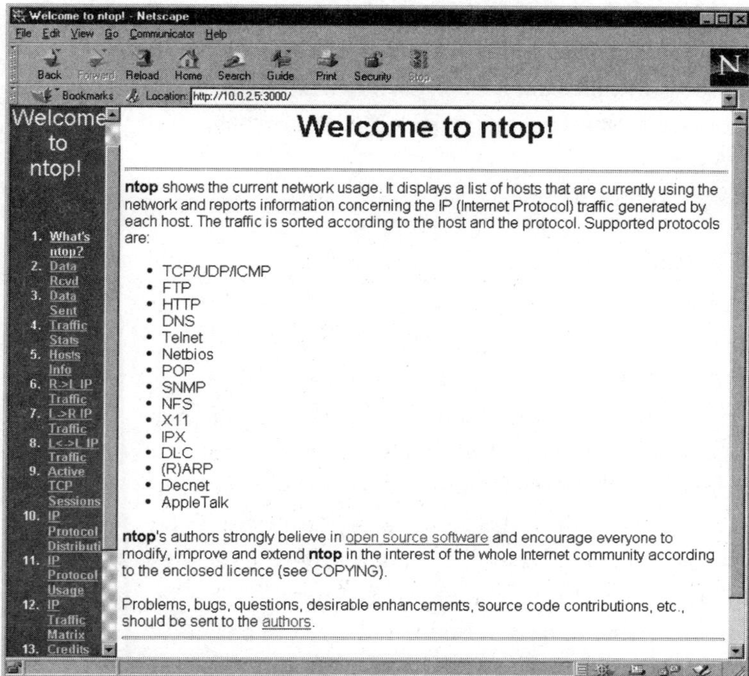

Figure 7.8 *Main NTOP Web Page.*

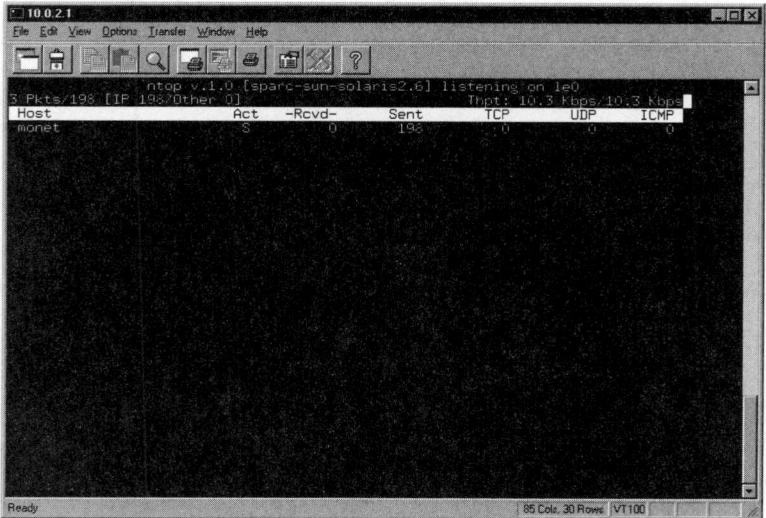

Figure 7.9 *Terminal Display Mode.*

Using Web Mode

To start `ntop` in Web mode, use the `-w` option followed by a port number. This is the port the client Web browsers will use to connect to the NTOP program. Thus, to start `ntop` on port `3000`, issue the following command:

```
ntop -w 3000
```

After the command has started, it displays the following output:

```
ntop: listening on le0
Warning: unable to read file '//.ntop'. No security will be used!
Waiting for HTTP connections on port 3000...
```

NTOP displays which interface it is using when more than one is installed on the system and it confirms the specified port used for incoming connections by browser clients. Also, it warns that it was unable to read the security file and, as a result, no security will be used. In this case, any client browser may connect to `ntop` and view the reports. Securing the reports will be covered later.

With Web mode, the main page is divided into two separate frames as shown in Figure 7.8. The frame on the left-hand side provides a list of report types that the user may select, while the frame on the right displays the actual selected report. The types of reports that NTOP supports include:

- Data Received
- Data Sent
- Traffic Statistics
- Host Information
- Remote to Local Traffic
- Local to Local Traffic
- Active TCP Sessions
- IP Protocol Distribution
- IP Protocol Usage
- IP Traffic Matrix

Note the most important NTOP reports are described in more detail below.

Data Received Report

This report shows network traffic that was received by the listed network hosts, sorted by network protocol type. This report displays a long table, as shown in Figure 7.10, that contains the active hosts, the amount of received data in kilobytes, the percent of network traffic received by system, and the amount of data network traffic broken down by network protocol type.

Network Traffic: Data Received

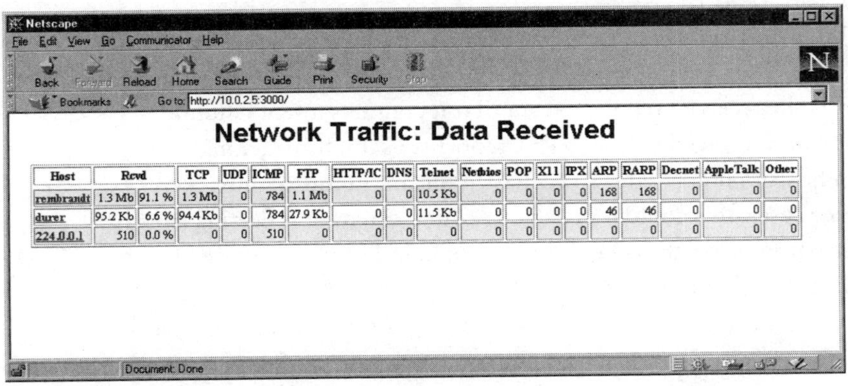

Host	Rcvd		TCP	UDP	ICMP	FTP	HTTP/IC	DNS	Telnet	Netbios	POP	X11	IPX	ARP	RARP	Decnet	AppleTalk	Other
rembrandt	1.3 Mb	91.1 %	1.3 Mb	0	784	1.1 Mb	0	0	10.5 Kb	0	0	0	0	168	168	0	0	0
durer	95.2 Kb	6.6 %	94.4 Kb	0	784	27.9 Kb	0	0	11.5 Kb	0	0	0	0	46	46	0	0	0
224.0.0.1	510	0.0 %	0	0	510	0	0	0	0	0	0	0	0	0	0	0	0	0

Figure 7.10 *Data Received Report.*

In this example, three hosts have been identified, including `durer`, `rembrandt`, and `224.0.0.1`. These are the active systems presently generating traffic on the network. However, in the case of `224.0.0.1`, the Sun system periodically polls this IP address (using ICMP) to determine if the multicast address is available. The NTOP software is recording this as a real host when, in fact, it is just the same system as `durer`.

This report shows the total amount of received traffic in the second column, expressed in bytes, kilobytes (Kb), or megabytes (Mb). Also, the received column shows the amount of traffic that each host received as a percent. In the example above, out of the listed systems, `rembrandt` was the recipient of the largest amount of traffic, which represents 91% of the total traffic transmitted on the network.

The next two columns show the total amount of data that were either TCP or UDP packets. In this case, TCP accounted for the lion's share of traffic. The remaining column includes total data received by protocols such as ICMP, FTP, TELNET, and others. Although this report contains only a small number of hosts, from a network performance standpoint it provides some very useful information. We can surmise that the FTP protocol is used more than any other protocol listed. This was determined by comparing the total FTP traffic with all other protocols.

Data Sent Report

This report shows the hosts that transmitted traffic on the network and is shown in Figure 7.11. The format of this report is the same as the received report, except that it contains a sent column instead of a received column. This report is useful for tracking down hosts that generate or receive significant numbers of packets. In some cases, this could represent a normal situation reflecting true traffic patterns; on the other hand, it could indicate some type of trouble. It could provide evidence of a misconfigured device or some other undesirable activity. For example, it is interesting to note that the host `rembrandt` transmitted a significant amount of data on the network using the NETBIOS protocol. This could be reason to suspect foul play, because the network being monitored is IP based.

Further, the number of ICMP packets seems rather high. This could indicate that a large number of `ping` requests are flooding the network.

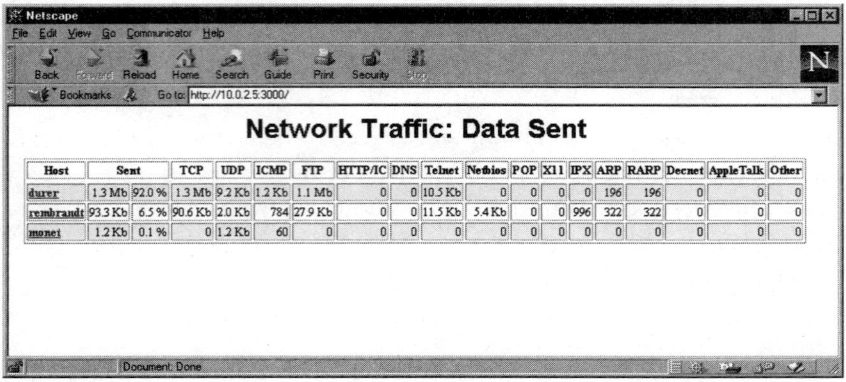

Network Traffic: Data Sent

Host	Sent		TCP	UDP	ICMP	FTP	HTTP/IC	DNS	Telnet	Netbios	POP	X11	IPX	ARP	RARP	Decnet	AppleTalk	Other
durer	1.3 Mb	92.0 %	1.3 Mb	9.2 Kb	1.2 Kb	1.1 Mb	0	0	10.5 Kb	0	0	0	0	196	196	0	0	0
rembrandt	93.3 Kb	6.5 %	90.6 Kb	2.0 Kb	784	27.9 Kb	0	0	11.5 Kb	5.4 Kb	0	0	996	322	322	0	0	0
monet	1.2 Kb	0.1 %	0	1.2 Kb	60	0	0	0	0	0	0	0	0	0	0	0	0	0

Figure 7.11 *Data Sent Report.*

Traffic Statistics Report

This report shows both overall traffic statistics and distribution of IP traffic by protocol type as shown in Figure 7.12. The first table on this page shows the following information:

- Total Packets
- Dropped Packets
- Total Traffic
- Total IP Traffic
- Total Non-IP Traffic
- Actual Throughput
- Max Throughput

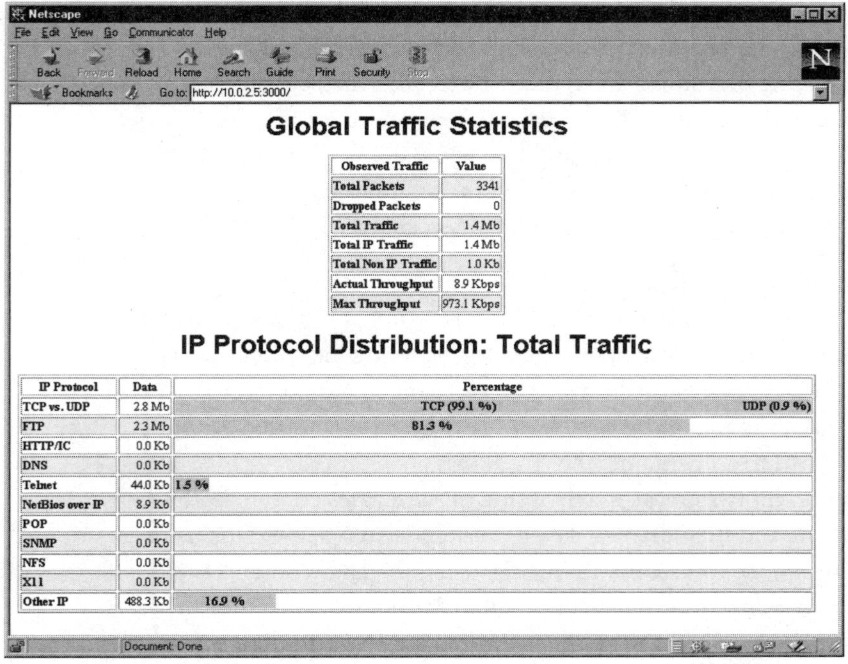

Observed Traffic	Value
Total Packets	3341
Dropped Packets	0
Total Traffic	1.4 Mb
Total IP Traffic	1.4 Mb
Total Non IP Traffic	1.0 Kb
Actual Throughput	8.9 Kbps
Max Throughput	973.1 Kbps

IP Protocol	Data	Percentage
TCP vs. UDP	2.8 Mb	TCP (99.1 %) UDP (0.9 %)
FTP	2.3 Mb	81.3 %
HTTP/IC	0.0 Kb	
DNS	0.0 Kb	
Telnet	44.0 Kb	1.5 %
NetBios over IP	8.9 Kb	
POP	0.0 Kb	
SNMP	0.0 Kb	
NFS	0.0 Kb	
X11	0.0 Kb	
Other IP	488.3 Kb	16.9 %

Figure 7.12 *Traffic Statistics Report.*

The `Total Packets` statistic represents the total number of frames captured on the interface that `ntop` has been monitoring since this monitoring was started. The `Dropped Packets` field indicates frames that were dropped due to processing constraints or filtering criteria. The `Total Traffic` field indicates the total amount of data that was read from the interface. This is the sum of both IP and non-IP traffic. The `Total IP Traffic` field shows the total amount of IP-based traffic, which will include, for example, all upper-level protocols such as ICMP and TCP. The `Total non-IP Traffic` statistic includes protocols such as IPX, AppleTalk, or others. Thus, if we have a mixed network of both IP and AppleTalk protocols, this field would be non-zero and contain the AppleTalk traffic portion. `Actual Throughput` measures the observed performance of the interface (packet reception), while `Max Throughput` is indicative of the theoretical performance based on the type of interface (such as 10 Mbit/s Ethernet).

The second table in Figure 7.12 shows the total IP traffic sorted by protocol. On the right is the protocol type with the total amount of data for that protocol. The left-hand side includes the visual representation of the data as a percent. The percentages include both TCP and UDP traffic. When viewed within the browser, the TCP usage is light blue, while the UDP traffic is light pink. For each TCP-based protocol, the amount of traffic is represented by the number and a graphical bar chart.

Host Information Report

This report provides additional information pertaining to the hosts found on the network. It includes the following columns: `Host Name`, `IP Address`, `MAC Address`, and `Nw Board Vendor`. Figure 7.13 contains a sample of this report. If the IP address of a host cannot be mapped to a hostname, the IP address is used in the `Host Name` column. This is the reason why some of the entries contain both hostname and IP addresses. The IP address field is self-explanatory and the `MAC Address` column (media access control) contains the hardware address of the host interface that sent/received network traffic. The final column contains the vendor of the interface hardware as derived from the last three bytes from the `MAC Address` field.

Notice the entries in the `Host Name` column are underlined. This is because these represent a link to another `ntop` report. This report provides additional information about the host that includes more detailed traffic information, IP history, and the current TCP sessions for the system. Figure 7.13 shows this report for the host `durer`. As you can see, some of the information presented in the report can also be found in the `Host Info` report as well. The `Info About Durer` section includes the following:

- IP Address
- MAC Address
- Nw Board Vendor
- Host Location
- Total Data Sent
- Broadcast Pkts Sent
- Multicast Pkts Sent
- Data Sent Stats
- Total Data Rcvd
- Data Received Stats

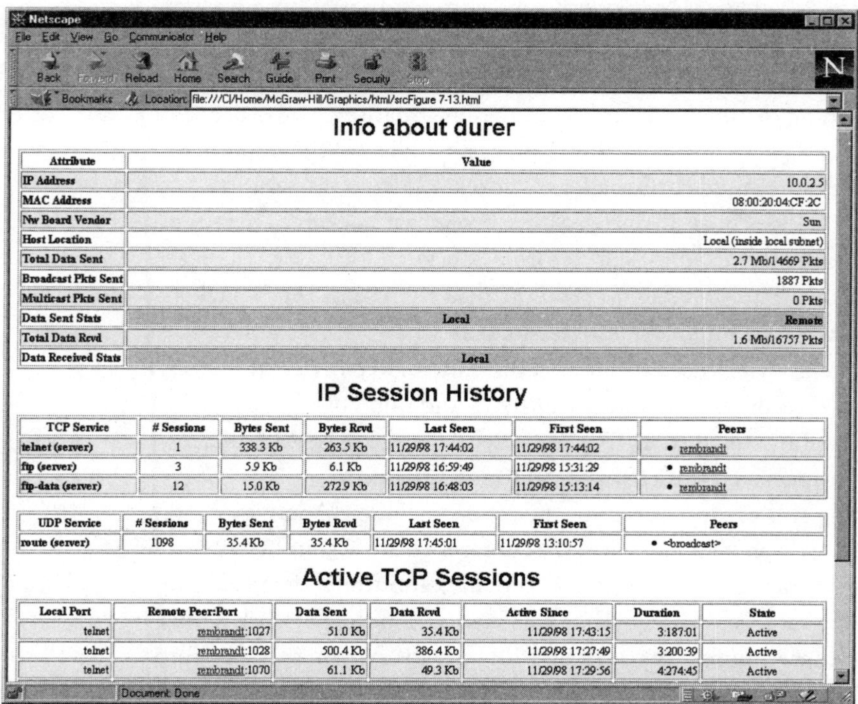

Netscape
File Edit View Go Communicator Help
Back Forward Reload Home Search Guide Print Security Stop
Bookmarks Location: file:///C|/Home/McGraw-Hill/Graphics/html/srcFigure 7-13.html
Info about durer
Attribute | Value
IP Address | 10.0.2.5
MAC Address | 08:00:20:04:CF:2C
Nw Board Vendor | Sun
Host Location | Local (inside local subnet)
Total Data Sent | 2.7 Mb/14669 Pkts
Broadcast Pkts Sent | 1887 Pkts
Multicast Pkts Sent | 0 Pkts
Data Sent Stats | Local | Remote
Total Data Rcvd | 1.6 Mb/16757 Pkts
Data Received Stats | Local
IP Session History
TCP Service | # Sessions | Bytes Sent | Bytes Rcvd | Last Seen | First Seen | Peers
telnet (server) | 1 | 338.3 Kb | 263.5 Kb | 11/29/98 17:44:02 | 11/29/98 17:44:02 | • rembrandt
ftp (server) | 3 | 5.9 Kb | 6.1 Kb | 11/29/98 16:59:49 | 11/29/98 15:31:29 | • rembrandt
ftp-data (server) | 12 | 15.0 Kb | 272.9 Kb | 11/29/98 16:48:03 | 11/29/98 15:13:14 | • rembrandt
UDP Service | # Sessions | Bytes Sent | Bytes Rcvd | Last Seen | First Seen | Peers
route (server) | 1098 | 35.4 Kb | 35.4 Kb | 11/29/98 17:45:01 | 11/29/98 13:10:57 | • <broadcast>
Active TCP Sessions
Local Port | Remote Peer:Port | Data Sent | Data Rcvd | Active Since | Duration | State
telnet | rembrandt:1027 | 51.0 Kb | 35.4 Kb | 11/29/98 17:43:15 | 3:187:01 | Active
telnet | rembrandt:1028 | 500.4 Kb | 386.4 Kb | 11/29/98 17:27:49 | 3:200:39 | Active
telnet | rembrandt:1070 | 61.1 Kb | 49.3 Kb | 11/29/98 17:29:56 | 4:274:45 | Active
Document: Done

Figure 7.13 *Host Report.*

The first three items were already discussed. The Host Location indicates that this host is contained within the subnet that ntop is monitoring. That is to say, the interface that ntop is monitoring from is on the same network as the host. Why is this important? It helps to know if this host is local or remote from the perspective of ntop, so that the additional information ntop reports is interpreted correctly. For example, the Data Sent Stats gives a graphical representation of the percentage of both local and remote traffic. This is very useful because it can be used to determine traffic patterns across an internet. In the case of the report shown above, approximately 90% of the traffic is local. Local traffic is blue and remote light pink when displayed on a color monitor. If this situation, for example, had been reversed, and 90% of the traffic was remote, it might be necessary to move durer to another remote network or limit access to this system from the remote location. Total Data Sent represents both the number of bytes and number of packets transmitted from durer.

The Total Data Sent statistic is a combination of broadcast and multicast expressed in both byes and number of packets sent. This is a true measure of what this host transmitted on the network, regarding the final destination of the information. The Broadcast Pkts Sent statistic, as its name suggests, indicates the number of packets that used the broadcast address (255) to transmit packets. This includes both IP and datalink broadcast packets. These types of packets are used to send information to all local devices on the network. The Multicast Pkts Sent field represents those packets used with the multicast address such as 224.0.0.1. As you can see, no packets were used to support this kind of network traffic. Total Data Rcvd shows the number of bytes and number of packets received by this system. The Data Received Stats field indicates that all received traffic was local to the system.

The IP Session section of the report includes IP activity that this host was involved with. In this case, both TCP and UDP traffic were recorded. The report also provides additional details about the higher level protocol that was involved in the network activity—that is, higher than either TCP or UDP. As you can see, both FTP and ROUTE services are listed and additional information regarding these services is provided. In the first table, the FTP activity shown includes the number of sessions (times) that service was active, the bytes sent/received, timestamp information, and which other systems (Peers) were involved in FTP sessions. In this example, both FTP sessions included the host rembrandt.

The other table contains the same information, but notice that the peer is labeled as <broadcast>. The reason the peer of this service is the broadcast address is because the service is the Unix routed command. The normal behavior of the route command is to transmit routing protocol information periodically on the network. This is why the number of sessions is relatively large. The fact that routed is running on this system should be no surprise because, when a system contains two network interfaces, generally IP routing is enabled by default.

The Active TCP Session section is also included within this report and is described in detail below. However, the only difference between this report and the main report is that this is a subset of the main report.

Local and Remote Report

The next three reports display IP traffic that is remote to local, local to remote, and local to local from the perspective of ntop. Each of the reports shares the same general report layout and format. These reports—R->L IP Traffic, L->R IP Traffic, and L<->L IP Traffic—show the following details:

- Hostname
- IP Address
- Data Received/Sent
- Total Traffic
- Data Received/Sent
- Bandwidth

Figure 7.14 shows a Remote to Local IP Traffic report only. Like the other graphs, these graphs list specific hostnames and IP address information. Also, they provide links to obtain additional host information as described previously. They also include two separate tables, one showing the individual traffic for each host, the other showing the totals for all hosts combined. In the first table, the `Data Received` and `Data Sent` statistics both contain two columns. The first column shows the amount of data that was either received or sent by each system and may be expressed in bytes, kilobytes (Kb), or megabytes (Mb). The second column shows the amount of traffic as a percent for all hosts listed in the table. The second table contains the `Total Traffic` column, which is a summary of both the `Data Received` and `Data Sent` columns from the first table. The next two columns, `Data Received` and `Data Sent`, are the sum of the columns with the same name in the first table. The `Bandwidth` column lists the effective bandwidth utilization as a result of the network traffic monitored.

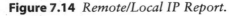

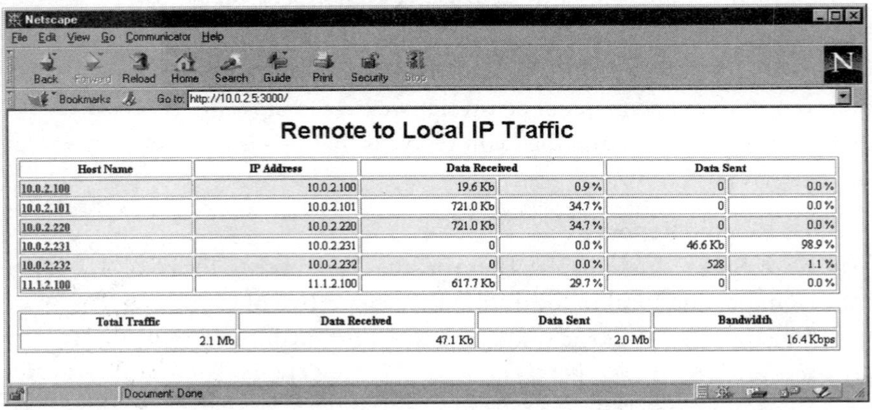

Remote to Local IP Traffic

Host Name	IP Address	Data Received		Data Sent	
10.0.2.100	10.0.2.100	19.6 Kb	0.9 %	0	0.0 %
10.0.2.101	10.0.2.101	721.0 Kb	34.7 %	0	0.0 %
10.0.2.220	10.0.2.220	721.0 Kb	34.7 %	0	0.0 %
10.0.2.231	10.0.2.231	0	0.0 %	46.6 Kb	98.9 %
10.0.2.232	10.0.2.232	0	0.0 %	528	1.1 %
11.1.2.100	11.1.2.100	617.7 Kb	29.7 %	0	0.0 %

Total Traffic	Data Received	Data Sent	Bandwidth
2.1 Mb	47.1 Kb	2.0 Mb	16.4 Kbps

Figure 7.14 *Remote/Local IP Report.*

Active TCP Sessions

The `Active TCP Session` report includes much of the information that can be obtained from the `netstat` command. However, it provides a much easier format in which to review the information as displayed in Figure7.15. In general, it provides a way to view the state of all TCP-based connections from both a client and server perspective. This report contains the following information:

- Client/Server Port Numbers
- Data Sent/Rcvd
- When the Connection was Initiated
- Duration of Connection
- State of Connection

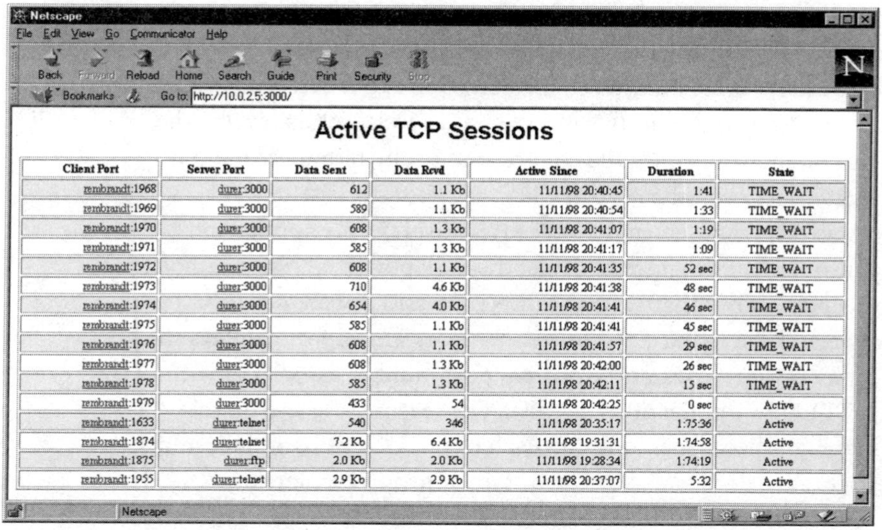

Active TCP Sessions

Client Port	Server Port	Data Sent	Data Rcvd	Active Since	Duration	State
rembrandt:1968	durer:3000	612	1.1 Kb	11/11/98 20:40:45	1:41	TIME_WAIT
rembrandt:1969	durer:3000	589	1.1 Kb	11/11/98 20:40:54	1:33	TIME_WAIT
rembrandt:1970	durer:3000	608	1.3 Kb	11/11/98 20:41:07	1:19	TIME_WAIT
rembrandt:1971	durer:3000	585	1.3 Kb	11/11/98 20:41:17	1:09	TIME_WAIT
rembrandt:1972	durer:3000	608	1.1 Kb	11/11/98 20:41:35	52 sec	TIME_WAIT
rembrandt:1973	durer:3000	710	4.6 Kb	11/11/98 20:41:38	48 sec	TIME_WAIT
rembrandt:1974	durer:3000	654	4.0 Kb	11/11/98 20:41:41	46 sec	TIME_WAIT
rembrandt:1975	durer:3000	585	1.1 Kb	11/11/98 20:41:41	45 sec	TIME_WAIT
rembrandt:1976	durer:3000	608	1.1 Kb	11/11/98 20:41:57	29 sec	TIME_WAIT
rembrandt:1977	durer:3000	608	1.3 Kb	11/11/98 20:42:00	26 sec	TIME_WAIT
rembrandt:1978	durer:3000	585	1.3 Kb	11/11/98 20:42:11	15 sec	TIME_WAIT
rembrandt:1979	durer:3000	433	54	11/11/98 20:42:25	0 sec	Active
rembrandt:1633	durer:telnet	540	346	11/11/98 20:35:17	1:75:36	Active
rembrandt:1874	durer:telnet	7.2 Kb	6.4 Kb	11/11/98 19:31:31	1:74:58	Active
rembrandt:1875	durer:ftp	2.0 Kb	2.0 Kb	11/11/98 19:28:34	1:74:19	Active
rembrandt:1955	durer:telnet	2.9 Kb	2.9 Kb	11/11/98 20:37:07	5:32	Active

Figure 7.15 *Active TCP Sessions Report.*

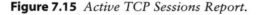

The `Client Port` column shows the remote system and TCP port used, which represents the remote end of the connection. The `Server Port`, which is the local end of the connection, also shows the system and TCP port. In Chapter 2, "Simple Network Management Protocol," we discuss how a TCP connection consists of four items: the remote IP address, remote port, local IP address, and remote port. With this report, we can observe the state of each connection. This is found in the `State` column and provides the current state of all TCP connections. The title for this report is a little misleading, because it suggests that only active sessions will be displayed. This report also includes those connections for which termination is pending. Note, in this example, that there are a number of TCP connections in the `TIME_WAIT` state. This state is entered after either side of a TCP session has been terminated. The large number of sessions in this state is due to the HTTP activity on this system. Because HTTP uses a large number of TCP connections, it is not uncommon to have many outstanding TCP connections pending termination on a Web server.

The `Data Sent` and `Data Rcvd` columns show the amount of data, expressed in bytes, kilobytes (Kb), or megabytes (Mb), that was sent/received by the connection. The `Active Since` field shows when (data and time) the connection was first initialized. Also, the `Duration` field shows the how long the connection was active. It is interesting to note that, when a connection is not active anymore from a TCP standpoint (it's in `TIME_WAIT` mode, for example), the duration increases until the connection is fully terminated and no longer appears on the report.

Also note that, when possible, `ntop` displays the application name of the service instead of just the TCP port itself. For example, the report shows that several TELNET sessions were active between the systems `durer` and `rembrandt`. The report displays the port as `telnet`, and not the normal port number associated with the TELNET application (i.e., `23`). The reason `ntop` can do this mapping is because it looks up each of the TCP ports it finds and searches the `/etc/services` file for an appropriate match.

IP Protocol Distribution Report

One of the most useful of all the `ntop` reports, the IP protocol distribution report shows the breakdown of network usage by higher-level protocols. It reveals the amount of data (sent/received) by protocol type, such as SNMP or FTP, as shown in Figure 7.16. This is an important observation, because this report clearly shows which applications are used the most in comparison with those used the least. The report contains three tables that include protocol distribution for `Local Traffic`, `Remote to Local Traffic`, and `Local to Remote Traffic`. Each section or table contains three columns, `IP Protocol`, `Data`, and `Percentage`. The `IP Protocol` column includes the higher-level protocols that `ntop` understands. Those protocols that `ntop` doesn't support are listed under the `Other IP` category. Each protocol has associated `Data` and `Percentage` columns, which relate to the amount of data, expressed in bytes and as a percent of data, in comparison to each of the other protocols.

Using the bar graphs contained within this report, it is relatively straightforward to identify network utilization by protocol or network application. For example, observe the second table shows that, out of all the IP traffic displayed, UDP usage was by far the most significant.

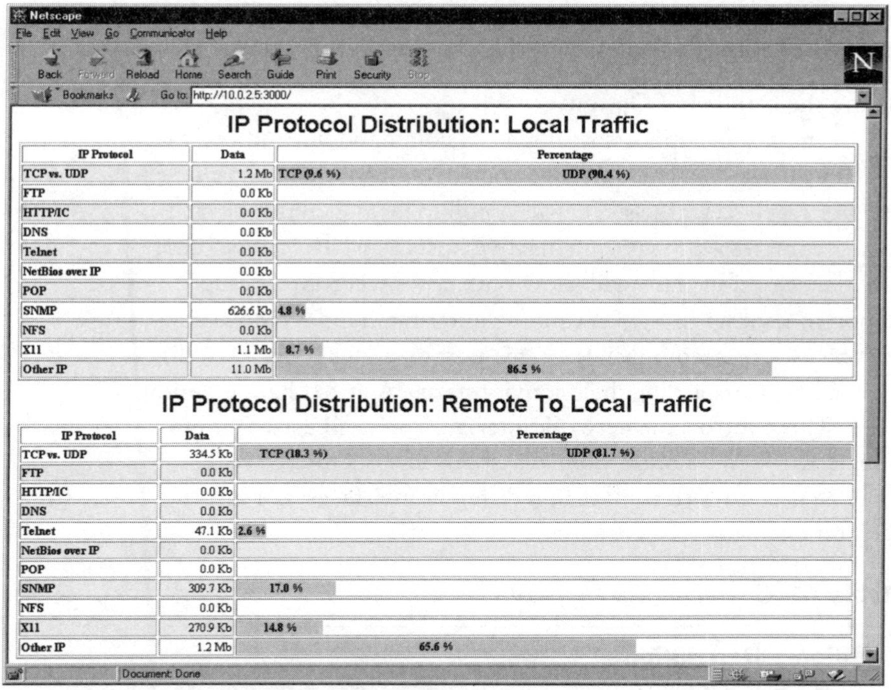

IP Protocol Distribution: Local Traffic

IP Protocol	Data	Percentage
TCP vs. UDP	1.2 Mb	TCP (9.6 %) UDP (90.4 %)
FTP	0.0 Kb	
HTTP/IC	0.0 Kb	
DNS	0.0 Kb	
Telnet	0.0 Kb	
NetBios over IP	0.0 Kb	
POP	0.0 Kb	
SNMP	626.6 Kb	4.8 %
NFS	0.0 Kb	
X11	1.1 Mb	8.7 %
Other IP	11.0 Mb	86.5 %

IP Protocol Distribution: Remote To Local Traffic

IP Protocol	Data	Percentage
TCP vs. UDP	334.5 Kb	TCP (18.3 %) UDP (81.7 %)
FTP	0.0 Kb	
HTTP/IC	0.0 Kb	
DNS	0.0 Kb	
Telnet	47.1 Kb	2.6 %
NetBios over IP	0.0 Kb	
POP	0.0 Kb	
SNMP	309.7 Kb	17.0 %
NFS	0.0 Kb	
X11	270.9 Kb	14.8 %
Other IP	1.2 Mb	65.6 %

Figure 7.16 *Protocol Distribution Report.*

Subnet Usage

This report shows high-level protocol or application service and both the client and server that participated in the traffic exchange. Figure 7.17 displays a sample report that shows that `FTP`, `TELNET`, `SNMP`, `FINGER`, `SMTP`, and `ROUTE` were active. Also, it lists both the clients and server that were using these protocols and services. The rea-

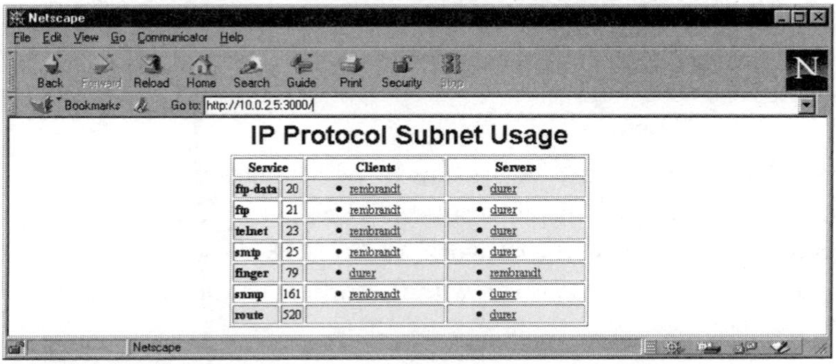

IP Protocol Subnet Usage

Service		Clients	Servers
ftp-data	20	• rembrandt	• durer
ftp	21	• rembrandt	• durer
telnet	23	• rembrandt	• durer
smtp	25	• rembrandt	• durer
finger	79	• durer	• rembrandt
snmp	161	• rembrandt	• durer
route	520		• durer

Figure 7.17 *Protocol Subnet Usage Report.*

son the ROUTE service doesn't have a client is that it uses a broadcast approach, thus removing the need for specific client connections.

Using the Command Options

The ntop tool supports a number of command line options as listed in Table 7.8. This software considers a host that hasn't generated or received traffic since its last poll to be an inactive host. If you are interested in viewing inactive hosts as well as active ones, use the -d option. This will show both types when generating reports. Also, when ntop is running in terminal mode, the -d key can be used to accomplish the same purpose. This is useful to display all hosts regarding their activity status. Another handy option is -i. This controls the network interface ntop will use to monitor the network. With multi-homed systems this is a must, because it may be necessary to run ntop on different interfaces, not just the default one.

Table 7.8 *Command Line Options*

Option	Description
-d	Shows all hosts, not just active ones
-l	Shows both local and remote hosts that generate network traffic
-i	Specifies an alternate interface to use
-n	Shows numeric IP addresses instead of names
-r	Controls the delay between screen updates
-p	Shows network traffic as percent
-w	Enables web mode

If you are interested in monitoring systems by percentage, use the -p option. This option will display traffic as a percent of total traffic for each system active on the network. Figure 7.18 shows what will be displayed when ntop is run with this option enabled.

Figure 7.18 *Traffic by Percent.*

Security of the Web Reports

If you are concerned about security with respect to the reports, no problem! The `ntop` tool supports a rudimentary, but very useful, security feature that can be implemented quickly and easily. When `ntop` is run, it searches the home directory of the user starting the process for a file called `.ntop`. This file may contain one or more names and associated passwords. When an entry is added to this file, the user is prompted with a login window as displayed in Figure 7.19.

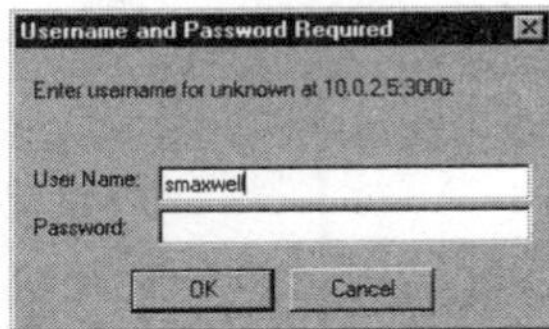

Figure 7.19 *NTOP Login Window.*

In most instances, it is reasonable that `ntop` be run as the superuser of the system. As a result, a `.ntop` file can be placed in the directory of the `/` (root) file system. To make it as secure as possible, ensure that the file is not readable, except by the superuser.

Assume that we wish to provide access to `ntop` for a handful of users. The following sample `.ntop` would serve our purpose:

```
netmgr private
tech-1 secret
smaxwell 1ghost99
acartwright 44 pleaseread
```

With these entries, any of the four users—`netmgr`, `tech-1`, `smaxwell`, or `acartwright`—can obtain access to the `ntop` reports, provided they each use the associated password string. Thus, `netmgr` would have to use `private and so on`. Clearly, this security feature is very simple, but it does have its weakness. Namely, someone could capture the login sequence with a probe or other device and obtain the name/password pair.

Using Terminal Mode

By default, `ntop` starts in terminal mode. The information presented with the Web interface is available in the terminal mode but, of course, the data is formatted differently. To review the different reports, `ntop` defines a number of keyboard commands that, when pressed, will alter the displayed report. The keyword command consists of a single letter without the enter key.

For example, the `h` command provides help for the `ntop` tool and displays a list of available keyboard commands. Thus, when `ntop` is running, pressing this key (without the return or enter) will display the following:

```
ntop v.1.0 for sparc-sun-solaris2.6 [libpcap version 0.4a7]
Written by Luca Deri <deri@unipi.it> and Stefano Suin <stefano@unipi.it>.
While ntop is running interactively, the following keys are active:
       'q' - quit ntop
       'r' - reset statistics
       'n' - toggle address format (num <-> sym <-> MAC <-> Nw Board Manifact.)
       'p' - toggle traffic values (vs. bytes)
       'l' - toggle hosts display (local subnet vs. all)
       'd' - toggle idle (idle vs. send/receive)
       't' - toggle sort (sent vs. received)
       'y' - toggle columns sort
       'h' - show this help
       ' ' - toggle protocol
Strike a key to continue...
```

The user is prompted to press a key to return to the main report screen. Even when `ntop` is displaying the help screen, it is still monitoring and collecting network traffic statistics. As you can see from the help screen, `ntop` shows the supported keyboard commands. The `q` command is used to halt the operation of `ntop`. The `^c` command sequence will accomplish the same thing.

NTOP Package Information

The NTOP software may be obtained from the Internet from this location:

```
ftp://ftp.unipi.it/pub/local/ntop/binary/ntop-1.0-solaris-2.6.gz
```

Also, additional information may be obtained at:

```
http://jake.unipi.it/~lderi
```

Conditions of Use

The following information appears in the `COPYING` file for this distribution:

```
NTOP LICENSE
Copyright (C) 1998 Luca Deri and Stefano Suin
ntop has been written by Luca Deri <deri@unipi.it> and Stefano
Suin <stefano@unipi.it> with the purpose to create a tool able
to effectively monitor networks. ntop belongs to the authors
(L.Deri and S.Suin) who allow you to use it according to the
license below (GPL2).
This license basically ALLOWS you to:
- use ntop for both educational and commercial purposes
- study, modify, redistribute ntop's source code.
- build new applications based on ntop.
What you CANNOT do with ntop is:
- charge a fee for using ntop except for the physical act of
 transferring a copy.
What you SHOULD do with ntop is:
- use and have fun with it, hoping it's useful for you
- send suggestions, bug reports, patches, enhancements to the authors
In other words you must keep ntop free of charge. If you have some
questions or if you plan to integrate ntop in a commercial
product (a.k.a you charge a fee for using the product) then you
must contact the authors.

Luca Deri <deri@unipi.it> and Stefano Suin <stefano@unipi.it>
Pisa, October 1998.
```

Installing the NTOP Package

The installation procedures for the NTOP software are included below. Please note that these instructions are based on using the 1.0 version of this package on the Sun Solaris platform. This package contains only the binary for the Solaris system. If you will be installing a newer version, these procedures may not be accurate or complete. In this case, consult the installation instructions that accompany the NTOP distribution.

1. Obtain the NTOP package from the site above or from the CD-ROM available with this book.

2. Uncompress the archive:

   ```
   gunzip ntop-1_00-solaris-sparc.gz
   ```

3. Use the Solaris `pkgadd` program:

   ```
   pkgadd -d ntop-1_00-solaris-sparc
   ```

4. Step #4 causes the `/opt/ntop/bin` to be created. This is where the `ntop` binary has been placed.

A

Tools at a Glance

The table below provides a quick summary of the tools and utilities described in the book. Pay particular attention to the Category columns as these will help you determine which of the three major elements of network management will best be served by the particular tool. The “Page #” column provides a quick index to the section of the book that describes the tool.

Tool	Description	Category			Page #
		Perform	Config	Monitor	
arp	Monitoring and Control of ARP Cache		✓	✓	88
fping	Fancy ping (see ping)	✓		✓	144
ifconfig	Interface Configuration		✓		95
ping	Determination of active device(s) on network	✓		✓	115
mibiisa	Sun MIB-2 SNMP agent	✓	✓	✓	185
mrtg	Network performance grapher	✓		✓	278
netstat	Network Statistics	✓		✓	106
ntop	Network Traffic Monitor	✓		✓	311
snoop	Packet Sniffer			✓	122
snmpbulkwalk	Enhanced SNMP retrieval			✓	250
snmpconf	Automated SNMP configurations		✓		270
snmpd	UCD SNMP agent			✓	204
snmpdelta	Formatting of SNMP data			✓	251
snmpget	Regular SNMP retrieval			✓	253

Tool	Description	Category			Page #
		Perform	Config	Monitor	
`snmpgetnext`	Retrieval of multiple SNMP objects			✓	254
`snmpnetstat`	Retrieval of network statistics from SNMP entity			✓	254
`snmpset`	Alteration of SNMP configuration information		✓		257
`snmpstatus`	Retrieval of important SNMP data			✓	261
`snmptable`	Retrieval of SNMP table data			✓	262
`snmptest`	Testing of SNMP connectivity			✓	264
`snmptranslate`	Translate SNMP MIB objects into more readable text			✓	265
`snmptrap`	Sending SNMP traps			✓	266
`snmptrapd`	Receipt of SNMP traps from network			✓	267
`snmpwalk`	Retrieval of either a group or entire MIB tree.			✓	268
`traceroute`	Display of routing paths	✓		✓	155

Index

The symbols in this index are sorted alphabetically by the symbol's name (ampersand, asterisk, at sign, etc.).

Symbols

A

D

E

F

G

K

L

M

S

T

Software and Information License

The software and information on this diskette (collectively referred to as the "Product") are the property of The McGraw-Hill Companies, Inc. ("McGraw-Hill") and are protected by both United States copyright law and international copyright treaty provision. You must treat this Product just like a book, expect that you may copy it into a computer to be used and you may make archival copies of the Products for the sole purpose of backing up your software and protecting your investment from loss.

By saying "just like a book," McGraw-Hill means, for example, that the Product may be used by any number of people and may be freely moved from one computer location to another, so long as there is no possibility of the Product (or any part of the Product) being used at one location or on one computer while it is being used at another. Just as a book cannot be read by two different people in two different places at the same time, neither can the Product be used in two different places at the same time (unless, of course, McGraw-Hill's rights are being violated).

McGraw-Hill reserves the right to alter or modify the contents of the Product at any time.

This agreement is effective until terminated. The Agreement will terminate automatically without notice if you fail to comply with any provisions of this Agreement. In the event of termination by reason of your breach, you will destroy or erase all copies of the Product installed on any computer system or made for backup purposes and shall expunge the Product from your data storage facilities.

Limited Warranty

McGraw-Hill warrants the physical diskette(s) enclosed herein to be free of defects in materials and workmanship for a period of sixty days from the purchase date. If McGraw-Hill receives written notification within the warranty period of defects in materials or workmanship, and such notification is determined by McGraw-Hill to be correct, McGraw-Hill will replace the defective diskette(s). Send request to:

Customer Service
McGraw-Hill
Gahanna Industrial Park
860 Taylor Station Road
Blacklick, Ohio 43004-9615

The entire and exclusive liability and remedy for breach of this Limited Warranty shall be limited to replacement of defective diskette(s) and shall not include or extend any claim for or right to cover any other damages, including but not limited to loss of profit, data, or use of the software, or special, incidental, or consequential damages or other similar claims, even if McGraw-Hill has been specifically advised as to the possibility of such damages. In no event will McGraw-Hill's liability for any damages to you or any other person ever exceed the lower of suggested list price or actual price paid for the license to use the Product, regardless of any form of the claim.

The McGraw-Hill Companies, Inc. specifically disclaims all other warranties, express or implied, including but not limited to, any implied warranty of merchantability or fitness for a particular purpose. Specifically, McGraw-Hill makes no representation or warranty that the Product is fit for any particular purpose and any implied warranty of merchantability is limited to the sixty day duration of the Limited Warranty covering the physical diskette(s) only (and not the software or information) and is otherwise expressly and specifically disclaimed.

This Limited Warranty gives you specific legal rights; you may have others which may vary from state to state. Some states do not allow the exclusion of incidental or consequential damages, or the limitation on how long an implied warranty lasts, so some of the above may not apply to you.

This agreement constitutes the entire agreement between the parties relating to use of the Product. The terms of any purchase order shall have no effect on the terms of this Agreement. Failure of McGraw-Hill to insist at any time on strict compliance with this Agreement shall not constitute a waiver of any rights under this Agreement. This Agreement shall be construed and governed in accordance with the laws of New York. If any provision of this Agreement is held to be contrary to law, that provision will be enforced to the maximum extent permissible and the remaining provisions will remain in force and effect.